W9-AMR-350

Transforming Borders

Transforming Borders

Chicana/o Popular Culture and Pedagogy

C. Alejandra Elenes

LEXINGTON BOOKS

A division of

ROWMAN & LITTLEFIELD PUBLISHERS, INC.
Lanham • Boulder • New York • Toronto • Plymouth, UK

Published by Lexington Books
A division of Rowman & Littlefield Publishers, Inc.
A wholly owned subsidary of The Rowman & Littlefield Publishing Group, Inc.
4501 Forbes Boulevard, Suite 200, Lanham, Maryland 20706
www.lexingtonbooks.com

Estover Road
Plymouth PL6 7PY
United Kingdom

British Library Cataloguing in Publication Information Available

Library of Congress Cataloging-in-Publication Data
Elenes, C. Alejandra, 1958–
 Transforming borders : Chicana/o popular culture and pedagogy / C. Alejandra Elenes.
   p. cm.
 Includes bibliographical references.
 ISBN 978-0-7391-4779-5 (cloth : alk. paper) — ISBN 978-0-7391-4781-8 (electronic)
 1. Hispanic American women—Education. 2. Feminist theory—United States. 3. Women in education—United States. 4. Critical pedagogy—United States. I. Title.
LC2670.E54 2011
 371.829'68073—dc22

                                                            2010034246

Printed in the United States of America

♾ ™ The paper used in this publication meets the minimum requirements of American National Standard for Information Sciences—Permanence of Paper for Printed Library Materials, ANSI/NISO Z39.48-1992.

Contents

Preface

The stories, images, and legends about La Llorona (the weeping woman), La Virgen de Guadalupe (the Virgin of Guadalupe), and Malintzin/Malinche have been an intrinsic part of my life, even when I did not give them much thought. Like so many other Chicanas and *mexicanas,* I have reclaimed and re-imaged them as feminist figures. As a little girl, I was told the patriarchal versions of these figures, and because of that, I had little room for them in my life. This is particularly the case with La Virgen de Guadalupe. I went to Catholic school with *Guadalupana* nuns in Monterrey, México. Every December 12th we had to offer roses to La Virgen.

In addition to having to take a crowded bus to the Church when it always seemed to be either too hot or too cold, we also had to endure the nuns' distortions of the meaning of Tonantzin/Guadalupe. She was never presented as an active Mother. The image we had of her was as the passive, meek, and obedient Mother of Christ. We had to bring our own flowers for the offering ceremony. The task of finding flowers, we were told, would be almost impossible to achieve. The nuns made us believe that it would be very difficult to find roses in December, because roses do not grow in the winter. However, God would help us. In the early elementary school years, I was always amazed that I was able to find beautiful roses in my mother's garden. Only as I grew up did I realize that in México roses grow in the winter. If the appearance of the flowers was not a miracle, could the rest of the story be untrue? What was the miracle, then?

I started to ask questions, impertinent questions. Although the nuns, who were far from amused, could not or would not answer my inquiries, neither could they contain them. It wasn't until I started working on this project—when I understood in my heart who Guadalupe/Tonantzin is, and why she is such an important figure for people of Mexican descent,[1] both from a religious and secular standpoint—that I reclaimed her into my life, but this time as a feminist icon. At different times in my life, I have also unknowingly deconstructed and reconstructed meanings of Malintzin/Malinche and La Llorona.

Part of the genesis of this project stems from the realization of and fascination with how cultural meanings are always changing. The relationship between culture and education, particularly the possibility of implementing pedagogies where Chicana identities can be explored and articulated in their complexity, is one I have been interested in for a long time—especially when these efforts are part of a larger social justice project. The representations, re-imagining, and deconstructions of La Llorona, La Virgen de Guadalupe, and Malintzin/Malinche exemplify how the fluidity of culture is necessary for the development of transformative pedagogies. Because these images cut across so many different discourses, they represent conflicts over meanings that societies struggle over. As such, they are excellent examples for the formation of pedagogical practices that seek to understand the complexity of cultural representations.

Transforming Borders: Chicana/o Popular Culture and Pedagogy is an interdisciplinary book that seeks to intervene and contribute to transformative pedagogies by adding Chicana/Mexicana voices into this important scholarly and activist endeavor. I engage this project from my borderland experience, as the product of two cultures, religions, languages, and nations. My identity as a *mexicana* and Chicana informed my interest in borderland theories. Throughout my life, I have constantly crossed linguistic, national, and cultural borders; it was, therefore, easy for me to gravitate toward a theoretical framework that offered a non-binary analysis. Gloria Anzaldúa's philosophy offered such analysis.

My schooling experiences and the stories I learned from family members triggered my interest in the relationship between culture and education. Educational institutions in the U.S. neglect, dismiss, and undermine cultural practices of people of Mexican descent. Yet, Mexicans and Chicanas/os deploy their cultural repertoire in order to express their worldviews and their positions within the social order. Through narratives, Mexicans and Chicanas offer teaching and learning strategies that speak about unequal social conditions. In this book, I bring the stories of La Llorona, La Virgen de Guadalupe, and Malinztin/Malinche to show a complex array of stories about colonialism, patriarchy, and social inequality; in doing so, I bring to the front Chicana's decolonial re-imagining of these narratives. I link these narratives to their pedagogical meanings and hope that Chicana feminist thought enters into transformative pedagogies' discourses in more significant ways.

NOTES

1. La Virgen de Guadalupe is an important cultural and religious symbol of people of Mexican descent who are Catholic. Today, this is the majority view; however, it is necessary to take into account that for Chicanas/os who were not raised Catholic the meaning of this icon is quite different. The image of Guadalupe is prevalent in barrios, cultural production and in political struggles. Thus, she enters into the formation of Chicana/o cultural identity as a cultural and political figure. Those who did not grow up with the process of indoctrination of her Catholic meaning that I received as a child ascribe to her quite different meanings. Given that an important argument I am presenting in this book is the need to understand Chicana/o identity in all its multiple manifestations, it is necessary to remember that Catholicism and Chicanismo are not necessarily associated. During the late 1970s or early 1980s, a series of TV announcements in Mexico (probably to raise funds for the construction of the new *Basílica*) carried the specious message that "*todos los mexicanos somos Guadalupanos*" (all Mexicans are Guadalupanos). We cannot equate the symbolism of Guadalupe as one for all people of Mexican descent. Even though she does symbolize secular nationalism and is Tonatzin, she is still intrinsically associated with Catholicism, and not all Chicanas/os come from a Catholic background.

Acknowledgments

Researching and writing this book has been, to say the least, a long and difficult process—yet a rewarding one. I have been blessed with the support of many friends, colleagues, and family members; without their aid and encouragement, I would not have been able to start and finish this book. I am indebted to so many people and it is my desire to do justice to their support.

I want to first thank the numerous Chicana feminist scholars, activists, cultural workers, and artists who initiated the process of reclaiming and transforming the meanings of La Llorona, La Virgen de Guadalupe, and Malintzin/Malinche. Their work inspired my study; I hope I can do justice to their artistic inspiration and scholarly productions. I thank Gloria Anzaldúa for her foresight in reframing Chicana feminism, borderland theories, identity/subjectivity, sexuality, and spirituality. I would not have understood the significance of Gloria's work without Norma Alarcón's advice—offered so many years ago—to pursue my intellectual interests and to examine Gloria Anzaldúa's philosophy, to "give her her due" and link her to the emerging work on Chicana feminist pedagogies. Words of gratitude to Ester Hernández and Consuelo Jiménez Underwood do not do justice to convey how much their support means to me. I thank Ester for taking time from her busy schedule to read drafts of my chapter on La Virgen de Guadalupe and for providing me with invaluable feedback that helped clarify key points in my analysis. Notwithstanding, all errors and misreadings are mine. I am so grateful to Consuelo Jiménez Underwood's support for my work and for human rights and social justice in Arizona. It is indeed an honor to reprint their work in this book. Special thanks to Joan Pinkvos at Aunt Lute for so generously granting permission to reprint Gloria Anzaldúa's poem "To Live in the Borderlands

Means You." I am particularly grateful to Naomi Quiñonez who allowed reprinting of her poem on La Llorona.

The research on La Llorona could not have been completed without the assistance from Dr. James S. Griffith, former director of the Southwest Folklore Center at the University of Arizona who generously opened his archives and let me examine his collection of oral histories on La Llorona. Monique Durham, at the Center for Southwest Research at the Zimmerman Library in the University of New Mexico, was very generous and supportive during my visit to examine the archives. I owe a debt of gratitude to ASU's Fletcher Library librarians who helped me so much in researching this book; deg farrely, Lisa Kammerlocher, Denis Isabel, Melisa Guy, and Allison Leaming. All these individuals and institutions enriched my work.

Mil gracias to the various graduate and undergraduate research assistants who diligently worked with me throughout the length of this project. During the early stages of this endeavor, Juan Guevara meticulously gathered information on La Llorona, La Virgen de Guadalupe, and Malintzin/Malinche. I thank you so much for helping me lay down the foundations for this book and I wish you life's best wishes. Marla Conrad thoroughly worked on the bibliography and offered stimulating intellectual conversation. I thank Danielle Ahlberg for proofreading and double checking citations and data, and doing a final fix on the bibliography. Jessica Sánchez carefully worked in preparing and fixing the manuscript to fulfill Lexington's specifications. Without all of your help I would have not brought this project to completion. Really!

Four editors helped move the project to print. Michael Sisskin, at Lexington Books, has been a very supportive editor. He came into the project at a moment I thought all was lost. I cannot say how much I appreciate his answering all of my questions, and for his patience when things got a bit slow. Eric Wrona was extremely helpful in the preparation of the book. Special thanks to Gwen E. Kirby who diligently worked on the final preparations to get the book to print. Thanks to Alan McClure at Rowman & Littlefield for helping find a suitable home for this book.

Throughout the years I have been blessed with the support of my *colegas* and *amigas* Dolores Delgado Bernal, Sofia Villenas, and Francisca Godinez who toiled with me in developing the field of Chicana feminist critical pedagogy. It was incredible to meet other Chicanas whose research is on critical education and Chicana feminist pedagogies and epistemologies. Dolores exemplifies the scholar activist and her work on Chicana feminist epistemologies has been a source of inspiration. Sofia Villenas deep intellect and ability to bring to light the complexities of everyday life to her scholarship is an inspiration as well; moreover, she has the ability to offer words of encouragement when one needs them the most. Francisca is an inquisitive scholar, gentle and generous soul, and a friend I can always count on. Her ability to explain complex methodologies has been of so much assistance to my students. She is indeed not only a great friend but a wonderful role model. I have learned so much from her.

Still there are others who extended to me their intellectual and moral support. Rosario Carrillo is an amazing scholar and *mujer*, who never loses sight of political priorities. Karleen Pendleton Jiménez is always expanding the meaning of geographic, racial, gender, and sexual borderlands. I give special thanks to Karen Mary Davalos who generously read drafts of chapter 4 and offered invaluable comments. I also thank Karen Mary for answering each one of my simple and naïve questions. My gratitude to my *comadres* Yolanda de la Cruz and Cleopatria Martínez.

There are so many individuals to thank at Arizona State University. This book would have not been finished without my dearest friends and colleagues from our Manuscript Group: Gloria Cuádraz, Shari Collins-Chobanian, Anna Guevarra, Eduardo Pagán, Luis Plascencia, and Michelle Téllez. I am extremely thankful to Shari for asking complex questions and raising issues that helped me look at a point from a very different perspective. I am sure she read more drafts of this book than she expected. Anna Guevarra, who now works at the University of Illinois, Chicago, helped me refine the transnational feminist framework and ground my analysis in material conditions. I miss so much the Friday Night Shift and hours of stimulating conversation. I cannot say how much I appreciate her interests in Malintzin/Malinche and her inquiries about what is coming next. Eduardo Pagán provided much needed feedback from a historian's perspective. Thank you so much for your questions on the *indigenista* movement. Luis Plascencia significantly helped me rethink how I looked at the México-U.S. border, immigration, and citizenship. Thanks to Michelle Téllez for her commitment to spirituality, activism, and autonomous movements. Finally, but certainly not least, my utmost gratitude goes to Gloria Cuádraz. I think that Gloria read almost every page of this manuscript and never hesitated in providing a critical eye toward theory and practice. She keeps me on my toes and always reminds me to get back to the ground when I venture too much into the abstract world of theory. This last year, Gloria and I worked together as the cochairs of the Arizona MALCS Institute. In working with Gloria, I learned the meaning of commitment and pulling up your sleeves and getting the work done when it is needed and no matter what the circumstances. I could not ask for a better partner in organizing a conference, especially under the difficult conditions in which we found ourselves. I thank Gloria so much for her friendship, we can tell it as it is, and at the end of the day, we get the work done and maintain our friendship. And thank you for the all the wonderful meals!

I thank New College Dean and Vice President Elizabeth Langland as well as Monica Casper, Director of the Division of Humanities, Arts & Cultural Studies (HArCS) for their support with a faculty development grant. I was fortunate to receive two Scholarship Research and Creative Activities grants from ASU West in the early stages of this research. Thanks so much to Bertha Álvarez Manninen for helping me when I got stuck burning a CD, and for being such a wonderful and joyful colleague. I express thanks to all my current and former women's studies colleagues: Celia Álvarez, Breanne Fahs, Astair Mengesha, Saira Quereshi, Jessica Share, Sarah Stage, and Cynthia Tompkins. I extend my appreciation to the HArCS staff Mary Bauer, Lucy Berchini, and Tracy Encizo, and I give thanks to Tosha Ruggles from the Graduate Programs Office.

My family has been my support over the years. My mother LaVerrne Steven has always given me unconditional love and support; she also taught me how to be a feminist. My sisters Cristina and Victoria Elenes always have words of encouragement. *Le doy las gracias a Cristina por preguntarme, ¿Cómo va el libro?* Victoria always reminded me of the environment's significance. I want to show my gratitude to my brother Federico Elenes for being a fellow writer and knowing the importance of historical memory. I am proud of all of my nieces and my nephew for becoming incredible creative human beings on their own: Claudia Cristina Hinojosa Elenes, Verónica Hinojosa Elenes, Patty Elenes de la Torre, Letty Elenes de la Torre, Ana Bader Elenes, and Andrés Bader Elenes. Olga, *¡Te doy las gracias por los chiles rellenos!* I am very grateful to my Los Angeles family: Enrique Castillo, Bel Hernández, Karina Castillo, Joaquín Miramontes, Alex Miramontes, Lupe Miramontes, and especially my mother-in-law, one of the strongest women I know, Amalia Miramontes. My love and gratitude goes also to Maria Pelly, Ricardo Pelly, Rami Pellly, and Daphnna Pelly Baranick.

I take time to honor all my loved ones who have traveled into the spirit world, especially my father Mario Elenes Gaxiola and his two sisters, *mis tías Chata y Luz. ¡Los extraño mucho!* I want to take the opportunity as well to remember Steve Casanova, who left us way too early.

My husband and life partner Manuel de Jesús Hernández-G. has offered me all the support, space, and love needed to finish this book. He gave me words of encouragement when I needed them the most. He puts up with my moodiness, mess, and taking over the kitchen table. Your love has sustained me and given me the courage to finish. I thank my stepson Xchel Hernández-Zendejas for offering humor when needed, babysitting, and for being an all around great guy and big brother. And finally, but certainly, not least, I thank my son H-Tubtún Hernández-Elenes for his love, patience, and humor. I thank you so much for being a great movie theater partner and loving the theater and filmmaking. I'm sorry for all the times I said, "not now *mijo*. I'm working on my book" and sent you on your own to do other things. I am so proud of your generous heart and creativity.

Introduction

Reconstructing the Self

Constructing New Pedagogies

Transforming Borders: Chicana/o Popular Culture and Pedagogy seeks to contribute to the emerging discourse on Chicana feminist pedagogies, epistemologies, and ontology (see Villenas, Godinez, Delgado Bernal & Elenes 2006, Elenes, Gonzalez, Delgado Bernal & Villenas 2001), with the hope to adjoin them to the scholarship on transformative pedagogies.[1] Chicana feminist thought and symbolic creative works produce knowledge that not only take into account the multiple subject positions that Chicanas and Chicanos occupy in U.S. society (and the globe) but that are also capable of enabling the formation of democratic subjectivities (for Chicanas/os and non-Chicanas/os alike) that interrogate and thus work to transform social inequalities. The analysis and critique of unequal social conditions and the struggle to change these also produce knowledge, alternative pedagogies, and ways of being in the world. I propose to name these Chicana feminist forms of knowledge production and its communicative processes border/transformative pedagogies.

Border/transformative pedagogies involve cultural politics that incorporate as social practices the construction of knowledge capable of analyzing unequal social conditions, power relations, and conflicts over meaning that ensue from these struggles. They offer a cultural critique of the material conditions of subaltern communities and invoke politics of change to transform society in order to become truly democratic. Border/transformative pedagogies are concerned with the production of meaning and democratic practices both inside and outside of schooling, however, in this book, I am focusing on the pedagogical potential of cultural productions by Chicana artists, writers, and other educational actors (Villenas 2006a) that have re-imagined three main female figures in Mexican and Chicana/o history, culture, and popular

1

culture: La Llorona (The Weeping Woman), La Virgen de Guadalupe, and Malintzin/Malinche.

The historical representation of three Mexican and Chicano mythical figures, La Llorona, La Virgen de Guadalupe, and Malintzin/Malinche are paradigmatic of the conflicts over the meaning(s) of Mexican and Chicana/o culture. As such, they offer alternatives for pedagogical practices that tend to essentialize and reify Chicana/o cultural practices. Chicana feminist theorists, writers, and artists such as Norma Alarcón, Gloria Anzaldúa, Ana Castillo, Sandra Cisneros, Ester Hernández, Consuelo Jiménez Underwood, Irene Lara, Alma López, Yolanda López, Emma Pérez, Laura Pérez, Chela Sandoval, and Carla Trujillo, to name but a few, have engaged in this process and are respectively re-claiming and re-creating the meanings of these three figures. At the same time, they are offering theoretical frameworks that inspire new work on Chicana feminist thought, pedagogy, and epistemology. As many Chicana theorists and critics have argued, re-claiming and re-imagining these three figures as feminist has been central in the formation of Chicana feminist thought (Blake 2008, Flores 2000, Sandoval, A. 2008).The symbolism of each of these figures is quite different because each represents different notions of patriarchal constructions of Mexican and Chicana womanhood.

The genesis of these figures can be traced to the sixteenth century; however, we can find the roots of their development in the indigenous Mesoamerican cultures (Elenes 1999). La Llorona is a ghost-like figure who cries for her children, supposedly after committing infanticide as revenge. She appears dressed in white and frightens people, particularly men and children. She also represents social injustice. The Virgin of Guadalupe is the dark-skinned virgin who shortly after the Spanish Conquest appeared to a humble Indian speaking Nahualt. She symbolizes Mexican and Chicano secular nationalism, life, hope, and protection. Malintzin/Malinche is the Indian woman who served as Spanish Conqueror Hernán Cortés' interpreter, lover, and mother of one of his children. Like Eve, she symbolizes the woman traitor and is blamed for the Conquest of México. These three figures are paradigmatic of borderlands discourses because they cross different discourses such as nationalism, patriarchy, and feminism. Their meanings are constantly shifting and can simultaneously invoke different and contradictory ideologies.

While in dominant Mexican and Chicano nationalist narratives these figures have been constituted in ways that disempower women and define femininity in traditional patriarchal norms (the Virgin/Whore dichotomy), women have not passively accepted such official and constrictive representations. Women have not only *resisted* such patriarchal scripts, but they have been active participants in the production of the meanings of La Llorona, La Virgen de Guadalupe, and Malintzin/Malinche in a variety of cultural productions such as oral narratives, art, poetry, essays, short stories, plays, films, and theory. Demonstrating that the writing of narratives and counternarratives of the three figures is not always a response to patriarchal representations, from the outset women have been active participants in the formation of the myths. Through the writing and re-writing of the meaning of Chicana/o culture, women are reconstituting Chicana/o and Mexican subjectivity and identity. A significant characteristic of the formation of these particular myths is that they are central in the conflict over meanings that can be, and often are, paradoxical. The contradictory meanings played out in the multiplicity of texts, images, and popular culture representing La Llorona, La Virgen de Guadalupe, and Malintzin/Malinche attest to the instability of these cultural meanings. Oscillating back and forth between its colonial and pre-colonial "origin" and its modern nationalist function, the representation of the three figures in Mexican and Chicana/o popular culture can invoke discourses as disparate as colonial, anti-colonial, patriarchal, nationalist, and feminist. Often, these even occur in the same representation, making these figures paradoxical representations and excellent sources for the formation of border/transformative pedagogies.

Conflicts over meanings result from distinctive ideological positions within different social actors and the power to decide which of these ideologies has more currency. Indeed, these conflicts represent different views on values, morality, spirituality, and social justice.[2] The dominant patriarchal, religious, and nationalist discourses about La Llorona, La Virgen de Guadalupe, and Malintzin/Malinche have had the power to construct the misogynists' meanings of these three figures; Chicana feminists' re-imagination of the figures has destabilized such meanings. In doing so, Chicanas demonstrate that the meanings of these symbolic and mythological figures that have endured for five centuries are not stable. This is an important point for critical educational and pedagogical discourses because the re-imagination and reconstruction of these figures help to construct a progressive, alternative, and radical Chicana subjectivity. Certainly, understanding Chicanas' subjectivity as active agents in their lives who are capable of offering a critique and struggle against multiple forms of oppression is necessary for progressive educational practices. Importantly, as well, is that they also destabilize essentialist constructions of Chicana/o subjectivity that have produced stereotypical notions of Chicanas/os as manifested in rubrics like "deviant," "inferior," or just simply *a problem.* Concomitantly, these pedagogical efforts also destabilize the myth of U.S. homogeneity by placing at the center of the analysis particular forms of Chicana/o popular culture.

Transforming Borders is situated within the cultural studies movement and draws from a variety of theoretical frameworks, particularly Chicana feminist theory, Chicana/o cultural studies, education cultural studies, and critical and feminist pedagogies. The aim of the book is to contribute to these theoretical frameworks by offering new alternatives for understanding Chicana/o culture and educational practices broadly defined and develop transformative pedagogies that center Chicana critical practices.

CHICANA FEMINIST PEDAGOGIES, POPULAR CULTURE, AND CRITICAL PEDAGOGIES

The fields of critical and feminist pedagogies have contributed to our understanding of democratic and transformative educational practices. Influenced by the work of Paulo Freire, pedagogical discourses seek to transform educational practices and undermine the hierarchy between the knower and the known (Lather 1991); the distinctions between "high" and "low" culture; and the context in which educational actors (Villenas 2006a) construct knowledge. Transformative pedagogical approaches envision their own methods as capable of enabling the formation of subjectivities that are liberatory. With a concern over the interrelationship between social structures (e.g., the economy or popular culture) and education, transformative education is concerned with social justice. Such social transformation must cut across the boundaries of race, class, gender, sexuality, nation, and language. Moreover, these discursive practices understand how cultural politics can be implicated in the formation of oppressive structures and in counter-hegemonic politics.

However, critical and feminist pedagogies have not systematically taken into account Chicana/o cultural practices. This is a point we made in the introduction to anthology *Chicana/Latina education in everyday life* when we argued that "while there is much excellent work in the field of education on critical pedagogy and feminist pedagogy, these have failed to include in meaningful ways the lives of Chicana/Latinas and specifically Chicana/ Latina feminist perspectives as theoretical tools" (Villenas, et. al. 2006, 3, see also Elenes 2001). Our concern over the lack Chicana/Latina voices[3] within critical pedagogy is similar to the discussion of the limited participation of African American and indigenous voices within the field (Allen 2006, Grande 2004, Kincheloe 2007).[4] bell hooks helps illuminate on why this is the case, and it is worthwhile to quote her at length:

> The scholarly field of critical pedagogy and/or feminist pedagogy continues to be primarily a discourse engaged by white women and men. Freire, too, in conversation with me, as in much of his written work, has always acknowledged that he occupies the location of white maleness, particularly in this country. But

the work of various thinkers on radical pedagogy (I use this term to include critical and/or feminist perspectives) has in recent years truly included a recognition
of differences—those determined by class, race, sexual practice, nationality, and
so on. Yet this movement forward does not seem to coincide with any significant increase in black or other nonwhite voices joining discussions about radical
pedagogical practices. (hooks 1994, 9–10)

Transforming Borders seeks to add to the body of critical and feminist
scholarship by centering the border/transformative pedagogies invoked in
Chicanas' deconstruction and reconstruction of La Llorona, La Virgen de
Guadalupe, and Malintzin/Malinche.

The relationship between pedagogy and popular culture can be seen in the
ways in which the latter is implicated in the production of knowledge. That
is, it is important to analyze pedagogy in its function as a cultural practice
in or outside educational settings. I am particularly interested in exploring
the connection between the representation in popular culture of critiques of
unequal social conditions, particularly of Chicanas and Chicanos, as expressions of the struggles against forms of domination and social power with
education and the formation of subjectivities. This is not a study that offers
specific curricular practices of the proper application of folklore and popular
culture in the classroom, but an exploration of the meaning and battles over
the representations of cultural practices in the imaginary of "the people" and
the formation of knowledge.

The relationship between popular culture and pedagogy is well articulated
by Giroux and Simon (1989) when they propose that "any practice which
intentionally tries to influence the production of meaning is a pedagogical
practice. This includes aspects of parenting, film making, theological work,
social work, architecture, law, health work, advertising, and much else. These
are all forms of cultural work" (249). They define pedagogy this way:

> *Pedagogy* refers to a deliberate attempt to influence how and what knowledge
> and identities are produced within and among particular sets of social relations.
> It can be understood as a practice through which people are incited to acquire a
> particular 'moral character.' As both a political and practical activity, it attempts
> to influence the occurrence and qualities of experiences. When one practices
> pedagogy, one acts with the intent of creating experiences that will organize
> and disorganize a variety of understandings of our natural and social world in
> particular ways. What we are emphasizing here is that pedagogy is a concept
> which draws attention to the processes through which knowledge is produced.
> (Giroux and Simon 1989, 239)

Education does not only occur in officially sanctioned spaces such as
schools and universities. Families, museums, churches and other religious

organizations, and the media, for example, are institutions constituted around acculturation and socializing practices, and as such have and enact pedagogical functions. As Ruth Trinidad Galván (2001) asserts, "everyday ways of learning and teaching that arise around kitchen tables, on church steps, in local stores, and in family courtyards" are "pedagogical forms" (606) Moreover, within a Mexican and Latin American context the word *educación* signifies more than schooling; this term implies the teaching and learning of socializing practices that introduces the young to community and family traditions necessary for the survival of the community, culture, and family (Elenes et al. 2001). *Educación* offers particular pedagogical practices given that they seek to influence the formation of subjectivity, but are also the result of community knowledge that has been transmitted and continues to be constructed over generations. Villenas and Moreno (2001) refer to *educación* as a "dialectical form of education because it is inclusive of what is thought and learned in all social spaces, including home and community" (674). Of course, community knowledge can be oppressive and liberatory. Therefore, from a feminist perspective, it is important to recognize that the transmission and construction of community knowledge can be implicated in patriarchy and oppression and with alternative and resisting meanings. In other words, cultural memory is not about maintaining static knowledge that does not change over time and is transparently transmitted, it also has the possibility of constructing alternative meanings of ancient knowledge and can work in the service of transformative and libratory practices.

Precisely because the representation of La Llorona, La Virgen de Guadalupe, and Malintzin/Malinche are contested terrain over the definition of appropriate and inappropriate womanhood, they are deeply implicated in the formation of Chicana feminist subjectivities. Exploring how the three figures function in these processes is a way of linking pedagogy with women's everyday experiences. This is the case because popular culture is a terrain of possibilities where the conflict over the construction of meanings of social or cultural events, for example, is played out. As Giroux and Simon understand it, "it [popular culture] may contain aspects of a collective imagination which make it possible for people to surpass received knowledge and tradition. In this sense, popular culture may inform aspects of a counterdiscourse which help to organize struggles against relations of domination" (245). Popular culture, then, refers to more than cultural productions or products (i.e., films, toys), but also to beliefs and practices of particular social groups or cultures. For Mukerji and Schudson (1991), it

> refers to the beliefs and practices, and the objects through which they are orga-
> nized, that are widely shared among a population. This includes folk beliefs,

practices and objects rooted in local traditions, and mass beliefs, practices and objects generated in political and commercial centers. It includes elite cultural forms that have been popularized as well as popular forms that have been elevated to the museum tradition. (Mukrji and Schudson 1991, 3–4)

Cultural politics, as Chicana feminist scholars Romero & Habell-Pallán (2002) remind us, are important in the struggle to resist oppression and power. Specifically, they argue, Latina/o popular culture "can publicly image new ways of constructing racial, ethnic, gendered, and economic identities" (7). The re-imagining of the three figures enters into the contested terrain of popular culture and envisions new ways of being for Chicanas/os. The incorporation of Chicana/o popular culture in educational practices also alters contemporary cultural practices. Clearly, border/transformative pedagogies understand popular culture as beliefs and practices of Chicana/o communities as malleable and changing over time. I am particularly interested in the representation of the three figures in oral histories, historical chronicles, popular beliefs, legends, religious practices, and the like; as well as in cultural products such as art, murals, key chains, telephone cards, tee shirts, et cetera. These cultural productions are sites where the conflicts over the construction of Chicana/o subjectivity are represented. Bringing such cultural practices to a variety of educational settings and analyzing the conflicts over their meanings is a pedagogical practice where knowledge is produced, and alternative subjectivities can be explored.

CHICANA FEMINIST THEORIES

When La Llorona comes to me
vulnerability turns compassion
the haunting melody of her song
wanders as wounded and random
as her legend through the rivers
and alleyways of my existence.
La Llorona—madre perdida
who searches eternally
the phantom murderess
who has killed her children,
the rejected mother
of desgraciados.
All-giving and all-loving
the all-forgiving part of my being
that is negated.

La madre bendita
La mujer fuerte
La puta madre
La soldadera
La india amorosa
La mujer dolorosa:
But who can understand
that a woman sentences to death
the child she brings
into the world.
La Llorona, the feminine
haunts us if we fear her
comforts us if we understand.
La madre who grieves
at bringing children into a world
that might destroy them
and will kill them.
La Llorona, contradiction
of life and death,
who sacrificed her children
to haunt the weak
and comfort the living.
La mujer sagrada
the defiled woman.
She makes her peace
with those who respect vulnerability
and draw from her strength.

(Naomi Quiñones, *La Llorona*)[5]

In this poem, Quiñonez captures the complexities of the legend of La Llorona by deconstructing discourses that define her as a revengeful mother to an interpretation of the difficulty women face in order to take care of their children and survive in the world. Quiñones reclaims La Llorona as a mother and prototypical feminist and liberatory figure. In doing so, she is contributing to Chicana feminist intellectual traditions in which theory[6] is built on the analysis of cultural productions that deconstruct and re-imagine the representation of La Llorona, La Virgen de Guadalupe and Malinztin/ Malinche, (e.g., Anzaldúa 1997, Alarcón 1983, 1989, Chabram-Dernersesian 1992, Candelaria 1980, Castillo 1994, Pérez, E. 1999, Pérez, L. 2006, Trujillo 1998). As politically speaking subjects, Chicana feminists' refashioning of these cultural icons involve cultural politics that offer a challenge to the material conditions that Chicanas/os suffer within U.S. capitalism and are integral aspects of border/transformative pedagogies.

The cultural politics engaged by Chicanas are struggles against oppressive policies that limit Chicanas' educational opportunities and are the legacy of decades of struggle of farm workers, cannery workers, welfare rights activists, students, mothers, and professionals. In her analysis of Malintzin, Norma Alarcón (1983, 1989) characterizes these reconstructions as Chicanas' giving birth to themselves. Chicana feminist theorists are re-defining their "selves" in alternative forms from Anglo-American, Chicano, and white feminist discourses. Therefore, they have emphasized the need to reconstruct the myths that have defined what it means to be Chicana.

In general, feminist writing in the 70s tended to work under the "assumption of a unified subject organized oppositionally to men from the perspective of gender differences" (Alarcón 1989, 86). This tendency generated the notion that women's oppression could be explained universally. Feminist theorizing in the 80s, 90s, and at the beginning of the twenty-first century demonstrates that boundaries and differences among women exist in such a way that "experiences cannot be contained under the sign of a universal woman or women" (Alarcón 1989, 87). These writings are destabilizing any notion of a static, unified, and essential subject, including female subjects. Similarly, Chicana feminist theorists and cultural workers' deconstruction of these figures and the analysis of alternative representations are unsettling to any illusion of an essential and universal Chicana/o subject. Therefore, for Alarcón, "it is through a revision of tradition that self and culture can be radically reenvisioned and reinvented" (71). Border/transformative pedagogies are intrinsically implicated in this process of renewal and re-birth. As Aida Hurtado (1989) writes, "socially stigmatized groups have reclaimed their history by taking previously denigrated characteristics and turning them into positive affirmation of self" (846). According to Chabram-Dernersesian, Chicana feminist cultural politics (1993) "altered the subject position of Chicanas in cultural productions, from distortion and/or censure to self-awareness and definition" (42). La Llorona, La Virgen de Guadalupe, and Malintzin/Malinche are powerful symbols that represent traditional patriarchal notions of appropriate and inappropriate womanhood.

The division of female identity into the virgin-whore dichotomy, that well-known, over-determined, and oversimplified yet powerful tool of patriarchy, is invoked in nationalist and Catholic scripts (Lara 2008a) on the three figures. For Anzaldúa, the true identity of each of these figures (or mothers, as she calls them) has been subverted for patriarchal purposes: Guadalupe, to makes us docile, La Chingada (Malinche), to make us ashamed; and La Llorona, to make us long-suffering people. Obscuring the true identities of these figures encourages the virgin/whore dichotomy (Anzaldúa 1987). As Chicana feminist theorist Norma Alarcón (1989) has well established, Guadalupe and Malinche are functions of each other (and so is Llorona). Their function in patriarchal representations exemplifies the division of women into "good" and "bad." In these re-interpretations, Chicanas go even beyond undoing these false dichotomies.

The radical politics invoked by Chicanas' reconceptualization is a result of the reality that for many, their creativity and inventiveness is in direct conflict with traditional female function (Alarcón 1989). Through these re-conceptualizations, Mexican American women are constructing an identity that is always in flux and invoking a political analysis that looks beyond the dual prescriptive roles of wife/mother, virgin/whore. *Las mujeres* are constructing subject positions that offer alternatives to the prescribed roles assigned by white dominant society, Chicano nationalism, or the white feminist movement, refashioning a political subject that contests such positions that keep her in the fields, assembly line, kitchen, or day care centers; or that views her as inevitable and passive "victim" of her male counterpart's *machismo*. As such, Chicanas become speaking subjects with blaring voices. Angie Chabram-Dernersesian writes, "The Mujer story is prefaced by another narrative of struggle in which we (brown people) challenge the you of dominant discourse in an effort to alter the relations of cultural production with alternative ethnic subjects" (1992, 92).

Chicana writers are employing female-speaking subjects who are exploring the subjectivity of women, and "often their writing takes as its point of departure 'woman's' over-determined signification as future wives/mothers in relation to the 'symbolic contract' within which women may have a voice on the condition that they speak as mothers" (Alarcón 1996, 220). Alarcón uses Kristeva's notion of "symbolic contract" to explain the ways in which womanhood is defined. Historically, Mexican and Chicano cultures have enacted and "enforced" such a "symbolic contract" by representing women in the dichotomous pattern of "good" vs. "bad," the virgin/whore dichotomy imaged in the three mythical figures. Mónica Russel y Rodríguez (1997) in her ethnographic study of Chicanas and domestic violence, suggests that "the ideological features used against Chicanas in abusive relationships are the very same symbolic forces used to construct all Chicanas as 'good' or 'bad'" (104). Demonstrating the violent, extreme consequences of such restrictive definitions of womanhood, Russel y Rodríguez argues that Chicanas who are not in abusive relationships and fail to challenge such conventions become unwittingly complicit in the abusive structure (104). As Norma Alarcón reminds us, "The female-speaking subject that would want to speak from a different position than that of a mother, or future wife/mother, is thrown into a crisis of meaning that begins with her own gendered personal identity and its relational position with others" (221). Paradoxically, Alarcón adds, this crisis of meaning can exist even for women who do not wish to speak other than as mothers/wives.

Chicana feminists, then, have not only removed themselves from the simplistic representation of virgin/whore and refused to play by those outmoded, essentialist, patriarchal rules, but in so doing they have constructed a particular form of feminist politics that subverts and undermines these representations. In this process, Chicanas' reclaim their indigenous meanings and spirituality.

With this development in mind, I propose that the subversions, undermining, and analysis and praxis that re-recreate La Llorona, La Virgen de Guadalupe, and Malintzin/Malinche as paradigmatic feminist figures are border/transformative pedagogies. While the patriarchal pedagogy invoked in the virgin/whore dichotomy dictates or presents proper notions of Chicana womanhood, the border/transformative pedagogies invoked in the re-constructions and counter-hegemonic practices present alternative Chicana subjectivities that are transgressive. Patriarchal nationalists' constructions of the three figures are, needless to say, pedagogies of passive sexuality and didactic scripts of appropriate female behavior. These are lessons about the consequences for women as individuals (La Llorona) and for the community (Malintzin/Malinche) when women transgress sexual mores; lessons that offer an adequate "role model" of appropriate behavior in the self-denied all loving mother (La Virgen de Guadalupe). The pedagogical practices involved in Chicanas' re-imagining La Llorona, La Virgen de Guadalupe, and Malinztin/Malinche are also about sexuality, but of transgressive sexualities and desire, and spirituality.

Border/transformative pedagogical practices are, as well, about Chicanas as speaking subjects with agency and creativity who are involved in political struggles against the subjugation of women based on sexual, race, class, and gender oppression. As such, these pedagogical practices are (or offer the possibility of enacting) democratic practices that seek to not only undo such oversimplified and over-determined definitions of womanhood, but that offer a more complex understanding of Chicana subjectivity. Given that La Llorona, La Virgen de Guadalupe, and Malintzin/Malinche are represented in a variety of historical, philosophical, literary, and popular culture texts, feminist re-constructions are also pedagogical practices that demonstrate how knowledge is constructed, contingent, and ideologically committed. These re-imaginings of La Llorona, La Virgen de Guadalupe, and Malintzin/Malinche are constructed in the interstitial spaces Chicana/o theorists have come to name the borderlands.

BORDERLANDS THEORIES AND CRITICAL PEDAGOGY

Border/transformative pedagogies benefit from borderland theories. As I have argued elsewhere (1997), the production and re-production of the discourse of the borderlands speaks a language of fluidity, migration, postcolonialism, and displacement: of subaltern identities. The borderland is the discourse of people who live between different worlds. It speaks against dualism, over-simplification, and essentialism. It is a discourse, a language, which explains the social conditions of subjects with hybrid identities. The contemporary conceptualization of borderlands speaks of the in-between cultural, geo-political, and identity spaces that displaced peoples "occupy." These discourses talk of movements of people back and forth between center and periphery, of the crossing and transgressing of borders. The discourses on La Llorona, La Virgen de Guadalupe, and Malintzin/Malinche have historically crossed national and disciplinary boundaries. Not only do the Borderlands represent the breaking of traditional boundaries between nations, but also of race, class, gender, and sexuality.

Chicanas and Chicanos have lived this peculiar in-betweenness of culture, language, and borders since the U.S. annexed México's northern territories in the mid-nineteenth century. It is not surprising, then, that scholars in disciplines as varied as cultural studies, critical pedagogy, feminism, and Chicana/o studies have adopted the discourse of the Borderlands, which Emma Pérez (1999) proposes is a cohesive theoretical lynchpin (see Villenas & Foley 2002).

Yet, the conceptualization of Borderlands is not new. The Eurocentric historian Herbert Eugene Bolton identified Borderlands as the geographical area of the U.S. conquered by the Spanish. Throughout the twentieth century, significant production of scholarship on the historical and socio-economic conditions of the México-U.S border has appeared (e.g., Fernández-Kelly 1983, Martínez 1994, Peña, M. 2007, Ross 1978, Ruiz & Tiano 1991, Sadowski-Smith 2002, Segura & Zavella 2007, Mattingly & Hansen 2006). Why, then, did the conceptualization of the borderlands gain so much currency in the last decades of the twentieth century? What are the geo-political circumstances and intellectual developments that motivate or inform the production of Borderlands discourses? *Transforming Borders* argues that contemporary conceptualizations of Borderlands results from postcolonial geo-political conditions, such as globalization, that "obligate" the movement of people from their place of "origin" to the "advanced" capitalist countries. These movements de-homogenize what were once considered homogeneous societies. Borderlands also are characteristic of postmodernity's advanced capitalism and flexible construction of identities. Finally, these theories result from intellectual "innovations" such as feminist theory, ethnic studies, postmodernism, and post-structuralism. Its popularity is due precisely to its ability to offer a flexible language and forms of conceptualization that articulate the complexities of so-called identity politics (race, class, gender, and sexuality) in the late twentieth and early twenty-first century in the U.S., without reifying such dynamics. Any discourse that seeks to capture these complexities will find it intriguing and productive to apply this metaphor.

The contemporary conceptualization of Borderlands owes much of its production to the work of Chicana and Chicano scholars. Starting with the publication of Gloria Anzaldúa's (1987) *Borderlands/La Frontera*[7] and Renato Rosaldo's (1989) *Culture and Truth,* the border as metaphor has appeared in many disciplines. In Chicana/o Cultural Studies, its influence is demonstrated with publications such as Ramón Saldívar's *Chicano Narrative* (1990) and *The Borderlands of Culture* (2006); Héctor Calderón and José David Saldívar's *Criticism in the Borderlands* (1991); Carl Gutiérrez-Jones'*Rethinking the Borderlands* (1995); José David Saldívar's *Border Matters* (1997); Alicia Gaspar de Alba's *Chicano Art* (1998); Arturo Aldama (2001) *Disrupting Savagism;* and Rosa Linda Fregoso (2003) *MeXicana Encounters: The Making of Social Identity on the Borderlands.* In addition to Gloria Anzaldúa's and Alicia Gaspar de Alba's work, Chicana feminist theorists and writers have contributed and applied this conceptualization as well, particularly in the work of Norma Alarcón, Corderlia Candelaria, Ana Castillo, and Sandra Cisneros.[8]

Within the field of education, progressive Chicana/o scholars have applied the conceptualization of the border and borderlands to offer new insights to the theorization of pedagogies and epistemologies (e.g., Bejarano 2005, Cline & Necochea 2006, Delgado Bernal 2006, Delgado Bernal, Elenes, Godinez & Villenas 2006, Elenes 1997, 2001, 2006, González, N. 2001, Romo & Chavez 2006, Pendleton Jiménez 2006, Villenas 2006b). Similarly, as the aforementioned scholars in cultural studies, education scholars have looked at the metaphors of crossing borders that are depicted in Chicana/o cultural theory, aesthetics, and popular culture. For education scholars, these metaphors do not only refer to the México-U.S. border, but of crossing borders along institutional (schools, the media, government), racial, gender, class, and sexual orientation lines. "As members of groups that simultaneously are located inside and outside social structures, including educational institutions, and historically marked by way of race, ethnicity, socio-economic status, language, and oftentimes citizenship, Chicanas/os and Latinas/os must navigate the contradictions of living between two or more worlds" (Elenes & Delgado Bernal, p. 73).

Critical pedagogy from the late 80s to mid 90s adopted the concept of the border, particularly in the work of Henry Giroux and Peter McLaren. A cursory examination of titles published between 1992 and 1995 demonstrates the contributions of Borderlands theory to educational theory and pedagogy. Books such as, Giroux's *Border Crossings* (1992); Giroux and McLaren's collection *Between Borders* (1992), McLaren's *Critical Pedagogy and Predatory Culture* (1995); bell hooks' *Teaching to Transgress* (1994), as well as Antonia Darder's work are some of the most significant. There is, then, an interrelationship between Chicana/o Borderlands and critical pedagogy's construction of border pedagogy. Both apply the concept as a metaphor, and both rely on each other to advance their respective theories. However, this interrelationship also raises the problematic of appropriation and erasure of difference. Of particular concern for this study is the lack of attention on the part of critical and feminist pedagogical scholars—except for a marginal representation of Gloria Anzaldúa's work—of the scholarship and writings produced by Chicana feminists. While Giroux and McLaren's work offers important insights into the workings of cultural studies, popular culture, and pedagogy, their analysis is limited in terms of Chicana/o popular culture and cultural productions; resulting in the apartheid of knowledge of transformative pedagogies (Sandoval 2000).

BORDER/TRANSFORMATIVE PEDAGOGIES AND RELATIONAL THEORY OF DIFFERENCE

Any pedagogical practice that centralizes Chicana/o culture and subjectivities cuts across race, class, gender, and sexual orientation; thus the border/transformative pedagogies I am proposing intervene through the boundaries of critical/feminist/multicultural/queer pedagogy. Because it centers on Chicana/o cultural practices and subjectivities, it recognizes that this analysis cannot be accomplished by isolating any single axis of analysis. Doing so contributes to the sexist, heterosexist, racist, and classist practices of conservative educational discourses, or even the sexist and homophobic practices, albeit liberatory, of cultural nationalism. This conceptualization is similar to Hernández's feminist transformative pedagogy, which "addresses difference in all its possibilities within power relations in a constant process of contestation against concrete oppressive practices" (1997, 19).

Border/transformative pedagogies propose that to adequately account for multiple subject positions encountered in contemporary classrooms and cultural practices, a relational theory of difference is necessary (Yarbro-Bejarano 1999). This relational theory of difference examines "the formation of identity in the dynamic interpenetration of gender, race, sexuality, class and nation" (Yarbro-Bejarano 1999, 340). Similarly, Chandra Talpade Mohanty argues that gender and race are relational terms, thus "to define feminism in purely gendered terms assumes that our consciousness of being 'women' has nothing to do with race, class, nation, or sexuality, just with gender" (Mohanty 1991, 12). Yet, the impetus to establish a primary source of oppression continues as, for example, McLaren's "revolutionary pedagogy" (2000, 2006) where he argues that class should be a primary focus of analysis.[9]

Even though by most accounts pedagogical discourses follow some form of understanding of difference, they do so in relation to a particular axis of analysis or subjectivity. While at this juncture most of these discourses would not endorse limiting its practices on a single axis, such as race or gender, for example, or to focus their pedagogical efforts to one particular subject position (i.e., gender), there is still a limiting integration of race, class, gender, and sexuality, and the outcome can be the apartheid of knowledge (Sandoval 2000). Indeed, even McLaren recognizes the need for the race, class, and gender "triptych" (2006, 87) although he is critical of it. Nevertheless, differences tend to be recognized in relation to dominant subjectivities in ways that privilege is left under-theorized. I will return to this point in chapter 6.

The difficulty with many pedagogical discourses is not necessarily that they have failed to take into account differences of race, class, gender, and sexuality. The issue resides in the under-theorization of historically unmarked categories such as "white," "male," "heterosexual," and "middle class" (Allen 2006). What is necessary is to recognize the unmarked categories as relational as well (e.g., "the heterosexual coded spaces of women's studies").[10] In Yvonne Yarbro-Bejarano's words, this means that "the theory is also relational within each binary set, for example, a man lives his masculinity through his cultural, sexual and class identifications, but also in relation to a certain construction of femininity which for the man is essential to his manhood" (430). Democratic pedagogical discourses need to theorize all subject positions, dominant and subaltern, and mark their registers. In doing so, it is indispensable to decenter the hegemony of the white, middle class, heterosexual, male subject as normative. It is necessary, as well, to recognize the multiple marginalities of people of color and those with hybrid identities.

Border/transformative pedagogies recognize that "Chicanas are inhabitants of the borderlands—the lands on the U.S. Mexican border, as well as the crossroads between cultures. They, themselves, inhabit multiple spaces between cultures, ethnicities, genders, and classes. They are outsiders and insiders; they inhabit the center and the margin; they are self and other; they are subject and object" (Martínez 1996, 116). It is precisely this marginal existence, what Saldívar calls a liminal condition, of Chicanas/os in institutional settings such as schools, media, and cultural centers that have marginalized them. For Chicanas/os, presence in such institutions is a paradoxical state of "belonging" and "not-belonging." Border/transformative pedagogies seek to remap pedagogical discourses by recognizing that the liminal characteristics of Chicanas/os are paradigmatic of the subject positions of people of color in the U.S. The language of the borderlands and concepts such as mestiza consciousness (Anzladúa 1987), new tribalism (Anzladúa 2002), third space feminism (Pérez, E. 1999) and differential consciousness

(Sandoval, C. 2000) with its flexible notion of identity, help decenter the dominant subject. Whether dealing with classroom or cultural practices, the multicultural realities of the U.S. attest to the need to recognize the multiple levels of difference that we encounter in any variety of pedagogical practices. For the most part, however, pedagogical discourses have not discussed how Chicanas/os' hybrid identities affect classroom or cultural practices. Border/transformative pedagogies must take into consideration the fluidity and multiplicity of subject positions encountered within its praxis.

Transforming Borders contributes to such a progressive and democratic educational vision and pedagogical practices by centralizing Chicana/o cultural productions that address border/hybrid identities. The narratives, cultural productions, artistic creations, oral histories, legends, et cetera representing various meanings of La Llorona, La Virgen de Guadalupe, and Malintzin/Malinche attest to the multiple histories, experiences, and standpoints of Chicanas and Chicanos. Because these representations are informed by (and at the same time inform) a variety of ideological positions, they are examples of the ways in which cultural productions can offer spaces for a critical analysis of the relationship between ideology and power.

In this sense, border/transformative pedagogy is concerned with the construction of knowledge as a cultural practice in which educational actors actively participate. This can be accomplished by setting up strategies that deconstruct, for example, the representation, construction, and re-construction of La Llorona, La Virgen de Guadalupe, and Malintzin/Malinche in relation to the construction of knowledge and the formation of subjectivities. What is important, then, is to explore the multiple meanings and struggles over the representations of cultural practices that deal with the formation of Mexican and Chicana/o cultural identities, and the sites of the struggles over these multiple meanings. The representation of these figures in the Mexican and Chicana/o imaginary are examples of how these struggles operate. This flexible understanding of knowledge can help students, teachers, cultural workers, and other educational actors demystify the production of knowledge. Viewing the struggles over cultural meanings is a way to highlight how culture is flexible and avoids the pitfalls of reifying culture and establishing prescriptive curricular and pedagogical practices.

The first two chapters of this book offer historical and theoretical overview of border/borderlands scholarship and the feminist conceptualizations that serve as the theoretical foundations for border/transformative pedagogies. Chapters 3, 4, and 5 deal specifically with each one of the figures; in each of these chapters I offer a genealogy of sorts of the historical and cultural significance of each of the figures. This helps to historically situate the myths and explain how the popular (often times) patriarchal meanings developed, and in doing so be able to situate Chicana feminist re-imaginings of La Llorona, La Virgen de Guadalupe, and Malintzin/Malinche. The concluding chapter proposes a new vision for transformative pedagogies.

Chapter 1, "From the Historical Borderlands to *Borderlands/La Frontera:* Border Studies and Borderlands Theorizing," offers a historical overview of the conceptualization of borderlands. To accomplish this, I clarify the distinction between border studies, the historical notion of the borderlands as a geopolitical space, and borderlands as a metaphor. I offer an historical overview of the borderlands school in U.S. history and how it influenced our understanding of the Southwest and Mexican American and Native American subordination. I then move to explain the significance of the México-U.S. border region and contemporary immigration debates. Finally, I offer an overview of Anzaldúa's borderlands, nepantla, and new tribalism.

Chapter 2, "Borderland Epistemologies, Subjectivity, and Feminism: Toward Border/Transformative Pedagogies," outlines Anzaldúa's philosophy and identifies three areas of her thought that are the foundations of border/transformative pedagogies. These three areas are *conocimiento*/epistemology, borderland subjectivities, and third space feminism. Anzaldúa's conceptualizations are non-binary and are contrasted with Western-based epistemologies. I outline the foundations of indigenous epistemologies, spirituality, borderland epistemologies, and third space feminism. I end the chapter by delineating the contours of border/transformative pedagogies.

Chapter 3, "La Llorona: Decolonial and Anti-Patriarchal Cultural Politics," offers a critical reading of oral histories documented in Arizona and New Mexico. In order to do so, I first provide a history of the Nahua and Western bases of La Llorona. I identify three aspects of the legend that signal its potential feminist readings: the scream, loss of children, and re-birth. I use Chicana feminist short stories such as Sandra Cisneros "Woman Hollering Creek" and Helena María Viramontes "The Cariboo Café" as a backdrop for my analysis of the oral histories. I conclude the chapter showing how the contradictory meanings of La Llorona are examples of border/transformative pedagogies.

Chapter 4, "The Virgin de Guadalupe: Spirituality, Desire, Consumption, and Transformation," applies transnational feminist theory to examine the process of commodification the image of La Virgen de Guadalupe has gone through. I contrast this with the work of Chicana artists, such as Yolanda López, Consuelo Jiménez Underwood, re-imagining Guadalupe as a labor activist and as a symbol for immigrant rights. Alma López and Ester Hernández focus on women's desire, agency, and spirituality. The chapter ends by showing how these expressions find voice in spiritual activism.

Chapter 5, "Malintzin/Marina/Malinche: Embodying History/Reclaiming our Voice," analyzes the representation and construction of *Malintzin/Malinche* in key historical texts that chronicle the Spanish conquest of Mexico. I offer a genealogy of sorts of the development of the trope of treachery, using as an example an analysis of the novel *Xicótencalt*. Using as a theoretical framework how gender ideologies operate in the formation of the trope of treachery, I analyze Chicana feminists' theorist re-imagining of Malintzin's life from a non-binary perspective and offer alternative readings that relate sexuality and survival. The border/transformative pedagogies enacted by Chicanas show how, through a recognition of Malintzin's desires and her survival strategies, we can develop borderland subjectivities through which we can reclaim Chicana voices.

The last and concluding chapter, "Re-Mapping Transformative Pedagogies: New Tribalism and Social Justice," uses the examples provided by border/transformative pedagogies to re-think notions of white privilege, universalization, and localized knowledges. Using the concept of apartheid of knowledge, I propose to apply Anzaldúa's notion of new tribalism to work along the axis of difference and privilege that will permit transformative pedagogies' discourses to work on a social justice agenda for all.

NOTES

1. Transformative pedagogies, including critical, feminist, queer, multicultural projects, are concerned with educational practices that seek to create social change free of inequality.

2. I refuse to concede the territory over values and morality to the religious right and to Catholic Church dogma. Values and morality are the basis by which individuals and societies make decisions on how to live life in harmony with the environment and with different individuals and social groups. As such, I believe that struggles for social justice such as feminism, civil rights, workers rights are based on morality and spirituality.

3. Some of the Chicana/Latina/o scholars' contributors to the field include Cynthia Bejarano, Cindy Cruz, Antonia Darder, Dolores Delgado Bernal, C. Alejandra Elenes, Francisca González, Adriana Hernández, Enrique Murillo, Jr., Karleen Pendleton Jiménez, Marcos Pizarro, Rudy Torres, Ruth Trinidad Galván, Henry Trueba, and Sofia Villenas, to name but a few.

4. Respectively, Allen and Kincheloe show concern over the lack of participation of African American and Indigenous scholars in the critical pedagogy field. Interestingly, they both believe that Latinos are well represented in the field; however, it is not clear who they are referring to. Allen offers a critique of Darder and Torres's contribution to the anthology *Critical Pedagogy Reader,* but Kincheloe does not

make any specific reference to Latinos or Chicanos. Neither cites any of the work by Chicana feminist pedagogy scholars, therefore, it is not clear who these Latino scholars are.

5. Quoted with permission from the author.

6. This section does not intend to provide an overview of Chicana feminist discourses and theoretical positions. Rather, I am contextualizing for this book the ways in which an aspect of Chicana feminist theorizing has resulted from the exegetical projects that look at Chicana cultural workers' re-imagining of the figures and how these re-constructions serve as the basis for the development of border/transformative pedagogies.

7. In the second edition of *Borderlands,* Gloria Anzaldúa makes it clear that she does not claim the invention of the concept of borderlands.

8. Other works on border that merit attention, most notably Jacques Derrida's work on borders, deal mostly with literary borders. Although his work precedes some Chicana/o writings, he did not influence either Chicana/o borderlands work or critical pedagogy. Emily Hick's work is also worth mentioning here. Her work has been influential in some of the works cited in this book; she is included in the discussion on borderlands in chapter 1.

9. McLaren vehemently argues that "revolutionary critical pedagogy" insists on "understanding social life from the standpoint of the strategic centrality of class and class struggle." Peter McClaren "Some reflections on critical pedagogy in the age of global empire," in *Reinventing critical pedagogy: Widening the circle of anti-oppression education,* eds. César Augusto Rossatto, Ricky Lee Allen, and Marc Pruyn (79–98) (Lanham: Rowmand & Littlefield, 2006).

10. For some examples on educational scholarship on the construction of whiteness see Michelle Fine, et. al. eds. *Off White: Readings on Race, Power, and Society* (New York: Routledge, 1997); Leslie Roman "White is a Color! White Defensiveness, Postmodernism, and Anti-Racist Pedagogy" in *Race, Identity and Representation in Education,* eds. Cameron McCarthy and Warren Crichlow (New York: Routledge, 1993),71–88; Peter McLaren, *Revolutionary Multiculturalism* (Boulder: Westview Press, 1997).

Chapter 1

From the Historical Borderlands to Borderlands/La Frontera

Border Studies and Borderland Theorization

> From borderlands to border texts, border conflict and border crossings to border writing, border pedagogy, and border feminism, the concept of "border" enjoys wide currency as a "paradigm of transcultural experience."
>
> Rosa Linda Fregoso (1993, 65)

The ubiquitousness of the borderlands during the waning decades of the twentieth century is captured in the above epigraph from Rosa Linda Fregoso. After the publication of Gloria Anzaldúa's *Borderlands/La Frontera* in 1987, and Renato Rosaldo's *Culture and Truth* in 1989, scholars in a variety of fields, including education, adopted the metaphorical conceptualization of the borderlands (Alvarez, Jr. 1995, Elenes 1997, 2006, Elenes and Delgado Bernal 2010, Keating 2005, Saldívar-Hull 2000). Why did the discourses of the borderlands gain such currency in the late twentieth century? Was it because these discourses were helpful in advancing theories that explained particular social phenomena? Or was it something that scholars embraced because it was "in style?" Chon Noriega, in a one page editor's introduction to the fall 1999 issue of *Aztlán*, literally (and humorously) illustrates this concern by repeating the word "millennium" 180 times, dividing the words into five columns and each making three blocks of text. On the bottom of the page he writes, "I guess they're done with the 'Border Crossing' craze, right?" (vii). Noriega does not tell us who "they" are; he leaves that up to the interpretation of his readers. But by ending the statement with an interrogative, he raises the possibility that whoever "they" are, "they" are not done with the border crossing; hinting to the relevancy of borderlands theories.

As many Chicana/o scholars and cultural workers have proposed, Chicanas/
os are in a continuous process of border crossing. Perhaps we can suggest
that it is mainstream scholars who can freely and without challenge pick and
choose when to cross borders, and are done with the "border-crossing craze."
This is not the case for many Chicanas/os who due to a history of colonialism
and U.S. expansionism—as the old saying goes—"did not originally cross the
border, but the border crossed them." The Chicana/o subject does not always
have the privilege of deciding whether to cross a border or not. It seems to
me that at the historical juncture at the end and beginning of the millennium, Chicana/os have no choice but to continue crossing borders and living
in the borderlands. Chicana/os will keep on writing, conceptualizing, and co-
existing in the borderlands because of the existence of the physical México-
U.S. border, as demonstrated in works published in the first decade of the
twenty-first century by scholars such as Cynthia Bejarano, Norma González,
Sonia Saldívar-Hull, Ramón Saldívar, Rosa Linda Fregoso, and myself to
name but a few. At the same time, we must continue to contend with ideologies that place peoples of Mexican descent as outsiders of dominant society.
It is precisely this "outsider within" (Collins 1998) status that created the
tension between living with concrete and metaphorical borderlands. As such,
the metaphorical conceptualizations of the borderlands are paradigmatic of
our condition of constantly crossing borders and of being between one, two,
three, or more cultures or social signifiers. The borderlands, I propose, are
empirical, ontological, and epistemological.

The concept of the borderlands is not new, in reality this is an area of scholarship that has existed throughout the twentieth century. What is different is how
the borderlands have been reconceptualized through the work of Chicana/o
cultural studies scholars, opening possibilities for the formation of border cultural politics that are capable of studying the concrete material border region
and the symbolic borderlands. In this chapter, I conceptualize the historical
development of the concept of the borderlands from its earliest formations as
a geopolitical and historical symbol in early twentieth century, to its recent
readoption as a symbolic and metaphorical signifier. I argue that it is in its
symbolic meaning that the borderlands influenced pedagogical discourse at the
end of the twentieth century, and continues to inform the conceptualization of
Chicana feminist pedagogies in the twenty-first century. Moreover, the struggles for immigrant rights and comprehensive immigration reform illustrate the
significance of the border and the borderlands for Chicanos/as and *mexicanas/
os*. If anything, the resurgence in nation-wide activism for a humane immigration reform and social justice in light of the passage in Arizona of Senate Bill
1070 (below I explain the scope of this legislation) demonstrate the significance
of the México-U.S. border for people of Mexican descent.

Tracing the "origins" of the concept borderlands is a complex task because there are multiple uses of the word and it spans many different discourses and disciplines.[1] In the first part of this chapter I trace the way in which the concept was developed in "Borderlands history."[2] Then, I look into the importance of the U.S.-México border region in the formation of the multiplicity of identity registers that are used to name people of Mexican and Latina/o descent in the U.S. Even though the focus of the book and of this chapter is on the metaphorical conceptualization of the borderlands, this idea would not have been possible if the border did not exist. After exploring the importance of the border region, I turn to the key analysis of the significance of Gloria Anzaldúa's conceptualization of the borderlands, nepantla, and new tribalism and their influence in borderland epistemologies.

HISTORICAL BORDERLANDS

The first conceptualization of the borderlands comes from the field of history. De León (1989) writes that there is a disagreement over what Borderlands history embraces, what regions it includes, and what time frame. For the most part, historians refer to the borderlands as the territory in the Continental U.S. that was part of the Spanish colonies (most of the current U.S. Southwest region and parts of the West, Louisiana, and Florida. The Spanish Colonial time frame starts in the fifteenth century and ends at the beginning of the nineteenth century). In general, as Oscar J. Martínez (1994) writes, borderlands are regions adjacent to a border (5). Thus, today most of us tend to think of the borderlands as the region along the México-U.S. border. Herbert Eugene Bolton, considered the father of borderlands history (De León 1989), defined the borderlands as "the regions between Florida and California, now belonging to the United States, over which Spain held sway for centuries" (quoted in Weber 1991, xiii). For Chicanas and Chicanos, then, the Borderlands are an important region because they encompass territory that was either part of or is near México.

Albert L. Hurtado (1995) believes that Constance Lindsay Skinner coined the term borderlands,[3] although credit is given to Bolton. From the nineteenth century to early twentieth century U.S. historians paid little attention to the U.S. southwestern region. When Herbert E. Bolton in the early twentieth century proposed that the study of the borderlands was necessary for U.S. history, he was hoping to transform the field. For as early as 1911 Bolton argued that it was important to study the Spanish possessions in what is now the U.S. because there was plenty of Spanish influence in North America (Bolton 1911/1964). Moreover, Bolton maintained that the neglect of the Spanish period in the West resulted from the East Coast bias in American history and the English colonialist perspective. Gerald E. Poyo and Gilberto M. Hinojosa (1988) argue that various U.S. scholars answered Bolton's challenge to study Borderlands history and move beyond the Eastern bias in U.S. history. Thus, the research and teaching of scholars such as Carlos E. Castañeda, Charles W. Hackett, Charles E. Chapman, and others, led to the development of a "formal field of study known as the Spanish Borderlands, which they hoped would be included in United States history" (Poyo and Hinojosa 1988, 396). In spite of Bolton and his disciples' work and place among notable U.S. historians, the borderlands school never gained major prominence in U.S. history textbooks and as a field of study. Rather, borderlands history maintained a marginal existence within history departments, some calling it regional history (Poyo and Hinojosa 1988), until its demise in the 1960s (except the work of Weber and Limerick) (De León 1989).

Scholars of Chicana/o and Native American studies agree that there are serious consequences about the way Bolton's borderlands school influenced the construction of knowledge about the U.S. southwest and "American" identity. Bolton's Eurocentric bias is reflected in his writings and contributes to the subordination of Mexican Americans and Native Americans. Even though his studies help rethink basic precepts of American history and open a field of study for understanding the importance of the borderlands region to the formation of not only U.S. history, but also to a more expansive notion of "American" identity, such reconceptualizations did not decentralize the hegemony of Eurocentric thought. Rather, they strengthened it.

The borderlands not only represent a significant geo-political region but also a place where particular notions of American culture and ideology are represented and enacted. The history of the borderlands region tells a story of how ideologies of racial superiority informed European and American expansionism, and that story continues to affect race relations in the U.S. Inherent in the way in which most borderlands histories have been written—in addition to Hollywood's romantic representation of the Cowboy and of rugged individualists who tamed the Wild West—is how the ideal of Manifest Destiny is viewed as a "natural" outcome. Bolton's rhetoric softens the impact that the Westward expansion and the U.S.-Mexican war had on Native Americans and Mexicans when he argues that the borderlands were a place where two European cultures met and fused. Chicana historian Deena González (1999) argues that the language used by historians reveals much about their viewpoints. Similarly, Antonia Castañeda (1990) asserts that historians reflect the gender, race, and class ideologies of their times. Therefore, Bolton's choice of words clearly situates his argument as one that erases Native and Mexican peoples' histories and influence on the borderlands (Bolton 1930/1991). Bolton also proposed that the Borderlands were a "zone of contact": "the scene of a long series of conflicts, ending in territorial transfers" (41). His historical description naturalizes the clash between Anglo Americans, Mexicans, and Native Americans by explaining "If these borderlands have left some unpleasant memories between two peoples, they are partly offset by the bonds of a common inheritance" (41). With this statement, Bolton not only ignores the high price Mexicans and Native Americans paid for this "common bond" but also articulates a normalization of Americanism and assimilation by presenting these concepts as the basis of the "common bond."

Bolton's work is marred by the belief in the superiority of the English over the Spanish (even though he expresses a somewhat romantic view of Spanish explorers) and Anglo-American industriousness over Mexicans' laziness (Castañeda 1990). In *The Spanish Borderlands,* Bolton adjoins his voice to the dehumanization of Native Americans by employing the signifier "savages" throughout his text. As Arturo Aldama (2001) documents, the word "savage" was used by European colonial powers to contrast Native peoples with the "civilized" European and later American. Thus, with such adjectives Bolton reproduces the hegemony of the perceived superiority of Europeans and, in the process marks indigenous peoples as "inferior others." Bolton's "pro-Spanish biases" (De León 1989) limited his understanding of Mexicans' role in the social, economic, and political development of the U.S. Southwest. Indeed, in his work, Bolton gives a cursory examination to the Mexican period of the region (1821–1848). As A. L. Hurtado (1995) proposes, "In combating the anti-Catholic and Anglophilic views of history that were common to his time, Bolton produced an Hispanophilic record of heroicized soldiers and missionaries who are out of place in our age. He emphasized the positive and lasting accomplishments of Spain, but ignored the terrible costs of European conquest for American Indians and Africans" (162). In *The Spanish Borderlands,* a book of approximately 295 pages of text, he dedicates two or three paragraphs to the Mexican period of the region, rendering it almost irrelevant.

Moreover, Bolton does not have kind words either for Mexicans, Californios or Native Americans. Let me quote a passage at length in his description of California, which illustrates his views of Mexicans (in this case Californios):

The land was too fertile; too much was done for them. Colonists were paid a salary for a term of years, given lands, stock, tools, in fact every necessity but the normal stimulus to labor. In California, where the climate compelled no measures of protection and the soil produced abundantly without urging, the spirit of *dolce far niente* possessed the settlers. Even the later coming of well-to-do families, who boasted the purest blood of Spain, made little change in the life of happy, sunny ease. Sheep and cattle increased, roamed the green valleys and found their own sustenance, with little effort on the part of their owners. Olive trees, introduced by the padres, flourished; and grain yielded from fifty to a hundredfold from a single sowing. Why work? Why be "progressive"? (Bolton 1921, 290)

Bolton's interpretation of the inhabitants of the borderlands and of the historical events that led to annexation of Mexico's northern territories serves as one more justification for U.S. expansionism. Bolton argued that Americans were more industrious than Mexicans and Native Americans and as a result of their "superiority" were entitled to lands that were not "well used" by Mexican and Native peoples. In this sense, Bolton does not waver from the official U.S. script that justifies manifest destiny nor its accompanied expansionism.

GENDER ON THE BORDERLANDS

Even a superficial analysis of early 1900s mainstream borderlands history shows that it is quite evident that male historians have disregarded the significance of gender and sexuality as historical concepts of analysis.[4] Indeed, in Bolton's writing, women are virtually absent from his text, except for a few lines given to the wives of Spanish-Mexican settlers in New Mexico and Arizona. Chicana and non-Chicana women's historians have initiated a process of historical writing that, in addition to focusing on women, also conduct a gender analysis (see Bouvier 2001, González, D. 1999, Heindrich 2005, Pérez, E. 1999, Ruiz 1998). These scholars follow the disposition of Chicana historians to stretch mainstream "analytical frameworks" of colonialism by "incorporating sex/gender domination and resistance within a colonial dialectic" (Pesquera and de la Torre 1993, 6). These analytical frameworks point that the mere absence of women makes any historical writing "incomplete," yet women's absences are even thornier when one considers how significantly the social construction of the meaning of gender intersects with race. That is, although Bolton barely mentioned women in his writings, he articulated his patriarchal ideology by ignoring women. At the same time, by elevating white male prowess as a conqueror he helped mark the gender and racial normativity and superiority of such subjects. This resulted in the manufacturing of the idealized hyper masculinity of white "settlers" of the region. Not surprisingly, many of the accounts of the "inferiority" of Mexicans and Native Americans are done in sexualized language through which the white male "liberates" indigenous women from the yoke of the men of their own culture. Chicana anthropologist Mónica Russel y Rodríguez (2000) argues that the U.S.-México War was a form of conquering the Mexican body. The way in which hegemonic borderlands historians have constructed their historical writing though female absence is a metaphor for the continuous colonization of the Mexican body and land. Indeed, as Rosa Linda Fregoso (1999) proposes, "there is a long tradition in Western thought of fixing the body of women as allegory for land and nation" (145). As I discuss in chapter 5, the body of Malintzin/Malinche was literally colonized by Cortés and symbolically in Mexican and Chicano construction of the trope of treachery.

A reading of the historical texts on the borderlands will lead the reader to believe that Mexican, indigenous, and Anglo women were passive and not active participants in the historical, cultural, and political making of the region. According to Antonia Castañeda, "Women, who (to the historians) were neither intrepid explorers, barefooted black-robed missionaries, nor valiant lancers for the king, do not figure in Spanish borderlands studies" (1990, 14). Women were active agents of history and there are numerous documents that show women's roles in the borderlands. However, many historians have simply not looked at the evidence (González, D. 1999). While for the most part the borderlands school ignored women, the few studies that include Mexican women mark them as racially inferior compared with the virtuous superior Anglo female (Castañeda 1990).

These gendered representations have a function in the foundation of dominant ideologies of race and gender. For the pedagogical arguments I am presenting in this book, then, understanding women's participation as active agents of history is not only important for the gender analysis such process represents, but it is also crucial to understand that the complexity of human relations—and the analysis we make of these—are part and parcel of the ways in which subjectivities are set and ultimately inform the economic and intellectual positions different groups occupy in arranged social hierarchies. Such positionality of different groups is encoded in the myths created by societies; therefore, they are represented in educational practices and curriculum. For example, in the U.S., the myth that Western thought exclusively created the philosophies that lead to progress, such as democracy, not only elevates European groups as more civilized and progressive, but also denies non-Western societies any contribution to such ideals. The construction of these myths tends to be done in sexualized language. Ultimately, these myths and ideals are linked with systems of knowledge and the substantive correct knowledge that an educated person should possess. As advocates of multicultural education have proposed, educational institutions in the United States have not systematically included non-Western knowledge in official curricula (Banks 1995, Sleeter 1996, Elenes 1997).

CHICANAS/OS AND THE
RECONCEPTUALIZATION OF HISTORY

The early borderlands historical school maintains hegemonic colonial social relations and their "normality," while Chicana and Chicanos' re-fashioning of such conceptualization of the borderlands are done in order to critique such unequal social and cultural relations. That is, Chicana and Chicano scholars are trying to create a decolonizing process through their historical (and other disciplinary and interdisciplinary) writings (Pérez, E 1999). For educational practices, the different meaning of the subjectivity of Chicanas/os, Anglos, and Native Americans has had and continues to have serious impact on students' success and failure. That is, the dominant historical writings presented in this chapter help construct the ideologies of cultural deprivation of Mexican children that have plagued many educational practices. These ideas of cultural inferiority continue to affect Chicana/o and Mexican students in public schools, demonstrated in low levels of high school graduation, and attacks on bilingual education, affirmative action, and ethnic studies (Pizarro 2005, Valencia 2002).

In spite of the pejorative views of Mexican and Native Americans there are affinities between borderlands and Chicana/o history, given that "both treat history of the Spanish-speaking peoples who trace their culture to the Iberian Peninsula and to the indigenous people of Mexico" (De León 1989, 356). Yet, Chicana/o historians have not identified with traditional borderlands historians because ". . . it pits their basic sympathies with the mixed-blood 'people' against the arrogance of the Spanish crown, the *conquistadores,* and the Catholic Church" (De León 1989, 357). Chicana/o history also tends to focus on how Mexicans operated within Anglo traditions and not so much on Spanish institutions (De León 1989). Influenced by the New Left and following a historiography methodology that refashions a history from a grass roots level, "Chicanoists either found Turner, Bolton, and Bannon irrelevant to their writings or consciously set out to take umbrage with the applicability of their 'elitist' interpretation to Chicanos" (De León 1989, 357).

The relationship between how histories are written, by whom, and under what circumstances informs how key historical concepts are elaborated and influence the development of national identities that have been detrimental, and continue to be so, to Mexican Americans. The formation of particular intellectual spaces where Chicanas/os have been able to re-write their stories is crucial for self-determination. The concept of the borderlands, viewed from this context, follows under the process of re-naming and giving new meaning to concepts that have been created in order to maintain subordinate positions. There is, I suppose, a sense of irony that Chicana/o cultural critics re-fashioned the conceptualization of the borderlands in order to develop theoretical frameworks that speak of our conditions from a historical and contemporary standpoint and from symbolic and concrete perspectives. In this sense, writing our own histories and correcting distortions, omissions, and outright stereotypical and racist representations of Mexicans in the histories of the borderlands has been extremely important and urgent. Moreover, as Patricia Nelson Limerick (1987) proposes, the study of the American West provides a crucial case study to understand race relations in the U.S., given that the region is quite diverse, including Native Americans, Hispanics, Euro Americans, African Americans, and, I would add, Asian Americans.

LINKING BORDERLANDS AND BORDER STUDIES

Although this book is primarily concerned with the metaphorical conceptualization of the borderlands, it is necessary to understand the different meaning of borderlands and border studies. In terms of this book and within the context of educational research, a cursory examination of the México-U.S. border region lets us understand how both terms and theories are related and how this link informs the multiplicity of identities that the designations "Mexican," "Chicana/o," "Mexican American," "citizen," "green carder or legal immigrant," and "illegal" signify. The focus and critique of cultural studies emphasis on the metaphorical borderlands at the expense of the border region and its material conditions are noteworthy (Fox 1999). Equally important is to point out that most studies on the border region have been conducted by social scientists studying economic development, immigration, history, activism, violence, or the drug trade (see Alvarez 1984, Bustamante 1992, Davidson 2000, Dunn 1996, Fernández-Kelly 1983, Martínez 1995, 1998, Mattingly & Hansen 2006, Peña 2007, Ruiz & Tiano 1991, Sadowski-Smith 2002, Segura & Zavella 2007, Téllez 2008, Vila 2000). The uniqueness of the border region necessitates the examination of the relationship between the region itself and the borderlands and between its history and culture. For it is precisely the creation of this lengthy border, approximately 2000 miles, that marks the beginning of the differentiation of people of Mexican descent according to the geopolitical area where they are born and/or reside. In this sense, the border region is a place where we can see how dynamics of race/ethnicity, class, gender, and sexuality affect and inform the construction of Chicana/o and *mexicana/o* identities.

I, like many other scholars, am making a distinction between border studies and the metaphorical use of the borderlands, that is, a distinction between the concrete and the symbolic border. Basically, a border is a clear demarcation of a boundary. It serves to mark the end and beginning of specific spaces. The borderlands usually are defined as the lands near an international boundary, but are also defined as the metaphorical divides among social groups. I do not necessarily think that understanding the borderlands in either way is problematic for each area of study, nor is it mutually exclusive. Rather, I believe that both approaches must build on each other; and both speak to the conditions of Chicanas and Chicanos. Fox (1999), for example, is critical of contemporary cultural theory non-specific post national imagery of the border region, yet she agrees that she is symptomatic of such trends. She also argues that not enough attention has been paid to the U.S. border region. I believe that the border region, the border itself, and borderlands as concrete margins, and in its metaphorical use have been paid attention both by social scientists and cultural critics, but in different ways. Part of the criticism of borderlands scholarship emphasis on the symbolic meaning is that it can neglect or deny the importance of the unique material conditions of the border region. Renato Rosaldo (1998) using the metaphor of "border theater" to explain border policy on the eve of the Gulf War in the early 90s, reminds us that the border "is simultaneously symbolic and material, constructed and violent" (635).

Moreover, we have to be careful to not confuse the meanings of the borderlands exclusively with studies of international border regions, because it also speaks for different types of boundaries along multiple identity markers such as race, class, gender, and sexuality. Critics of the clear division between the concrete and symbolic border seem to forget that one of the Chicano pioneers in the study of the border region was Américo Paredes whose 1958 study *With his Pistol in his Hand* studied the culture of the border from an interdisciplinary perspective (see Saldívar, R. 2006). As Sonia Saldívar-Hull reminds us, Américo Paredes' work signals the beginning of the study of the México-U.S. border from historical, cultural, and geographical perspectives.[5]

If the border region itself is better understood from this interdisciplinary viewpoint, then, border identities must also be recognized as multiply constructed and negotiated. Pablo Vila's (2000)[6] ethnographic study of the manner in which border residents use social categories, metaphors, and narratives to make sense of the "other" demonstrates that border identities and cultures are multiple, contradictory, and sometimes painfully negotiated. Vila concludes that identity markers (i.e., "Chicano," "Mexican," "Anglo") must be written in the plural. He follows theoretical perspectives in Chicana/o and feminist studies that propose that identities are constructed, in part, through negotiations of how "others" define subaltern identities. Thus, Vila argues, Chicana/o identity must be in a constant process of redefinition, resistance, and accommodation, yet culturally specific. In this sense, Vila's conclusion is very much in tune with Chicana feminists' theorization of identity (see Alarcón 1990, Bejarano 2005, Chabram-Dernessesian 1994, Fregoso and Chabram 1990, Hernández, E.D. 2006, Quintana 1996, Rivero 1995, Torres 2003). Vila's study provides insights into how the complex and painful process of identity formation goes beyond categories of race, class, gender, and sexuality, but also according to social context and location. It is precisely because identities are always in process, contextual, negotiated, multiple, and yet culturally and locally specific, that in order to understand the process of subjectivity formation of Chicanas and Chicanos, we need to understand how they are related to the specific history of the México-U.S. border as well as how this serves as a metaphor for the condition of in-betweenness that so many Chicanas speak of. That is, to understand the metaphorical conceptualization of the borderlands as articulated by Anzaldúa, it is necessary to understand the complex history and contemporary situation along the México-U.S. border.

THE BORDER REGION

The current two-thousand-mile border dividing México and the U.S. is the result of nineteenth century U.S. expansionism that led to its status as a world power. The history of the México-U.S. border illustrates the permeability of the border and how it has been riddled with tensions and violence since its formation. According to Oscar Martínez (1995) the results of the U.S.-México War shaped the destiny of both countries. The U.S. was able to extend its territory through dollar diplomacy and the use or threat of force, where México could not stop the advances of a stronger and more powerful nation's "Manifest Destiny" (Martínez 1995). The border region is actually one that is marked by power differentials where the U.S., because of its economic strength, imposes more power over its southern neighbor (Alvarez, Jr. 1995). The U.S.-México border region is unique in that two nations that are so different in cultural, economic, and political terms must share a large geographical space that suffers from social, economic, and environmental problems. This border is both a symbolic and concrete manifestation of the separation between so-called first and third world. As Mexican sociologist Jorge A. Bustamante writes, "to be at the border is to be on top of a fence that looks at two different lands that are neighbors" (1992, 486). But what one sees on the top of this fence is, quoting Gloria Anzaldúa, "*una herida abierta* where the Third World grates the first and bleeds" (1987, 3). The edge between these two nations is a place where respective national ideologies impose their prejudices (Bustamante 1992).

Generally speaking, the term "Border," especially among nations, implies a clearly marked area that is concrete and static and is "traditionally defined as international boundaries between nation-states" (Alvarez, Jr. 1995, 449). The function of such margins is to demarcate the outer limits among peoples, nations, and property. And their purpose is to designate who can legitimately enter and occupy such spaces. In the case of international boundaries, borders mark where one country ends and the other begins, and in so doing indicate the appropriate place members of certain social groups can or must occupy. We tend to think of borders and boundaries as fixed; however, marking jurisdiction of nation-states is not as clear cut as many would like to believe. For example, U.S. jurisdiction is not limited to spaces inside its borders. The U.S. borders are not limited to the northern (Canada) and southern (México) boundaries; the U.S. has states (Hawaii and Alaska) that lie outside those boundaries. Additionally, and critical for this theoretical discussion, the U.S. has territories outside those boundaries such as Puerto Rico.[7] Nevertheless, in the specific case of the México-U.S. border, it serves as a literal and symbolic place where hierarchical ethnic differences between Mexico and the U.S., as well as among people of Mexican descent, take significant meanings. In order for people, goods, and services to cross a border, they must possess the appropriate documents and carry goods that are permitted to pass through. Moreover, the México-U.S. border, in addition to setting the boundaries between the two countries, serves as a literal and symbolic place where the meanings of citizenship begin to shift.

The México-U.S. border region is noteworthy because as many scholars, writers, and cultural critics argue, this is a region in and of itself with its unique characteristics (Alvarez, Jr. 1995, Bustamante 1992, Davidson 2000, Martínez 1995, 1998; Vélez-Ibañez 1997, Vila 2000). One of the key attributes of this region is how the border serves as a place where the registrars "illegal" and "legal" acquire extremely important quality of life meanings. Since 2001, there have been numerous reports on the conditions on the México-U.S. border. For example, in the summer (before the attacks on 9/11) the U.S. national media showed much interest on the region and produced and published almost daily reports on the border region. *Time Magazine* called this *Nueva Frontera, Amexica.*[8] Much of this attention occurred due to increased deaths of undocumented immigrants, mostly in the Arizona dessert, tensions among residents on both sides of the border region over illegal immigration and U.S. treatment of undocumented crossers, drug trafficking and violence, environmental concerns, NAFTA, and exploitation of workers, especially women, in the maquiladora industry, and the murder of women in Cd. Juárez and Chihuahua City in the northern state of Chihuahua in México.

The border is a clear marker of all that separates the U.S. and México: advanced capitalism from the developing world and a place where the clash, construction, and contestation over the meanings of nationalist ideologies begin to manifest. On the U.S. side, citizenship is codified (in a semiotic and not necessarily legal sense) according to someone's race or ethnicity,[9] and the brown body is suspect of not being legitimate. Yet legislation such as SB 1070 criminalizes undocumented migrants in Arizona by allowing police to ask for documentation after a stop when there is "reasonable suspicion" that they are in the state illegally. For example, in Arizona Maricopa County, Sheriff Joe Arpaio has been conducting sweeps of "undocumented" workers in predominantly Mexican communities and, not surprising, most of the migrants he arrests are of Mexican or Latin American origin. This criminalization of the brown body is paradigmatic of U.S. dominant discourses over definitions of who is or is not "American." These discourses are not only expressed by those who are marked as bona fide "real Americans," but also symbolically and concretely by individuals of all racial and ethnic backgrounds—including people of Mexican descent whose ancestors (even as close as parents and grandparents) at one point in their lives were also undocumented immigrants—have allied themselves with U.S. nationalist dominant ideologies.[10]

The tensions over such criminalization of the movement of people to the U.S. are linked to the economic demands of advanced capitalism that are operating worldwide: the seeking of the ever cheaper labor force. The development of maquiladora industry in Mexico's northern border since the 1960's and augmented by the signing of the NAFTA agreement in 1994, has created enterprises that increase their profits by paying very low wages to a mostly young female workforce (Iglesias Prieto 1997, Peña 1997, Public Citizen's Trade Watch 1996, Téllez 2005). In some cases, wages in maquiladoras are so low that workers cannot afford basic necessities such as decent housing, food, water, indoor plumbing, and electricity in México (Davidson 2000, Téllez 2005). The maquiladora industry has not helped with the economic development of the region. Indeed, in 2002—and even more in 2009—the border regions of both countries suffer from high unemployment rates due to the downturn and recession in the U.S. economy. The U.S. population is purchasing fewer consumer goods, obligating some maquiladoras to close or to consolidate production into one plant. However, there are clear indications that some industrialists are moving their plants to other areas such as Indonesia and China where they can find even cheaper labor.

Nevertheless, lured by economic necessity, as well as the fear of violence in México and Latin America, and an ever-increasing need for cheap labor on the part of the U.S., many people decide to immigrate to the U.S. Because of current U.S. immigration policy, poverty, and lack of education, immigrants cannot secure the proper documentation that will permit them to enter the U.S. legally. After making crossing in California and Texas more difficult, many would-be immigrants opt to cross the border through Arizona with devastating results. The human rights organization No More Deaths documents that "since 1998 more than 4000 migrants—men, women, and children—have lost their lives in the deserts of the U.S.-Mexico borderlands trying to make their way into the United States" (No More Deaths facebook 2009). This number includes one of the worst catastrophes in which 14 people died in May 2001 after the smuggler who was guiding them left them near Yuma, Arizona to fend for themselves with little or no water, at triple digit temperature, and without proper clothes and shoes. The response on the part of the U.S. to tighten the border by building iron and virtual fences, increasing the number of border patrol agents, the use of advanced technology such as night vision goggles, cameras, sensors, and stadium lights, and a series of "operations" aimed at stopping easy illegal crossings such as El Paso's "Operation Blockade," San Diego's "Gatekeeper," and Nogales' "Safeguard" led to tragic results. In this harsh environment, ICE and DEA have not been able to stop either undocumented immigrants or the drug trade (Fox 1999, Davidson 2000, Vila 2000). Some argue that all that the increased surveillance of the border has done is aid in the exploitation of workers in the maquiladoras in México (Davidson 2000) and of undocumented workers in the U.S. Carlos Vélez-Ibañez (1997) proposes that this situation is based on the "commodification of Mexicans," which was historically manifested in their exploitation in dual-wage labor, low wages, prohibition to join labor unions, lack of education, linguistic exclusion, assimilation and Americanization, and today in the "informal" underground economy.

After an increased tightening of the border, due to terrorism and the subsequent down turn in the economy, in 2002 the number of Mexican immigrants seemed to have dwindled. The economy somewhat recuperated between 2004 and 2006, and at the height of the housing boom the number of migrants increased, and unfortunately, also those who lost their lives crossing the desert. The recession of 2008 and 2009, and harsh anti-immigrant environment and laws, have affected the number of migrants crossing the border. Even with less possibilities for work in the U.S., safety, educational campaigns in México and in the border, Central Americans and Mexicans are risking their lives crossing a border that hopefully will take them to low wage jobs in the U.S.

The seemingly democratic changes in México that led to Partido Acción Nacional (PAN) Vicente Fox's election in 2000 as the first non-PRI president in more than 60 years did not change border policy. The contested election of

Felipe Calderón in 2006, who is also a member of the PAN, has made matters worse as his implementation of the Mérida accords virtually declared a war on the drug cartels that has proven deadly. In June 2009, the Obama Administration unveiled a plan that "will devote more resources to fighting Mexican drug cartels and use new technology to thwart them while trying to quell the U.S. demand for drugs that fuels the violent gangs" (Korte 2009, A4).[11] It remains to be seen if the "new" strategy will help curb drug violence.

The Fox administration made it a priority to modify U.S. immigration policy to open doors for Mexican immigrants; this policy is an indication that México needs immigrant labor in the U.S. as much as the U.S. needs it. Mexican immigrants send approximately 9.3 billion dollars a year in remittances, becoming one of the main sources of revenue for many Mexican communities (Hernández 2003). Even though the Fox administration's efforts to change U.S. immigration policy was due more to economic needs in México, there still was a concern about human rights and safety of Mexican immigrants who die crossing the border.

It is estimated that there are 12 million people living in the U.S. without proper documentation. Entrance varies, some as I already mention, cross the México-U.S. border[12] often times with deadly consequences; while others have visa violations. During the early months of the Bush Administration, there was hope that the U.S. would engage in comprehensive immigration reform. Even though George W. Bush's two terms in office were marred by extreme conservative politics, including the wars on Afghanistan and Iraq and the meltdown of the economy, from the beginning of his administration he was in favor or immigration reform. The events of 9/11 derailed the possibility of legislative reform; during his first term in office he left immigration policy intact and towards the end of his second term switched toward enforcement. Nativists and xenophobic sentiments historically have influenced immigration policy in the U.S. After 9/11, anti-immigrant views grew due to a combination of the fear of terrorism and the globalization of the economy. These anti-immigrant and protectionist voices do not seem to represent the majority of the population's views, but they are loud and powerful.[13] For example, former CNN commentator Lou Dobbs in 2001 was expressing his concerns over unethical corporate practices as those of ENRON and about outsourcing. But soon he switched his critique to "illegal" immigration and corruption in México and continued to be the theme of his daily program *Lou Dobbs Tonight* until his resignation amid criticism of his anti-Mexican rhetoric.

In 2006, millions of people protested in the U.S against H.R. 4437 that would have classified unauthorized immigrants or anybody who helped them enter or remain in the U.S. as felons. The bill did not pass, but created a chilling effect on people who have made their lives in the U.S. and had little or no possibility to regularize their immigration status. The marches and organizing in favor of immigrant rights created a wider debate of the need to overhaul immigration law and create a path to legalization. In 2007, the McCain-Kennedy bill was introduced in Congress and would have required new investment in border security and technology. Also, one of the provisions of the bill would allow "illegal" immigrants already in the U.S. to regularize their status after paying a fine, staying employed for a prescribed period of time, and paying back taxes. The bill failed—after much critique of it on conservative talk radio—and with a presidential election on the horizon, Congress did not try again.

Xenophobic anti-immigrant forces in Arizona lead by State Senator Russell Pearce helped pass SB 1070, which was signed into law by Governor Jan Brewer and is a similar piece of legislation as H.R. 4437. SB 1070 makes it a crime to be in the State of Arizona without proper documentation and authorizes police to ask for documentation when stopping an individual the police officer finds that there is "reasonable suspicion" that the individual is in the U.S. illegally. The legislation also makes it illegal to transport undocumented residents (even family members), and the public can demand that the police enforce the law. As with H.R. 4437 there has been a nation-wide mobilization to rescind S.B. 1070, to pressure Congress and the Obama administration to pass just comprehensive immigration reform. Additionally, there is a targeted boycott of Arizona to pressure the business community to take action against S.B. 1070.

Pearce is not done yet with his anti-immigrant legislation as he is saying that he will propose legislation countering the Fourteenth Amendment of the U.S. Constitution and deny citizenship to children of "illegal" immigrants born in the U.S. In an e-mail Pearce forward to his supporters from someone else it reads: "If we are going to have an effect on the anchor baby racket, we need to target the mother. Call it sexist, but that's the way nature made it. Men don't drop anchor babies, illegal alien mothers do" (Wessler 2010). Clearly, the ideology behind anti-immigrant legislation goes beyond maintaining the rule of law; it is about reducing the number of people of Mexican and Central American descent in the U.S. Anti-immigrant groups such as the Federation for American Immigration Reform (FAIR)—which helped draft SB 1070—have had a long association with eugenics and curtailing the reproductive rights and freedoms for women of color, especially Mexican and Puerto Rican women. Sociologist Elena R. Gutiérrez documents in her book *Fertile Matters* there is an overlap between nativism and immigration. Dr. John Tanton, founder of FAIR and U.S. English, linked population growth and immigration. Gutiérrez documents that Tanton was concerned that the growth in the immigrant population would undermine any effect to the limit of the

U.S. population growth. Xenophobia coupled with demographic changes is at the center of legislation such as SB 1070. Rachel Maddow in her MSNBC program astutely also showed the links between FAIR, Tanton, racism, and S.B 1070.

Unfortunately, Congress and the Obama administration are working very gingerly on immigration reform. As of the time of this writing, there are discussions in Congress on immigration reform, yet President Obama said that S.B. 1070 is misguided has not used his power and leadership to pressure Congress to move the legislation, even though he recognizes the need (but perhaps not the urgency) and made a campaign promise that he would work to pass immigration reform his first year in office. With the passage of health care reform legislation after a one year battle, it is time for Congress to direct its attention to immigration reform. The only piece of legislation currently in Congress is The Dream Act which was introduced in the House and the Senate on March 26, 2009. The Dream Act has two major provisions: (1) It will permit immigrants who have grown up in the U.S. to apply for a temporary legal status and become eligible for U.S. citizenship if they go to college or serve in the U.S. military; and (2) It will eliminate a federal provision that penalizes states that provide in-state tuition without regard to immigration status. Noteworthy as well is the Schumer-Graham proposal for immigration reform composed of four pillars: (1) a biometric social security card; (2) strengthening border security; (3) a process for admitting temporary workers; and (4) the implementation of a tough path to legalization. Senator Graham pulled from the legislation because he does not have support from any other republican. Amidst the voting for health care reform and tea party protesters, thousands participated in a pro-immigration reform rally in Washington, D.C. And the next week there were similar marches in Los Angeles. Clearly, there is pressure on Congress and the Obama administration to work towards immigration reform.

The current debate over immigration reform is more than a legal debate; it is an ideological debate about U.S. national identity and the meaning of who is an American. Many who are vehement in their views against immigrant rights use the discourse of the "rule of law" to articulate their position. The "rule of law" is only a ruse that marks their anti-immigrant ideology. In Arizona (a state that is considered "ground zero" for immigration debates) former Maricopa County Attorney Andrew Thomas and Sheriff Joe Arpaio, State Senator Russell Pearce, as well as the Minuteman, argue that they are not against immigrants or Mexicans, but that they must follow the rule of law and apprehend, try, and convict law breakers. However, Thomas and Arpaio have spent millions of dollars (which continues even as the County faces a budget deficit) conducting raids against "undocumented" workers and not enforced warrants of those accused of committing serious felonies such as murder. In the final analysis, the anti-immigrant rhetoric expound by Tancredo, Dobbs, Limbaugh, Thomas, Arpaio, and the Minuteman are expressions of the fears of the browning of America. This leaves people of Mexican descent, regardless of what their passports say or whether they have adequate documentation, in a liminal stage where they are neither Mexicans nor Americans. This is the condition that Gloria Anzaldúa theorizes in her conceptualization of the borderlands, Nepantla, and New Tribalism.

BORDERLANDS: NEPANTLA

Gloria Anzaldúa's *Borderlands/La Frontera* has become one of the more circulated texts not only on Chicana/o conceptualizations of the borderlands, but also of Chicana feminism. As an autobiographical text that Anzaldúa calls *autohistoria* (Keating 2005, Saldívar-Hull 1999), *Borderlands* transcends and transgresses academic and non-academic boundaries.[14] In doing so, Anzaldúa takes us into a new dimension in the conceptualization of the borderlands in that she deals with the specific México-U.S. border, as well as with psychological, sexual, and spiritual borderlands that are not necessary specific to any geopolitical region. As Kevin Concannon (1998) proposes, Anzaldúa conceptualizes the borderlands beyond an "essentialist" definition of the border as something that "seems always to be there, only in terms of being crossed or inhabited" (342). Rather, she "draws on the constructedness of border" in order to speak of "the formation of a border consciousness" (433). The borderlands that Anzaldúa speaks of are far from being a reification of the border. In Norma Alarcón's (1996/2002) words, the "borderlands are spaces (. . .) continuously in the making" (116). Clearly, Anzaldúa moves beyond geographical spaces to symbolic and metaphorical ones in her elaboration of the borderlands.

While *Borderlands/La Frontera* is not the first Chicano text to speak of the border either in its geographic specificity or in its metaphorical sense, it is certainly the first that offers a view of the border and the borderlands from "a woman-identified-woman" perspective (Saldívar-Hull 1992). Moreover, following Anzaldúa's explanation, it is the only text that speaks of spiritual borderlands. *Borderlands/La Frontera,* as a text, defies any type of definition in terms of genre; it is, as Anzaldúa notes, "a mosaic pattern, an Aztec-like weaving pattern" (66). According to the author, she realized that as she was writing that she had "preoccupation with the deep structure, the underlining structure, with the gesso underpainting that is red earth, black earth" (66). Defying traditional Western lineal thought, the book "inscribes a serpentine movement through different kinds of *mestizaje* that produce a third thing that is neither this nor that but something else . . ." (Yarbro-Bejarano 1994, 17). In Sonia Saldívar-Hull's (1992) words, the book is "a *mestizaje:* a postmodern mixture of autobiography, historical document, and poetry collection" (211). Through this mixture of genres, identity formations, and destabilization of accepted forms (either literary or social), Anzaldúa lays the groundwork for the development of Chicana feminist epistemology that germinates from a mestiza consciousness that straddles between cultures, languages, in-between spaces; that is, that recognizes that ambiguity is part of a state of-being-in the world and that opens the possibilities of constructing feminist politics in a third space (see Delgado Bernal 1998, Saldívar-Hull 1999). As I will elaborate further in chapter 2, Anzaldúa's mestiza consciousness has been quite influential in the advancement of Chicana feminist pedagogies (see Dolores Delgado Bernal 2001, 1998, Elenes, et. al. 2001, Elenes 2001).

Anzaldúa's conceptualization of the borderlands is linked with land. In the first chapter of the essay section, Anzaldúa introduces her definition of the borderlands by claiming/establishing "ownership" of the land. Anzaldúa reports that the land along México-U.S. border belonged to Indian people, and will return to their hands in the future but does not specifically elaborate in what form.[15] The last chapter of this section ends with a similar statement arguing that the land will return to indigenous peoples. Unmistakable anti-colonial politics are established by marking the geographical borderland space as indigenous land. At the same time, she proposes that any discussion and understanding of borderlands and Chicana/o identity must be tied to indigenous identity. Mexican and Chicana/o indigenous background is central, not peripheral, to Anzaldúa; her own identity is tied with Mexican and Indian traditions.[16]

From the outset, Anzaldúa makes it clear that her conceptualization of the borderlands has more than one meaning. Nevertheless, the México-U.S. border is prominently featured in her writings, even though Anzaldúa expands the definition of the borderlands beyond reified meanings. In the preface of the book (all editions) she explains that the borderlands she is talking about are connected to the specific México-U.S. border. However, she clarifies that she expanded the definition beyond geo-political to include psychological and spiritual borders that are not specific to the southwest or even to Chicanas/os. Anzaldúa differentiates between the concept of the borderlands and borders. Borders are specific dividing lines, clear demarcations of spaces that belong to different groups, and that should not be crossed. "Borders are set up to define the places that are safe and unsafe, to distinguish *us* from *them*. A border is a dividing line, a narrow strip along a steep edge. A borderland is a vague and undetermined place created by the emotional residue of an unnatural boundary. It is in a constant state of transition" (3). For Anzaldúa, the borderlands must be understood as the interstices among identities, as in-between liminal spaces where ambiguity[17] reins. Because the border between México and the United States is an unnatural boundary created by the manifest destiny ambitions of the latter, the inhabitants of the borderlands are the marginalized, the "prohibited" and "forbidden." The borderlands are where all of those who are not considered "normal" live: "the squint-eyed, the perverse, the queer, the troublesome, the mongrel, the mulatto, the half-breed, the half dead" (3). As such marginal spaces, the socio-economic conditions in the borderlands are generally appalling. This is the case of the México-U.S. border. Anzaldúa reminds us, for example, that the lower Rio Grande Valley is one of the poorest areas of the U.S., and some of the poorest people in the U.S. live there. These conditions are also present in inner city barrios and ghettos and in Native American reservations.

The existence of borderlands' physical and symbolic spaces is the result of power relations between dominant structures and ideologies and those outside of such formations. Borderlands are marginal territory and the territory of the marginal. Anzaldúa best explains her understanding of borderlands in the poem "To Live in the Borderlands Means You":

To live in the Borderlands means knowing
    That the *india* in you, betrayed for 500 years
    Is no longer speaking to you,
    That *mexicanas* call you *rajetas,*
    That denying the Anglo inside you
    is as bad as having denied the Indian or Black;
Cuando vives en la frontera
    people walk through you, the wind steals your voice,
    you're a *burra, buey,* scapegoat,
    forerunner of a new race,
    half and half—both woman and man, neither—
    a new gender; "
To live in the Borderlands means to
    put *chile* in the borscht,
    eat whole wheat *tortillas,*
    speak Tex-Mex with a Brooklyn accent;
    be stopped by *la migra* at the border checkpoints;

                                          (Anzaldúa 1987, 194)

In this poem, Anzaldúa talks about multiple subject positions that defy a single unitary definition of identity, subjectivity, and culture. While living in the borderlands requires (or involves) accommodation to new cultural practices, it is also tied with socio-economic conditions. Living in the borderlands means being affected by racial politics and discourses, positioned within a segmented labor market, and new cultural practices. If to live in the borderlands means to be stopped by *la migra* at border checkpoints, then, as we can well document, not everyone is treated equally in these checkpoints. People with brown skin are looked upon with suspicion by the border patrol.

Anzaldúa adapted the Nahuatl concept of nepantla to further explain the state of in-between. In later works (Anzaldúa 2002, Keating 2005, Lara 2005) she said that she preferred the term nepantla, which is the Nahuatl word for the land in the middle. In AnaLouise Keating's (2000) book *Interviews/Entrevistas*, Anzaldúa proposes that *Nepantla* might be a better way to conceptualize her epistemology and ontology than borderlands. In the same volume, in an interview with Inés Hernández-Ávila, Anzaldúa says, "I use the concept of nepantla to describe the state or stage between identity that's in place and the identity in progress but not yet formed" (177–8). Clearly, for Anzaldúa the borderlands, or *nepantla,* refer to geopolitical spaces, but also construct alternative models and understanding of Chicana feminist identity and subjectivity.[18]

For Anzaldúa, nepantla is a transformative space that is an "unstable, unpredictable, precarious, always-in-transition space lacking clear boundaries" (1). Nepantla describes with more clarity liminal spaces between worlds, where the multiplicity of social positions and subjectivities encounter each other. Concomitant with imagining such a transitional space, Anzaldúa speaks of bridges that can connect the borders that separate different groups. Feminist philosopher Mariana Ortega (2005) beautifully explains nepantla as "the very experience of those who live an in-between life because they are multicultural, multivoiced, multiplicitous, because their being is caught in the midst of ambiguities, contradictions, and multiple possibilities" (79). Those who are committed to making possible connections among groups of people, Anzaldúa calls nepantleras.

A transformative project must recognize the differences among racial, gender, class, sexual orientation, religious groups. The challenge is to recognize differences without letting them separate us, and, in doing so, respect those differences. In order to facilitate these transformative strategies, Anzaldúa proposed to reflect "on the hybrid quality of our lives and identities—todas somos nos/otras" (2002, 3). "Nos/otras" uses the Spanish word "nos" (us) and "otra" (the other), to sound like the Spanish feminine plural "nosotras" (us women). In doing so, she acknowledges the reality that the relationship between women of color and other groups are complicated by historical divisions among "us" and "them," and with nos/otras "we recognize commonalities, the humanness in the other" (Lara 2005, 43). In her effort to create new labels that were not exclusive of Chicanas, Anzaldúa developed the term new tribalism, by which "we define who we are by what we include" (Anzaldúa 2002, 3). According to education scholars Cinthya Saavedra and Ellen Nymark (2008), new tribalism "is about how we/you/they can witness how we are all in each other. Although the concept of tribalism might seem like the ghettotization of ideas and concepts, on the contrary, it is about all of us (you, us, they) in the tribe" (268). Border/transformative pedagogies benefit from new tribalism in that they seek to intervene within a multiplicity of subjectivities and cultural practices. That is, while border/transformative pedagogies are situated within Chicana cultural practices, these are not only for the benefit of Chicanas and Chicanos. But rather, they take on the challenge of recognizing and honoring differences, yet making every effort not to create hierarchies.

CONCLUSION

The symbolic and metaphorical meaning of the border is central to borderland theorization because they are informed by the historical conditions that gave birth to the Mexican American communities in the United States. The border is key for U.S. history as well, as José David Saldívar (1997) argues in agreement with Rafael Pérez-Torres (1995) that the appropriation of the borderlands by "U.S. culture indicates how enmeshed the American frontier field-Imaginary continues to be in our culture" (Saldívar 1997, xiii). But in order to not lose sight of the relationship between history, culture, and material conditions, it is necessary to understand the border in both its real and metaphorical meanings. Yes, everyone at different times in their lives crosses real and symbolic borders, nevertheless for people of Mexican descent in the United States are defined by the existence of the U.S.-México border and immigration policies. Border/transformative pedagogies take their inspiration from borderland scholarship.

In order to understand the significance of the borderlands not only for my pedagogical discourses, but for Chicana and Chicano studies scholarship, I first offered a historical overview of borderland scholarship. The conceptualization of the borderlands in Chicana and Chicano cultural studies looks at the México-U.S. border as an allegory that helps explain the social, cultural, political, and economic condition of people of Mexican descent in the U.S. The border is significant because its existence is the result of U.S. expansionism in the nineteenth century that continues to mark the social position of Mexicans and Chicanos in the U.S.

But the México-U.S. border and the borderland speak of the condition of in-betweenness of people of Mexican descent. Gloria Anzaldúa's conceptualization of the borderlands, nepantla, and new tribalism offers a theoretical framework that is capable of understanding the differences among social groups in two ways: One, recognizing the heterogeneity of people in the U.S., and two, by not letting these differences create rifts among many of these groups. In the next chapter, I will outline how Anzaldúa's conceptualization in terms of it epistemological and ontological contributions, serve as the contours of border/transformative pedagogies.

NOTES

1. The complexity of the task required limiting the parameters or scope of the analysis; because the term was first used in historical writings, I needed to be cautious of not getting side tracked by the historical content of the works under analysis. While I find that it is interesting and important to understand the history of the U.S. Southwest, or México's northern territories (depending on whose point of view we are talking about), my interests in engaging in this research was to understand how the concept of the borderlands became so important to the works of critical pedagogy.

2. I am not in any way engaging in a comprehensive exegetical analysis of such scholarship—that is beyond the scope of this chapter and book. My focus is on how historians' viewpoints influenced the ways in which they constructed their own notion of the subjectivity of different social actors, and how these identity markers gave way to hegemonic pedagogies of race/ethnicity, class, gender and sexuality that continue to inform many educational and curricular practices. For most early twentieth century borderlands historians articulated their definitions of Mexicans and indigenous peoples as inferior to white Anglo-Saxon males and, thus, serving the interests of white America.

3. Constance Linsday Skinner was a freelance writer hired by Allen Johnson, editor of the Chronicles of America Series at Yale University Press to liven up Bolton's dry prose in 1919. Evidently this was more or less common practice, particularly with this series that aimed at a popular audience. Bolton's and Skinner's (although she is not credited as co-author) book was titled *The Spanish Borderlands*. (See A.L. Hurtado 1995).

4. While Bolton is symptomatic of historical writings of the beginning of the twentieth century that ignore women's contribution, I am not arguing that he should have conducted a feminist or gender analysis he never intended to do. What I propose is that while it is perhaps "understandable" that many male historians did not include women because they were part of typical andocentric writings, this does not mean that the exclusion of women from history did not have consequences for women's subordination. That is, I am not proposing that Bolton should have been a feminist or that we can use late twentieth century feminist theory "backwards" and critique historians who did not use these concepts before they were developed. However, as many feminist historians and theorists have demonstrated, the exclusion and distortion of

women in history and other writings do have consequences for women's lives and education.

5. See footnote on p. 176, *Feminism on the Border.*

6. Vila's study is an important contribution to the understanding of the difficulties of negotiating identity in situations where hegemonic discourses are constantly marking people according to power relations' scripts. Understanding the relationship between social structures, power, and the way in which people give meaning to their lives and limitations in terms of mobility (both social and across the border) and safety (fear of crime and drugs) to provide but two examples, is critical to appreciate how the informants in Vilas' study constructed their identities in ways that differentiated themselves from "others." A superficial reading of Vilas book might give the impression that all dwellers of the border region have equal access to power and that all of their designations of the "other" as problematic have equal weight. Nevertheless, Vila does demonstrate that it is not possible to talk about a homogenous border region—a point he makes in his critique of Anzaldúa, Rosaldo, and García Canclini. However, Vila's lack of cultural knowledge of northern Mexico's Spanish and culture is manifested in various "interpretative mistakes" of identity formation, "othering," and translations. For example he translates "feo, prieto y chaparro" as "ugly, "nigger," and "short." While, "feo" is indeed ugly, and "chaparro" is short; "prieto, which means "dark-skinned" and is indicative of internalized skin color hierarchies, does not have the same racist connotations that the slur "nigger" has.

7. It is important to note as well that the U.S. and some of its agencies, such as the Drug Enforcement Administration (DEA) and U.S. Customs (such as those in Canadian airports) have jurisdiction outside U.S. territory. Yet even though these institutions are outside the U.S. territory, they still operate as if they were in the U.S. Thanks to Luis Plascencia for this insight.

8. See "*La Nueva Frontera*/The New Frontier" *Time,* June 11, 2001, 157 (23), pp. 50–79.

9. While at this historical juncture U.S. citizenship cannot be awarded or denied on the basis of race, by practice people of "Hispanic" descent (or who might "look" Hispanic) can be presumed to be "illegal aliens" by ICE. The July 1997 raids in Chandler, AZ where the local police aided the then INS in identifying undocumented individuals by stopping brown-skinned individuals is a clear manifestation of how Mexicans and other brown-skinned peoples are not necessarily considered U.S. citizens. The "undocumented sweeps" that Sheriff Joe Arapaio conducts in Maricopa County, Arizona are another example.

10. The situation for undocumented immigrants is getting worse. Among the many consequences of the tragic events on 9/11, immigrants in general, but undocumented in particular, have been used as a scapegoat for the terror attacks. Many conservative thinkers and personalities have asked for tightening the border, especially cracking down on Mexican immigrants. Even though it is clear that undocumented immigrants and/or Mexicans were not involved in those attacks and that the real culprits were legally in the U.S. Indeed, families of undocumented workers who lost their lives or those who lost their jobs at the World Trade Center will not receive any of the funds

that were raised for the victims after the attacks. Ignoring how much these events affected the Latina/o communities in the U.S. and Latin America, anti-immigrant advocates have used the fact that those who perpetuated the terror on 9/11 were not U.S. citizens, to further their anti-immigrant policies.

11. The Obama Administration is committing more resources to fight drugs. It remains to be seen whether this strategy will be successful or continue the violence that is plaguing México. However, at least Washington is recognizing that U.S. high appetite and consumption of drugs is part of the problem. I hope the U.S. shifts its strategy to invest in prevention and treatment that might be able to curb drug consumption.

12. In this book I am focusing on migration from México and other Latin American countries. However, I do want to point out that not all migrants who come to the U.S. with or without documents are Mexican or Latin American. There are migrants from all over the world in the U.S. who have entered under a variety of circumstances.

13. I find it interesting and intriguing that among the 2008 Republican Presidential primary candidates, those who expressed a strong position against immigration were some of the first to drop out of the race, such as Tom Tancredo. Given that the anti-immigrant voices were so loud, I was sure those would be the candidates who would surface soon and secure the nomination. But the opposite occurred and Senator John McCain, who co-sponsored the McCain-Kennedy Bill, was the nominee.

14. Gloria Anzaldúa is one of the best-known Chicana feminist theorists and writers. *Borderlands* is a combination of autobiography, critical essay that includes academic footnotes, poetry, and written bilingually without "proper" translation. These characteristics make the book unique and not strictly academic. Moreover, Anzaldúa did not have "proper academic credentials" such as a Ph.D, which she received posthumously. She was a graduate student at the University of California, Santa Cruz in the English Department at the time of her death. Santa Cruz renowned program History of Consciousness rejected her as a doctoral student because she did not have the proper theoretical breath required of their students. Her book, however, is studied in the program, and some of the faculty have dutifully quoted it. See Keating (2000).

15. Some argue that the increase of population of Mexican descent in the Southwest and California is a form of recuperating the lost land.

16. See Patricia Penn-Hilden. "How the Border Lies: Some Historical Reflections" In *Decolonial Voices,* pp. 152–176, for an excellent critique of Chicano/a appropriation of Native American traditions. She does not critique Gloria Anzaldúa per se, nor am I necessarily arguing that Anzaldúa is symptomatic of this trend. It is necessary, nevertheless, to be cautious of the ways we as Chicanas/os might appropriate Native-American, especially Aztec, symbolism, that reproduce colonialists mentalities.

17. Ambiguity, as I understand Anzaldúa's use of the term, refers to multiple identities and in-between spaces, but not confusion. One can find solace in knowing and accepting such ambiguity and be happy with it. This understanding of ambiguity moves away from traditional Western modern thought that views static unified identity as normative.

18. Identity and subjectivity are interrelated. Identity represents the shared characteristics among individuals that distinguish them as part of a group. Subjectivity refers

to "the conscious and unconscious thoughts and emotions of the individual, her sense of herself and her ways of understanding her relation to the world." Chris Weedon, *Feminist Practice and Poststructuralist Theory* (New York: Blackwell, 1987), 32. For Chicanas, then, Chicana feminist identity is related to their membership among groups such as "Chicanos/as," "Women," "Lesbian," *or* "working class" (among many others), and the ways in which membership on these different social groups inform how they think and feel, that is, make sense of the world. Subjectivity and identity are co-constructed by individuals and society. Thus, identity and subjectivity are always in process.

Chapter 2

Borderland Epistemologies, Subjectivities, and Feminism

Toward Border/Transformative Pedagogies

Anzaldúa's philosophy has been influential in the development of Chicana/o feminist critical education, pedagogy, and epistemology. Her conceptualization of the borderlands, mestiza consciousness, new tribalism, and spiritual activism has certainly inspired me to develop border/transformative pedagogies because they offer a conceptual framework capable of navigating the complexities of social relations, cultural practices, and education. A key configuration of Anzaldúa's philosophy, especially borderlands theory, is to work against dualistic thinking; however, this is not easy as we are oftentimes bound and limited by binary thinking (Keating 2008, Villenas 2010). Therefore, borderland theories do not ignore the existence of dialectical opposites but recognize that they are produced to maintain hegemonic practices (Mignolo 2000). For Chicanas/os this theorization takes into account the multiplicity of subjectivities that they experience in the U.S. as a racialized group, but also in terms of class, gender, and sexuality. Moreover, I argue in this book, borderland sensibilities are influential in a multiplicity of cultural productions, including some that re-imagine La Llorona, La Virgen de Guadalupe, and Malintzin/Malinche. In this sense, borderland theories contribute to decolonizing practices and can act in education, media, and all possible spaces where and when culture becomes a question of power, domination, and liberation (Mignolo 2000, 235).

Borderlands discourses recognize that Chicanas/os, although marginal members of society, are still socialized into dominant ideologies. Borderland epistemologies absorb and displace hegemonic forms of knowledge into the perspective of the subaltern (Mignolo 2000). They offer a way to move away from assimilationist and anti-assimilationist discourse in that it recognizes that there are traces of different cultural practices among various

47

social groups. For example, borderland theorization takes into account that Chicanas/os, while maintaining their Chicana/o cultural identity, have traces of U.S. mainstream culture (see Villenas 2010). At the same time, borderland theories affirm everyday cultural practices as systems of knowledge, teaching, and learning.

This is why, a new generation of Chicana/o critical education scholars[1] in the 1990s and 2000s interested in placing Chicana/o cultural practices at the center of their inquiries initiated a process of rethinking Chicana/o educational research (Elenes, González, Delgado Bernal, & Villenas 2001) following some of the concepts developed by borderland theorists, especially Anzladúa, and by borrowing concepts from Chicana/o studies, women's studies, and cultural studies. These scholars provide a broader understanding of educational practices inside and outside formal educational institutions (Bejarano 2005, Delgado Bernal 1998, 2006, Demas and Saavedra 2004, Dicochea 2006, Elenes 1997, 2002, González 1998, Murillo, Jr. 1999, Pendleton Jiménez 2006, Saavedra & Nymark 2008, Villenas 2006, 2010, Villenas & Foley 2002). Borderland educational scholars implement alternative methodologies that include everyday modes of knowledge, and from a variety of sources.

My conceptualization of border/transformative pedagogies is in tune with the work of borderland, cultural studies, and Chicana feminist scholars. However, the main inspiration comes from the framework developed by Anzaldúa in her two most significant works *Borderlands/La Frontera* (1987) and in *This Bridge We Call Home* (2002), but also in other essays. I find three conceptual interventions in Anzaldúa's work that are helpful for the development of border/transformative pedagogies and Chicana feminist thought. These three areas are *conocimiento*/epistemology, borderland subjectivities, and third space feminism.

In this chapter, I first elaborate on the main conceptualizations of these three theoretical interventions. I then move to explain the contours and foundations for the development of border/transformative pedagogies.

CONOCIMIENTO/EPISTEMOLOGY

Recent work by feminists of color honor the knowledge that "ordinary" women produce based on their everyday experiences and cultural knowledge (Delgado Bernal 1998, Ladson-Billings 2000, Villenas 1996). These innovative feminist scholars have named this cultural knowledge epistemological; thus reclaiming a philosophy term granted to the credentialed. Chicanas have looked at the work of Anzaldúa as one of the sources for the effort to construct Chicana feminist epistemologies (Delgado Bernal 1998). In general, epistemology is understood as a "theory of knowledge" (Alcoff and Potter 1993, 1). Gloria Ladson-Billings (2000) recommends defining epistemology as a "system of knowing" (257), which is intimately linked with worldview. Ladson-Billings suggests that there is double move in the formation of systems of knowing: an individual's standpoint about the world is influenced by the knowledge one has and the knowledge one is capable of having is influenced by an individuals' worldview. That is, Ladson-Billings makes it clear that social position influences what one knows, how one comes to know, and even what one is capable of knowing.

Chicana feminist epistemologies are similar to "endarkened feminist epistemologies" (Dillard 2000, 662) which point at the intimate relationship between experience and knowledge[2] and are rooted in Chicanas' everyday cultural knowledge. Therefore, Chicana feminists' epistemologies are "concerned with knowledge about Chicanas—about who generates an understanding of their experiences and how this knowledge is legitimized or not legitimized" (Delgado Bernal 1998, 560). These insights are associated with history, politics, culture, race, class, gender, and sexuality. Much of the epistemological outlook of Chicanas is rooted in their history of oppression experienced in the U.S and México and their negotiations with patriarchy in the society at large as well as at home. This epistemology finds expression through Chicana/o cultural productions that articulate the meaning people make of their own lives in relations to structural forms of oppression and resistance.

Dolores Delgado Bernal (2006) has proposed that Chicana feminist pedagogies "are partially shaped by collective experience and community memory" (114) and that these experiences and memories are taught in the form of legends, *corridos,* and storytelling. Just as these cultural productions are examples of Chicana feminist pedagogies, they also articulate Chicana/o epistemologies. For example, Pizarro (1998) writes that the *corrido* is one of the oldest cultural productions that transmit Chicano values, "and continues to be a means of passing on history for a people who rely heavily on the oral tradition" (64). Similarly, speaking from an African American tradition, Dillard (2000) proposes, that "life notes" (personal narratives constructed in letters, stories, journals, poetry, music, et cetera) embody "the meaning and reflections that consciously attend to a whole life as it is embedded in socio-cultural contexts and communities of affinity" (664). While Chicana feminist epistemologies "borrow" from African American "endarkened" epistemologies, they are "grounded in the unique life experiences of Chicanas" (Delgado Bernal 1998, 561). Thus "Chicana feminist epistemology arises out of a unique social and cultural history, and demonstrates that our experiences as Mexican women are legitimate, appropriate, and effective in designing, conducting, and analyzing educational research" (563). In this light, popular cultural productions on La Llorona, La Virgen de Guadalupe, and Malintzin/ Malinche are examples of epistemological outlooks.

Based on these understandings of epistemology, I will analyze how Anzaldúa constructs her epistemology or *conocimiento* (the Spanish word for knowledge), the unique ways in which she understands, explains, and contests the world.[3] Her epistemology is embedded in her experiences in the borderlands and her spirituality, and as Keating (2008) reminds us, in Anzaldúa's "metaphysics of interconnectedness" (60). Moreover, Keating proposes Anzaldúa drew from "indigenous philosophies, Eastern thought, psychic literature, and her own experiences, she maintained her belief in a fluid, cosmic spirit/energy/force that embodies itself throughout—and *as*—all existence" (60). Anzaldúa's epistemological project is to articulate a vision from the margin that is the basis for theorization about Chicana/o experience (or any subaltern and marginalized groups in society) due to their subordinate position in society. At the same time, she also wished to act as a bridge among different groups (Anzaldúa 2002). Anzaldúa's epistemology is from "below," from *los de abajo* (Pizarro, 1998) and is rooted in community memory linked to indigenous worldviews. Anzaldúa's theorizing tells us that there is a different way of seeing and understanding the world based on the (dis)advantaged position Chicanas/os occupy in U.S. society. It is through *la conciencia de la mestiza*/mestiza consciousness, new tribalism, nepantla, and spiritual activism that Chicanas enact their epistemological positions and, as I elaborate below, are the foundation of borderland subjectivities.

Anzaldúa's epistemology offers an important critique of, and separates from, Western thought. By invoking cultural memory of ancient knowledges, borderland epistemologies work to displace some of the legacies of Western modernist thought, particularly the colonial legacy of universalizing European knowledge and culture as the belief that it had the function as the civilizing force of the world and as the masters of scientific advancement. Based on the ideas of the Enlightenment, Eurocentric Western thought created a hierarchy of how knowledge could be produced and by whom: European women and non-Western peoples were not seen as capable of producing high-level knowledge and science. In such a viewpoint, highly educated European and Euro-American males produced science, art, and philosophy (although influenced by ancient classic Greece and Rome), while the rest of the world (including the poor and women) produced folklore. And even though the subject of Western thought and knowledge production was clearly embodied (male), the legacy of Western thought is a disembodied person who produced high-level thinking and knowledge. Borderland epistemologies offer a different course of thought that seeks to radically depart from Eurocentric thinking. Borderland epistemology does not seek to be included as an "honorary" Western subject. Rather, borderland epistemologies offer a "different way of thinking," and are "a machine for intellectual decolonization" (Mignolo 2000, 45).

Anzaldúa argues as well against Western "logic" where systems of knowledge are organized as binary opposites such as male/female, white/black, and oppressor/oppressed. In Western "logic," these terms are mutually exclusive, and analyses of social relations are seen in dialectical process where the distinctions and relations between these opposites are understood as static. Chela Sandoval (2000) proposes, "Conquered and dominated groups can be incorporated into dominant society, even when this happens negatively by distributing their possibilities onto its binary rationality" (151). Yet, as Sandoval explains, sometimes the subordinate undermines this process. Borderland theorists understand social relations as extremely complex and non-binary, and contend that racial/ethnic, gender, and gay/lesbian/bisexual/transgender groups in the U.S. occupy a space between the margin and the center of society that permit them to offer a new vision, a new way of thinking.[4]

By reclaiming the ancient knowledge that indigenous groups in the Americas produced, and through her deconstruction of the dehumanization of Native peoples, Anzaldúa offers the foundations of a Chicana feminist architecture that has helped advance Chicana feminists epistemologies. Unlike Western philosophy, Anzaldúa does not separate between mind and body, theory, art, everyday knowledge, popular culture, and spirituality. In her (2002) essay "now let us shift . . . the path of conocimiento . . . inner work, public acts" she writes about her belief that we are witnessing a feminization of knowledge, which provides a major shift in the understanding of what constitutes knowledge. "a shift away from knowledge contributing both to military and corporate technologies and the colonization of our lives by TV and the Internet, to the inner exploration of the meaning and purpose of life" (541).[5] Clearly, for Anzaldúa, this new form of *conocimiento* is intrinsically linked to spirituality.

Anzaldúa's epistemological project is situated with a critique of the legacy of colonialism, which is in part manifested in the acceptance of Western thought by colonized people. A problem for Anzladúa is how Western epistemologies encouraged the split of mind, body, and spirit. Thus, Chicanas and other subaltern peoples are split between spirituality, rationality, body, and soul. Chicanas, mestizas, and nepantleras are constantly shifting out of habitual formations: from single goal reasoning to divergent thinking. This shift is characterized by a movement away from set patterns and goals and toward a holistic perspective, "one that includes rather than excludes"

(Anzaldúa 1987, 79). This is a central aspect of "spiritual activism," which connects the mind, body, soul, and spirit. For Anzaldúa, "spiritual tools" help us to deal with political and personal problems (2002, 570). Spiritual activism is an integral aspect of the metaphysics of interconnectedness of all aspects of life; spirituality connects one with the world, with one's ancestors and descendants, and contemporary relations. At the same time, spirituality is a way of understanding one's (or a community) position in the world and working toward the transformation of social inequality. In this sense, as Keating so eloquently expresses, "spiritual activism is spirituality for social change, spirituality that posits a relational worldview and uses this holistic worldview to transform one's self and one's worlds" (2008, 54).

In order to regain mind, body, and spirit, it is necessary to start the process of decolonization. Anzaldúa exhorts Chicanas/os to "stop importing Greek myths and Western Cartesian split point of view and root ourselves in mythological soil and soul of this continent" (68). Thus, Chicanas' re-imagining of La Llorona, La Virgen de Guadalupe, and Malintzin/Malinche are ways of developing alternative Chicana feminists systems of knowledge. *Conocimiento* does not devalue spirituality, rather it "elevate[s] it to the same level occupied by science and rationality" (Anzaldúa 2002, 542). When Anzaldúa works on this process of recuperation, she takes us back to Nahua philosophy and culture by focusing on the symbolism of black and red ink as *escritura y sabiduría.* "They [Aztecs] believed that through metaphor and symbol, by means of poetry and truth, communication with the Divine could be attained, and *topan* (that which is above—the gods and spirit world) could be bridged with *mictlán* (that which is below—the underworld and the region of the dead)" (69). It is precisely by creating a new mythos, that is, to change the way we perceive reality and our relation to the world and the spirits, the way we see ourselves, and the way we behave, that la mestiza creates a new consciousness.

Anzaldúa's project reclaims indigenous forms of knowledge, particularly Nahua female deities, such as *Coatlicue, Tonantzin,* and *Coyolxauhqui,* among others, as symbolic figures. Her strategy is to reconstruct Aztec icons into "new feminist threads" (Saldívar-Hull 2000, 65). Key in her theorization is how she "appropriates" *Coatlicue.* In Mesoamerican cultures,[6] *Coatlicue* was the creator goddess; she was mother of the celestial deities, of *Huitzilopochtli* (God of War) and of, *Coyolxauhqui* (She With Golden Bells, Goddess of the Moon). Robelo (1951), following Chavero, believes that *Coatlicue* is *Cihuacoatl,* the woman-snake, who is the mother of the first pair from which humanity descends and proposes that *Cihuacoatl* gave birth to the twins *Huitzilopochtli* and *Quetzalcoatl.* To understand these associations, it is important to remember that Aztec philosophy was based on dualism, sometimes even contradictory ones. There are those who believe that *Cihuacoatl* and *Tonántzin* are associated and that they represent different sides of a duality. According to Anzaldúa (1987), the Mexica-Aztecs male domination split the female self from the female deities. With such a split completed, *Tonántzin* becomes the good mother and *Coatlicue, Chimalma,* and *Cihuacoalt,* the dark side (Lara 2008). John Bierhorst in *History and Mythology of the Aztecs: The Codex Chimalpopoca,* documents that approximately in 1430 the Mexica elite, in order to strengthen their control and influence, decided to "burn the old pictographic histories" (1). Many argue that the replaced histories gave accounts that were favorable to the Mexicas and their imperialistic practices (Lara 2008a). Based on Bierhorst's view, we can suggest that this is why the Mexica version of the birth of *Huitzilopochtli* prevails as the most common and acceptable version of Aztec and Nahua thought. In the Mexican version of *Huitzilopchtli*'s birth, *Coatlicue* became pregnant with *Huitzilopchlti* without having relations with a man. The story says that when *Coatlicue* was sweeping the temple, she picked up a feather and put it in her apron. Through this feather she was impregnated. When *Coatlicue*'s other children found out she was expecting, they got jealous and conspired to murder *Huitzilopchtli,* but he prevailed (Robelo 1951). The legend says that when *Huitzilopchtli* was born as a grown man, in revenge, he brutally murders and dismembers his sister, *Coyolxauhqui,* who was the leader of the conspiracy against him (Carrasco 1990, Contreras 2008, Lara 2008a).

The Aztec's myth of *Huitzilopchtili*'s birth was foundational for their cosmovision (Carrasco 1990) and is indicative of how patriarchy and imperialism manifested in the Aztec Empire. The interest that Chicana feminists give to the Aztec version of *Coalticue* and *Huitzilopchtli*'s birth is due to its misogynistic function, especially *Coyolxauhqui*'s violent death and dismemberment. The myth of the birth of *Huitzilopochtli* is a symbol for the struggle for women's rights because this version of the myth is marred with patriarchal symbols and violence against women (Moraga 1983). Pedagogically, myths have a pivotal role in epistemological formations. As this discussion of the how the Aztecs re-interpreted Mesoamerican traditions demonstrates, myths can be, and often are, reconstituted for political and ideological purposes. In the case of the Aztecs, they reconstituted myths in ways that parallel their imperialistic ambitions and used them as ideological tools for domination.

The re-imagining of myths can serve different purposes, including libratory, and are not always oppressive. In this sense, this is what Anzaldúa does when she re-claims and re-imagines Nahua deities such as *Coatlicue,* by urging Chicanas to enter what she calls the *Coatlicue* state. This state disrupts the smooth flow (complacency) of life. Because *Coatlicue* has a life-giving and life-taking ability as the goddess of birth and death, she can give and take life away. These are the intrinsic abilities of women and explain why historically females have been feared. Anzaldúa re-imagines *Coatlicue* as a transitional figure that can takes us from the darker sides of the psyche towards nepantla. *Coatlicue* is symbolic of the underground aspects of psyche. The *Coatlicue* state is what propels the soul to do its work, to make soul, increase consciousness, "Our greatest disappointments and painful experiences—if we can make meaning out of them—can lead us toward becoming more of who we are. Or they can remain meaningless. The *Coatlicue* state can be a way of life" (46). The *Coatlicue* stage helps us develop an active agency that permits us to act upon the world and oppressive forces in this world. The *Coatlicue* stage does not let us be complacent. We need *Coatlicue,* Anzaldúa believes, to slow us so our psyche can assimilate previous experiences and process changes.

Anzaldúa is reclaiming *Coatlicue* from the Aztec/Mexica versions, which were not shared by other Mesoamerican groups that preceded them. Not only did the Mexicas burn the old books, but much of what we know about Mesoamerican cultures is tainted by Spanish influences that were not generous in their interpretation of indigenous cultures. As Chicana feminist scholar Irene Lara (2008a) points, the version we have of *Coatilcue's* pregnancy and defense of her murderous son is suspiciously Christian and reminds us that "given that most Nahua documents were destroyed and the knowledge we have about ancient Nahua culture is laden with Christian colonial and Nahua male bias, it is challenging to discern pre-transculturated Nahua beliefs and practices" (102). This exemplifies how myths are malleable and whose constitution, reproduction, and perseverance are done in the service of particular ideological positions. Through this re-claiming of Aztec female figures, Anzaldúa is laying down a Chicana feminist path. Her project must be understood as symbolic. She is not proposing historical, anthropological, or archeological scientific studies of Aztec worldview and cosmovision. For Yvonne Yarbro-Bejarano (1994) the "appropriation redefinition of *Coatlicue*" is done in the "service of creating a new mythos" (15). Keating (2008) proposes that by looking into the past, Anzaldúa is looking toward the future.

Conocimiento comes from opening all your senses, and "attention is multileveled and includes your surroundings, bodily sensations and responses, intuitive takes, emotional reactions to other people and theirs to you, and most important, the images your imagination creates—images connecting all tiers of information and their data" (Anzaldúa 2002, 542). Anzaldúa makes it clear that *conocimiento,* gaining consciousness, is not easy. Actually, it is a painful process because it requires connecting "inner acts" and "public acts." Indeed, the *Coatlicue* stage is like a detour when your mind, body, and spirit are not aligned, but it is where transformation can take place.

While in *Borderlands* Anzaldúa developed her theories of Chicana subjectivity as mestiza consciousness, she understands that categories and labels can be both liberating and constraining. Her call to *conocimiento* is to cross bridges and widening borders that can help us to be free from constraining categories. This process leads to the *Coyolxauhqui* consciousness; in order to become whole, we need to put together the fragments of our identities and spirit that have been dispersed as a result of injustices. The path of *conocimiento* that Anzaldúa proposes is a path to transformation, which permits you to view "life through the third eye, the reptilian eye looking inward and outward simultaneously, along with the perception of the shapeshifting naguala, the perceiver of shifts, results in conocimiento" (2002, 542).

BORDERLAND SUBJECTIVITIES

Anzaldúa's feminism is intrinsically tied with her experiences of multiple marginality as a border woman, a lesbian, her working class background, and self-identified mythical leanings and spirituality. Subjectivity refers to the conscious and unconscious sense of self and position in the world (Weedon 1987), and the ways in which we act upon the world is agency.

For Anzaldúa, the genesis of Chicana/o identity, mestizaje, was born in 1521 during the Spanish Conquest of México (5). La *mestiza,* as a borderlands inhabitant, creates her borderlands culture and identity: *mestiza consciousness.* Anzaldúa merges symbolic, cultural, and spiritual perspectives to formulate her notions of borderland subjectivities. Above all, Anzaldúa informs us, mestiza consciousness is *una conciencia de mujer* (women's consciousness), a consciousness of the borderlands. This consciousness understands how Chicanas move in and out of different worlds and cultures, by occupying interstitial spaces: "*la mestiza* is a product of the transfer of the cultural and spiritual values of one group to another" (Anzaldúa 1987, 78). For Anzaldúa, la mestiza has the ability (and necessity) to walk between and among cultures; she is "all cultures at the same time" (77). Being caught between different cultures and traditions that keep her back, la mestiza is in a constant struggle. Ambiguity and the ability to be flexible, to incorporate all aspects of mestizaje are the hallmarks and strong points of mestiza consciousness. Dolores Delgado Bernal (2001) asserts, "the term mestiza has come to mean a new Chicana consciousness that straddles cultures, races, languages, nations, sexualities, and spiritualities—that is, living with ambivalence while balancing opposing powers" (626). Rigidity, Anzaldúa informs us, for la mestiza, means death, so la mestiza cannot hold concepts in rigid boundaries. Mestiza consciousness is not the sum or synthesis of parts, but a third element.

> The new *mestiza* copes by developing a tolerance for contradictions, a tolerance
> for ambiguities. She learns to be an Indian in Mexican culture, to be Mexican
> from an Anglo point of view. She learns to juggle cultures. She has a plural
> personality, she operates in a pluralistic mode—nothing is thrust out, the good
> the bad and the ugly, nothing rejected, nothing abandoned. Not only does she
> sustain contradictions, she turns ambivalence into something else. (79)

Therefore, mestiza consciousness enacts multiple consciousnesses. This multiple consciousness is similar to that described by W.E.B. Du Bois as dual
consciousness, but takes it a step further because it moves beyond a binary
of dual consciousness (Martínez, T. 2002). Cultural memory and one's social
location is a path toward knowledge. This path of knowledge includes the
multiple positions Chicanas occupy in society; this is why Anzaldúa writes
that lesbianism is a path of knowledge, but of course, race, class, gender, age,
and spirituality are also conduits of knowledge.

Through mestiza consciousness, Anzaldúa develops a theory of consciousness that sets a "new paradigm for theorizing difference but also addresses
aspects of identity formation for which theories of subjectivity alone are
unable to account" (Yarbro-Bejarano 1994, 14). This Chicana feminist
process requires Chicanas to be conscious, that is to have knowledge of
their history, and indigenous roots.[7] Jacqueline Martínez (2000) argues that
consciousness and experience are directional; they are a "movement toward"
(8). "The contents of consciousness and experience are always *contingent,
situated,* and *existential"* (Martínez 2000, 9). Anzaldúa's endeavor, as
well as many other Chicanas, particularly Chela Sandoval, understands the
Chicana feminist project as one where agency and multiple subject positions
are constructed through an understanding and awareness of lived experience.
As most Chicana feminists' politics, Anzaldúa's is intrinsically tied with
embodied everyday lived experience. It is "theory in the flesh" (Anzaldúa and
Moraga 1981) and not an abstract philosophical discussion (Ortega 2001).
This is also a theory of agency because Chicanas do not stumble by accident
into their analysis; rather, it is arrived at through experience and consciousness, and they act to create social change. This is why Anzaldúa argues it is a
process marred by resistance to consciousness because it can be painful and
to expose vulnerabilities can be paralyzing. Nevertheless, this consciousness
is necessary for it is through awareness that there is growth. The power to
change, to know a power greater than the conscious "I" is the inner self, and
this is key for feminist consciousness.

For Anzaldúa, the shadow beast and *la facultad* articulate the source of
feminist rebellion. *La facultad* is the ability to "see in surface phenomena the
meaning of deeper realities, to see the deep structure below the surface" (38).

Women, gays and lesbians, people of color, outsiders, and immigrants are dominate societies' outcasts: those who do not feel "psychologically or physically safe in the world" (38) develop this ability. The experience of oppression and marginalization can lead people to make in-depth conclusions about their circumstances and develop the ability to see deeper structures. *La facultad* is a survival tactic based on experiences of oppression. Sonia Saldívar-Hull (2000) suggests that it "can be interpreted as a spiritual extra-sensory perception, what New Mestizaje has in fact developed is the ability to rupture the belief systems that have been presented as ancient truths and accurate histories" (65–6). However, it is not a static form of consciousness that is automatically shared by all members of an oppressed community. Norma Alarcón (2002) argues that the shadow beast works as a "recodified Lacanian unconscious, 'as the discourse of the Other' and as an Althusserian Imaginary through which the real is grasped and represented" (120–1). The shadow beast helps the Chicana subject to fight back against "cultural tyranny." Yvonne Yarbro-Bejarano (1994) believes that the shadow beast links the serpentine imagery with the *Coatlicue* state, embracing both positive and negative poles (20). Anzaldúa explains that the shadow beast is that part of herself that refuses to take orders—to obey authority. It is a part of her that hates constraints, even self-imposed ones.

The Shadow Beast and *La Facultad* are feminist strategies that Chicanas can use in order to create their own space, subjectivity, and self. Anzaldúa advocates that Chicana feminists uncover alternatives for women that are not necessarily outside of the culture, but that are not conformist and accommodationist. Anzaldúa seeks to "carve and chisel her own face," and to create her own culture with "my [her] own feminist architecture" (*Borderlands* 22). The foundations of this feminist architecture are germinated from indigenous ancestry.

The theoretical and metaphorical framework offered by Anzaldúa opened a conceptual space from which to understand Chicana identity as multiply constituted. This reconceptualization of Chicana identity is crucial for my analysis. The border identity proposed by Anzaldúa recognizes race, class, gender, and sexual discontinuities within Chicana/o communities. Like many other feminists of color, Chicana feminists follow principles of intersectionality, "advancing notions of hybridity which challenge the distinction between self and community, between Mexican and American, a Chicana feminist perspective disrupts dualisms by identifying the co-existence of seemingly contradictory ideas" (Flores 2000, 695). That is, a border/hybrid identity "recognizes the presence and synthesis of many cultures" (Torres, R. 1998, 178). The everyday experiences of women give form to Chicana feminist theory and practice (Flores 2000). What these alternative discourses offer is to open a third analytical space—Emma Pérez's (1999) "third space feminism"—that moves us beyond static understanding of identity, institutions, culture, and agency from rigid dialectical scrutiny to a multifaceted examination. In nepantla, binaries collapse and recognize the fluidity of identity categorizations; therefore, race, class, gender, and sexual orientation, while important categorizations, do need be understood as flexible and move beyond conventional labeling (Anzaldúa 2002). This does not mean that these categorizations are not significant, but that we must recognize them as contingent, changeable, and contradictory. That is, they can be liberating, but they can also be oppressive.

THIRD SPACE FEMINISM

Feminist politics are central in discussions of subjectivities and agency. Feminism refers to women's struggles to gain their rights in society; for Chicanas, it involves struggles against unequal gender, race, class, and sexuality ideologies in the U.S. and México. Chicana feminism is then a national and transnational struggle and offers a feminist praxis. That is, the process by which one puts into action the theories that frame one's works.

Border/borderland discourses influence Chicana feminism at the same time that the latter also has been instrumental for the development of borderland theories (Elenes & Delgado Bernal 2010). Sonia Saldívar-Hull's (2000) elaboration of "feminism on the border" offers a feminist praxis by acknowledging the urgency of acting on political issues that exploit and oppress Chicanas globally, nationally, and within Chicana/o communities and cultures. These include reducing sexism and homophobia in Chicana/o communities, confronting institutional racism, fighting against economic exploitation, and grappling with demands from traditional patriarchal Chicano and Mexican cultures. Saldívar-Hull's proposal follows a borderland standpoint non-binary analysis that offers a new form of thinking and activism and intervenes in multiple fronts academically in everyday life. For Saldívar-Hull notes that "Chicanas' dialectical position as feminists on the border demands different strategies for filling in the gaps of a suppressed history, not only as working class women of Mexican descent but as women, [both] lesbians and heterosexual" (Saldívar-Hull 2000, 34). Therefore, "feminism on the border" deals with "material geopolitical issues" that redirect feminist theory to address the "multiplicity of experiences" of Chicanas in solidarity with Third World feminists. This point is crucial for the development of border/transformative pedagogies.

Saldívar-Hull's feminism on the border seeks to explain and honor the experience and knowledge produced by Chicanas in their heterogeneity.[8]

Following the theoretical advances made by Cherrie Moraga who, in her 1983 book *Loving in the War Years,* linked Chicana theory and feminism with Third World feminism as a "global theory of power," Saldívar-Hull insists on examining the hegemonic dichotomy between the first and Third World. Accepting hegemonic dominant ideologies serves to separate women who are politically committed from coming together for a common cause. "As our alignment with women of the Third World indicates, our subject position exists in the interstices of national borders" (Saldívar-Hull 2000, 55). Therefore, Saldívar-Hull's feminism on the border makes alliances between Chicanas (and other women of color) in the U.S. and Latin American feminism.

Feminism on the border is akin to the alternative to binary systems of thought such as the concept of third space. The third space is the liminal/ interstitial space articulated by Chela Sandoval (1991, 1998, 2000), Homi Bhabha (1994), and Emma Pérez (1999). It is in this third space where the gaps between the unspoken and unseen unfold (Pérez, E. 1999). Indeed, Anzaldúa's understanding of mestiza consciousness creates a third space where a new feminist consciousness emerges and is enacted.

Within Chicana feminist theory, the inspiration for the development of third space theorizing comes from Sandoval's theory and methodology of oppositional and differential consciousness, who in turn was influenced by Anzaldúa's theories. In breaking with Western binary systems, Sandoval has identified five categories on which oppositional consciousness is organized: (1) equal rights, (2) revolutionary, (3) supremacist, (4) separatist, and (5) differential forms of oppositional consciousness (2000, 44). The first four categories, Sandoval informs us, can be understood as tactical essentialism. That is, while they are oppositional and resist dominant ideologies, they are still bound by Western discursive practices because they react to dominant practices. It is when oppositional movements proceed to the category of "differential consciousness" that they start to create a new way of thinking and praxis. Sandoval defines differential consciousness as a "kinetic motion" (44) that permit to function within, yet beyond, the demands of dominant ideology and as such offer far-reaching strategy by offering discourses and tactics on their own terms that not are not merely responding in opposition to existing discourses. As doing so might seem to help alleviate multiple forms of oppression and offer temporary solutions, but they do not change the dominant discourse formations. Differential consciousness offers new terms of discourse. This politicized oppositional identity requires "a specific methodology that can be used as a compass for self-consciously organizing resistance, identity, praxis and coalition building under U.S. late-capitalistic conditions" (2000, 62). Sandoval argues that differential consciousness is structurally analogous to Derrida's *difference* and Barthes' abyss" or third meaning; however, what differentiates Sandoval's theory is that oppositional consciousness is connected to oppositional social movements (i.e., feminist, civil rights, and gay and lesbian): its decolonial politics.

Following Chela Sandoval's differential consciousness, Emma Pérez proposes that third space recognizes the mobility of identities between and among varying power bases. This third space is a decolonial process and, according to Pérez's theorizing, it is a theory of agency where Chicanas self-consciously negotiate opposing ideologies. The decolonial imaginary is a theoretical tool for uncovering hidden voices of Chicanas that have been relegated by colonial categories as silent and passive. Pérez explains her concept of decolonial imaginary as a shadow, as the figure between the subject and the object on which it is cast, moving on through an in-between space (6). This decolonial imaginary helps rethink history—because Pérez is writing about history, but it can be expanded to other disciplines—"in a way that makes Chicana/o agency transformative" (5). The decolonial imaginary "is that time lag between the colonial and postcolonial, the interstitial space where different politics and social dilemmas are negotiated" (6). Therefore, when Chicana/o history, narratives, and cultural productions are written/ produced from an interstitial space—the third space—they are the product of a different way of thinking.

Engendering history and cultural productions happens in a similar way, according to Pérez. In colonial thought, women's activities went unseen and unthought by colonial forces. Yet women's voices persisted whether acknowledged or not (Pérez, E. 1999). Pérez argues that colonial categories of analysis are incomplete and distorting because they have suppressed the voices of the Other (men and women of color), however, the fact that they have been suppressed does not mean that Chicanas/os, for example, have not had a voice, or have not told their story. Sonia Saldívar-Hull (2000) argues that part of a Chicana feminist practice is the "insistence to speak for ourselves" (55). The task of decolonialism, what borderlands discourses urge us to do, is not to recover the silenced voices by using hegemonic categories of analysis, but to change the methodological tools and categories to reclaim those neglected voices. That is, it is not enough to add, for example, women's voices to old historical categories; rather what we need is to create new discursive practices. This undertaking is done to demonstrate that through this theory of agency, alternative and oppositional voices exist. For example, the feminist and women-centered narratives and cultural productions on La Llorona, La Virgen de Guadalupe, and Malintzin/Malinche must be understood beyond their function of revising patriarchal myths, but as alternative voices that have existed from the genesis of the myths. Such a strategy is not aimed at ignoring that these myths have also been articulated by patriarchal discourses; it is necessary to also look into "the gaps, lapses, and absences in the masculinist discourses that have written women out of their historical agenda" (Saldívar-Hull 2000, 53). This is why Pérez proposes that feminism as a methodological tool unleashes systems of thought from restrictive categories, the categories of modernity in which Chicana history has been trapped (22).

The methodology of the oppressed does not belong to a single population, but to the subordinate who seek empowerment (Sandoval, C. 2000, 152). Third space feminism, which is equivalent to borderlands feminism, calls upon "syncretic forms of consciousness." This is the form of feminist politics that interrupts white feminist binary politics and contributes to the formation of categories and principles where there is mobility between races, genders, sexes, cultures, languages, and nations (Sandoval, C. 1998). As a discourse that refused to be trapped by categories, but which at the same time recognizes that these labels affect women's experiences and their material conditions, third space feminism recognizes the need for these categorizations as contingent. In this sense, these feminist politics do not follow a color or gender-blind policies, but the notion of new tribalism that Anzaldúa endorses.

TOWARD BORDER/TRANSFORMATIVE PEDAGOGIES

The three interwoven themes that serve as the basis for my interpretation of Anzaldúa's work—*conocimiento*/epistemology, borderland subjectivities, and third space feminism—are central for the analysis of the pedagogies of La Llorona, La Virgen de Guadalupe, and Malintzin/Malinche, and for the development of border/transformative pedagogies. As popular cultural forms, these legends are examples of the relationship between everyday culture and knowledge. The myriad of cultural productions depicting these three figures represent a multiplicity of disparate discourses that can explain, critique, offer alternatives, and/or support traditional definitions of Chicanas and *mexicanas*. Borderlands theoretical frameworks provide exegetical analytical tools that elucidate on the multiplicity and contradictory representations of the three figures. Sonia Saldívar Hull (2000) identifies the work of mestiza consciousness as that of a "feminist historian" that documents and reinterprets history by re-deploying historical symbols and recasting them as new myths. The cultural production on La Llorona, La Virgen de Guadalupe, and Malinztin/Malinche are borderlands stories in that they connect multiple forms of subjectivity and transcend national borders. They are inherently representative of mestizaje. Chicana feminists' re-imagining of the three figures and are also examples of spiritual activism because they offer an avenue to take subjectivity as a whole and as a source of transformation.

Chicana feminist emphasis on the significance of everyday experience of women is fundamental in reconstructing borderland subjectivities and in the development of border/transformative pedagogies. Feminist theorizing has long recognized that women's stories show "how personal experience contains larger political meaning[s]" (Latina Feminist Group 2001, 3). Experience and community memory often times serve as the bases for the process of constructing knowledge. As José David Saldívar reminds us, the discourse of the borderlands is an invitation to "redraw the borders between folklore and the counterdiscourses of marginality, between 'everyday' culture and 'high' culture, and between 'people with culture' and 'people between culture'" (1997, 17). Border/transformative pedagogies, then, help us understand that the cultural productions from *las de abajo,* including the productions since the sixteenth century on La Malinche, La Virgen de Guadalupe, and La Llorona have served to maintain a culture that might seemed vanished. Borderland discourses' emphasis on the everyday life is intrinsically tied with the relationship between experiences of colonization, decolonization, marginalization, immigration, racism, homophobia, and patriarchy.

In order to advance educational research (and hopefully a practice) that benefits Chicanas/os, it is necessary to promote multifaceted conceptualizations that move beyond binary and dialectical analyses of education. The multifaceted perspective developed by borderland scholars helps to simultaneously examine how dominant practices negatively affect Chicana/o education and how the Chicana/o community has struggled against such practices in efforts to transform educational institutions and pedagogy. Border/transformative conceptualizations offer different and more complex understanding of Chicana/o subjectivity and agency than those usually articulated by liberal and conservative educational discourses. It also expands the meaning of education to include everyday popular cultural forms.

Borderland theories do not look at power in a one-dimensional way, rather they take into account how institutions and individuals adapt to different historical moments and ideologies. As I have showed, proponents of borderland theories look at the enactment of power in complex, multidirectional ways. Borderlands scholars believe in active agency, and they recognize that although individuals are influenced by dominate ideologies, they do negotiate among competing ideologies. The notion of hybridity that is so common for borderland theories recognizes that people and institutions do not simply accept or reject ideologies in purely deterministic ways. Instead, we find that there are traces of different ideologies in all sides of the political spectrum. What borderland theories seek to do with this understanding is to offer an alternative to traditional educational research that provides mono-causal analyses of education in favor of educational research that offer the type of "another thinking" elaborated by Mignolo and Arteaga.[9]

As several Chicana/o education scholars have documented, the belief that Chicanas/os', and other people of color's, culture is at fault for their lack of educational attainment has, and continues to influence much of the educational policy aimed at "improving" Chicana/o education (Cuádraz 2005, Delgado Bernal 1999, García 2001, Donato 1997, Valencia 2002). The analyses of the ways in which dominant discourses inform policy are essential to develop different ways of understanding education. Borderland theories combine an analysis of definitions of identity from dominant and subaltern perspectives and the historical relations between U.S. mainstream with people of Mexican descent. Therefore, they are applying *los conocimientos* articulated in mestiza consciousness, nepantla, borderland subjectivities, spiritual activism, and third space feminism.

As I discuss in chapter 1, dominant historical discourses and popular culture have helped institutionalize and reproduce hegemonic notions of U.S. history that subordinate people of color. It is equally important to bring into the discussion Chicana/o cultural productions that have been developed outside the normative spaces of education and culture. It is not enough to document the ways in which Chicanas/os and other people of color have been excluded and distorted from educational discourses and practices. It is important to also show that marginalized groups have resisted and offered alternatives to such domination. Marginalized communities find ways to express their ideas, often times in popular culture. In Chicana/o communities, these manifestations are represented, for example, in corridos, storytelling, narratives, myths, and legends that document the ways Chicanas/os make sense of their life in the U.S.[10] Indeed, cultural studies scholars such as José David Saldívar (1995) propose that subaltern cultures should be incorporated in the education of future generations if we are to decenter dominant notions of American cultural studies. Saldívar believes that one way to accomplish this is by studying Chicana/o popular cultural productions such as music, literature, and performance arts as legitimate forms of knowledge production and pedagogy.

In this historical juncture, it is still necessary to counter cultural deficit views because of the phenomenon of developing "popular" educational policy in the ballot box (i.e., anti-bilingual education propositions in California, Arizona, Colorado, and Massachusetts) and conservative critiques of ethnic and women's studies (see Cline, Necochea & Rios 2004).[11] Educators and researchers that are offering alternatives to these conservative and to liberal approaches as well, often times find themselves in the position of articulating their position in contrast to the dominant views of Chicanas/os as inferior. Critical educators are to a certain extent responding to the realities of the "raw racism" that underlines conservative and liberal approaches to education. Borderland theories offer alternative theories, methodologies, and epistemologies to avoid the pitfalls of essentialism, conservatism, and relativism. Following these approaches, border/transformative pedagogies do not jettison analysis of the material conditions that affect the quality of life of Chicanas/os and are central for social justice issues, and adhere to the epistemologies, subjectivities, and feminist projects articulated by Gloria Anzladúa, Emma Pérez, Sonia Saldívar-Hull, and Chela Sandoval that I have outlined in this chapter.

The contours of border/transformative pedagogies are the following:

- Border/transformative pedagogies recognize that the existence of the México-U.S. border is central in understanding the experience of people of Mexican descent in a variety of social institutions, including schools and popular culture. By expanding the understanding of the significance of the border in the concrete material conditions of people of Mexican descent in the U.S. and its metaphorical meaning, the borderlands helps understand how the boundaries among different social groups also affect their experiences. Therefore, border/transformative pedagogies are concerned with history, how it is constructed, and how its construction affects the power relations involved in how we come to believe what knowledge is, how it is legitimated, and how it gets transmitted.
- Thus, the pedagogies of La Llorona, La Virgen de Guadalupe, and Malintzin/Malinche are involved in the construction of knowledge/conocimiento and in its dissemination in a variety of pedagogical formation. The cultural workers/education actors involved in re-inscribing the meaning of these figures are creating alternative epistemologies centered on feminist ways of being in the world, and in doing so, reconstructing their meanings, thus enacting Chicana feminist pedagogies.
- Such enactment demonstrates the significance of Chicana feminist borderland subjectivities and agency by recognizing that cultural workers/educational actors produce knowledge that is critical of the material conditions that subordinate Chicanas, and struggle to change those conditions. Chicanas, who engage in borderland subjectivities, refuse to take a position of passive victims of oppression, but rather become activist agents who are seeking to transform their society in the service of social, gender, and spiritual justice.

- Spiritual activism is a significant tool for the formation of border/ transformative pedagogies because it recognizes people's subjectivity as a whole and as a source of transformation. Chicana cultural workers/ educational actors' commitment to social justice connect feminist praxis, spirituality, and education.
- This process of enacting such agency and spiritual activism is based on subjectivities that result from multiple forms of oppression based on racialization, immigration, sexuality, gender, and class, among many others. At the same time, it recognizes that these categories are tenuous and have a colonial history.
- Even though my elaboration on border/transformative pedagogies in this book centers on popular culture, these can be enacted in a variety of institutional settings including schools. That is, in general, educational practices can also enact border/transformative pedagogies (see Elenes 2006) to make schools, universities, community centers, museums or other cultural institutions become transformative institutions where complex histories, epistemologies, agency, and subjectivity are taken into account.

In the same way that borderland education scholars understand education as a process of teaching and learning in formal and informal school settings, border/transformative pedagogies are interested in analyzing and understanding the informal settings that give voice to the three Mexican mythical figures: La Llorona, La Virgen de Guadalupe, and Malintzin/Malinche. By showing how border/transformative pedagogies are enacted in the alternative and deconstructive strategies utilized by Chicana feminist cultural workers, in the next three chapters I analyze the pedagogies associated with each of these figures. While my focus is most on how can we understand the meanings associated with these figures from a borderland symbolic perspective, it is important to recognize that the genesis of the three figures was during the Spanish conquest of México. As the Spanish moved their conquest north to what is today the U.S. and brought with them people of Aztec descent, the legends were brought with them. After Mexican independence from Spain and after the U.S. annexed Mexico's northern territories in the nineteenth century, and as people of Mexican descent have immigrated to the U.S. in the twentieth and twenty-first centuries, they continue to bring the legends with them. Therefore, the legends experience a process of transculturation. At the same time, Chicanas/os also maintain alive the legends, myths, and cultural meanings associated with La Llorona, La Virgen de Guadalupe, and Malintzin/Malinche. Thus, for Chicanas/os, the three figures are central in their cultural productions.

NOTES

1. By critical education scholarship, I am referring to works that use a variety of theoretical frameworks that include, but are not limited to, borderland and border theories, critical race theory, feminist theory, postmodernism, and poststructuralism. These scholars use a variety of methodologies, yet most follow qualitative research methods to examine issues that affect Mexican American education. What make these works critical, in addition to the theoretical and methodological approaches, are their engagement with social justice and a yearning to impact social change.

2. Dillard racialized the Enlightenment metaphor as illumination, but proposes that knowledge produced by racialized groups as endarken to illustrate the embodiment of knowledge.

3. In more recent publications, such as *this bridge we call home* and interviews with various feminist scholars including AnaLouise Keating and Irene Lara, Anzaldúa elucidated that working with different groups was important to her, and of her weariness about nationalistic politics that make working on alliances difficult. This is an important aspect of Anzaldúa's work, and I will return to this point in chapter 6. Yet, Anzaldúa maintained her Chicana identity, and how she viewed this identity and how it was a source for her philosophy is my interest in this book, hence my focus on Chicanas.

4. While endarken epistemologies specifically address how people of color construct knowledge based on their social position, one could argue that borderland epistemologies might seem narrow and too localized. Rather than viewing this worldview exclusively based on social position, I believe that anybody who takes a position against domination and in the service of social and gender justice and is willing to work to bridge the divides that exist among social groups can enact borderland sensibilities.

5. Anzaldúa's point that we should disconnect from electronic devices from time-to-time is well taken. However, I want to point out that technology can also have a liberatory function. For example, activists use the Internet and social media to communicate along the globe. International relief organizations are using cell phone text messages as fundraising tools as exemplified with the relief efforts for Haiti and Chile.

6. See Carrasco for an explanation of how the Aztecs adapted their beliefs from Olmecas and Toltecas.

7. Knowledge of indigenous past is necessary to develop decolonial practices. Arguably, not everyone will or should follow indigenous worldviews. While some believe (e.g., Contreras 2008, Keating 2008) that Anzaldúa romanticized *indigenismo* in *Borderlands,* it is important to remember that since the Spanish colonization of the Americas, indigenous peoples and their symbolic production and spirituality have been devalued. Therefore, it is important for Chicanas/os and Mexicanas/os to understand their indigenous past in order to move toward decolonial standpoints.

8. Sonia Saldívar-Hull unwittingly reifies the working class. This commitment to the working class is understandable because many Chicana theorists originate from

the working class, and the need to theorize the relationship between social location and experience. Yet, not all self-identified Chicanas come from the working class. This point is important because borderland theories recognize that experience is linked to social location. Chicanas' from different class locations, and those who have experienced class mobility, might have a different epistemological outlook. Additionally, if borderland theories are to take into account the differences within the Chicana/o community, it is imperative to recognize and theorize class differences. I believe that this reification of the working class is due to the political commitments of the Chicano movement and Chicana feminism. After all, the majority of people of Mexican descent in the U.S. are working class. Moreover, I would venture to argue that a good number (if not the majority) of Chicana and Chicano academics have their class origin in the working class. However, by the time these individuals are able to publish their theories, they have experienced class mobility in terms of education, income, and access to power (albeit limited).

9. One of the criticisms in general to progressive theories of education is that more often than not the alternatives to dominant educational practices are done within the confines of theory and between the covers of books and journal articles. That is, there are very few real life examples of progressive practices. I am afraid that this is the case as well with borderland theories, especially at the K–12 level. The problem is that conservatives have much control over the elementary and secondary school system, where it is much more difficult to enact the desired changes. This is not for the lack of trying, as many community groups try to implement changes. In higher education we have been able to see more changes due to the relative autonomy that faculty have in developing and teaching courses. Moreover, the policy in many universities that faculty are in charge of the curriculum (while not always true) does leave venues for faculty and students to demand and implement changes. This is how women's studies and ethnic studies programs and departments came into existence. This point is important because, while I am arguing in favor of developing alternative and new educational theories, I know they have not been implemented as much as I would like to see them. There is still a lot of work that needs to be done to create such change, but perhaps as we struggle against conservative and liberal educational policies, we can think of ways in which progressive educational ideology can be presented to the public at large in ways that will make sense to them.

10. I am not proposing that all popular culture developed by Chicanas/os and Mexicans in the U.S. are different forms of thinking. Rather, following a border-lands perspective, as I will demonstrate in the next three chapters, Chicana/o popular culture are quite contradictory and can and do simultaneously offer alternatives to traditional thinking and reproduce forms of oppression such as sexism, racism, classism, and homophobia. Another important point to take into account is that people of Mexican descent are staunch consumers of U.S. popular culture. A visit to Disneyland or a trip to any Disney movie demonstrates how much Mexican American children enjoy such popular cultural forms of expression.

11. HB 2281, passed by the Arizona legislature and signed by Governor Jan Brewer, bans ethnic studies courses in public and charter schools (see chapter 6 for

an explanation of the scope of the bill). The law specifically targets Tucson Unified School District's Raza Studies Program. Former State Superintendent of Public Instruction Tom Horne has pushed for this legislation over the years. In 2010 it was sponsored by Arizona Representative Steve Montenegro. Horne, Montenegro, and other conservatives such as anti-immigrant Senator Russell Pierce call ethnic studies "harmful and dysfunctional." The attacks on ethnic studies ignore the fact that students enrolled in the program have higher test scores on the AIMS test (Arizona standardized test used for No Child Left Behind purposes). (Pat Kossan, *The Arizona Republic*, retrieved on line at http://www.azcentral.com/community/phoenix/articles, June 17, 2009.)

Chapter 3

La Llorona

Decolonial and Anti-Patriarchal Cultural Politics

A girl fell in love with a high society man. They married and had two children, but his family didn't approve. He brought her to the hacienda, but after a while didn't love her anymore so he send her away. Then he re-married a woman of his class but could not have children, so he went looking for his children. The girl refused to give them back, so the night before the husband came for the children she took them to the river and drown them. For a long time she roamed the river and cried. After she died one could hear her crying. She had gone crazy and regretted her act. One hears the cries of La Llorona near the river. (Center for Southwest Research "Baughman Collection," University of New Mexico)

La Llorona represents mother earth, the all-sorrowing mother of an entire people to the Mexicans. It is difficult to tell when legends first appeared, for she was well known by the Aztecs of Cortez' time as she is known to the Mexicans of today. There are stories that her wailings were heard for weeks throughout the villages of Mexico before the landing of Cortez. She always foretells a disaster, rarely of a personal nature. It is something that will affect the entire village, like the death of their priest; an entire area, like the coming of an earthquake; or an entire nation, like the death of a president. There is rarely an earthquake that the old women do not say, oh yes, I knew it was coming, I heard La Llorona the other night. She was very active during the era of Pancho Villa and of Benito Juárez. (Oral History of La Llorona, Center for Southwest Research, University of Arizona)[1]

I have a vague memory from my early childhood of the first time I heard my father tell me the story of La Llorona. I believe I was about 5 years old, and my family was driving around the outskirts of Mexico City, near *El desierto de los Leones,* a beautiful hill-top forest between México City and el Estado de México. I remember my father was telling us stories of some pranks he

69

had done with his friends when they were young men in their late teens or early twenties. One prank, or perhaps a dare, involved entering a cemetery in the middle of the night. According to my father—and as it is typical in some versions—La Llorona appeared to the young men in the cemetery. When they "saw" her they ran out of the cemetery as fast as they could. The version of the legend of La Llorona my father told me that day, and in many subsequent re-tellings, was the well-known version of a young maiden who kills her children as revenge against their father who had done her wrong. As I have thought about this story over the years, I truly believe he made it up and was using it as a way to tell us the story of La Llorona. The part of the story that I clearly remember was that La Llorona was looking for her lost children and she would take any one she could find. The lesson was not lost on my very young mind: "If I don't behave, La Llorona will come and take me! Probably to a horrible scary place such as cemetery so I must behave well and obey my parents." My father's strategy worked, the pedagogy of La Llorona is still not lost on me.

The legend of La Llorona expresses border/transformative pedagogies manifested in popular culture. My purpose in this chapter is to examine the pedagogies of La Llorona through an analysis of oral histories of the legend in Arizona and New Mexico. Through these oral histories, we can see how ordinary people, particularly women, have been active participants in the creation of alternative meanings of La Llorona by criticizing women's subordinate position both in the U.S. and in México. As a backdrop for my analysis, I offer a critical examination of how Chicana feminist theorists and cultural workers have deconstructed and re-imagined La Llorona.

LA LEYENDA DE LA LLORONA

For almost 500 years, people of Mexican descent have transmitted the legend of La Llorona. Mexican and Chicana/o parents, mostly mothers,[2] have told the legend to their children, and these children will continue to tell it to their own offspring, whether they believe in its veracity or not, usually with the purpose of making children obey their parents. Of the three mythical figures that I am analyzing in this book, La Llorona has a clear pedagogical (some call it didactic) function. The teachings and learning involved in the telling of the story vary according to the version presented; hence the pedagogical function of the legend also varies. The most conventional narrative of La Llorona reproduces traditional values such as obedience and responsibility: children should obey their parents; fathers should not drink and leave their families; women should accept traditional notions of womanhood and sexuality. Any deviation of these norms will result in catastrophe, particularly the death of children. While early critiques of the legend of La Llorona on the part of Chicana and mexicana feminists centered on its patriarchal meanings, I believe that different connotations and diverse versions of the story have existed from the inception of the legend. Women have not only *resisted* its patriarchal implications, an in-depth analysis of the variations of the legend demonstrates that La Llorona is a much more complicated story because from its genesis it has included critiques of patriarchy and colonization.

Symbolically, through La Llorona, women can undermine the contradictory position they must contend with in a patriarchal society that venerates motherhood but subordinates women and tends to neglect children. La Llorona has endured for so many years in part because it is an intricate legend that evokes multiple and contradictory ideological and political meanings. The legend changes according to who is telling the story, as well as where the story is told, and under what circumstances. There are literally thousands of variations of the narrative that have been recorded in the U.S. and in México, as exemplified in the two versions cited in the beginning of the chapter.

Stories of infanticide are almost universal (e.g., Medea, *The Joy Luck Club*, *Beloved*). The loss of a child's life is disturbing because it is the loss of a future, of a life not lived to its potential. Most cultures hold up to the value and hope that children will have the opportunity to grow up and achieve their potential in order to contribute to the well-being of the society. Therefore, it is very difficult to accept the death of children. In part, this is why the loss of children is marred by symbolism that goes beyond a life not fulfilled; it can be associated with a culture's annihilation as in the case of conquest. One of the characteristics and consequences of colonialism is the violent imposition of the culture of the colonizer.[3]

Infanticide is, unfortunately, a common occurrence; it has existed since biblical times and continues in contemporary societies. Not withstanding idealistic notions of motherhood, mothers have killed their own children not only in legend but in real life, too. In the U.S., in recent years we have witnessed cases of contemporary women (Lloronas) who have killed their children in similar ways that the legendary Llorona. For example, Andrea Yates of Houston, Texas, drowned her children in her bathtub because she did not believe that she was a good mother, almost a decade before Susan Smith also drowned her children by strapping them in their car seats and pushing her car into a lake—and then proceeded to claim she was carjacked by a black man. Smith supposedly killed her children because her boyfriend would not marry her because he did not want the responsibility of a family. These two images of (in these cases white) mothers shocked the nation because they run counter to the stereotypes and idealization of motherhood constructed through conservative family values rhetoric in vogue since the 1950s. While some might empathize with Andrea Yates if she is ill, there is only scorn for Susan Smith.[4] Because infanticide has and continues to exist, many societies create legends about infanticide.

In the legend of La Llorona, conflicts over the meanings of appropriate female behaviors are played out. Starting in the sixteenth century, not long after the Spanish Conquest of México and continuing throughout the Mexican colonial period, the emergence of the Mexican nation-state and a new colonial intervention after the U.S. "annexed" México's northern territories, La Llorona (in its multiple variants) responds to such changes. La Llorona is commonly known as a story of infanticide, sexuality, betrayal, and/or social injustice. But the legend can also be understood as a decolonial practice that demonstrates the agency of Mexican and Chicana/o populations to re-create popular culture in ways that symbolically counteract colonial interventions, classism, sexism, and racism, and at the same time reproduce patriarchal ideology (Carbonell 1999). "Often the context of the stories is conquest, colonization, and violence against subaltern peoples" tells us historian Linda Heidenreich (2005, 35). Given that La Llorona is a complex legend, it can symbolize social injustice when the meaning ascribed to it refers to the unequal material conditions that Chicanas and Mexicanas endure under capitalism, patriarchy, and colonialism; it can symbolize patriarchy when applied to enforce traditional sexual mores. It is a story that endorses pedagogy of appropriate female sexuality and punishment, male responsibility, and sobriety.

It is precisely in these multiple meanings of La Llorona that we can analyze the legend as border/transformative pedagogy and third space feminism. La Llorona is a pedagogical practice because in its multiple variations the narrators purposefully try to influence meanings of appropriate or inappropriate womanhood and motherhood. The changing meanings of La Llorona are produced by everyday constructions of popular culture, thus making the legend a democratic narrative. As José Limón (1990) argues, unlike the narrative about the Virgin of Guadalupe, where there is an official Catholic account, La Llorona is a democratic narrative, for officially sanctioned and truthful descriptions of La Llorona do not exist (423) and everybody can create his or her own story. Women usually transmit the legend; therefore, they have created many of the contradictory meanings associated with La Llorona. In particular, because La Llorona is a democratic narrative, we find many conflicting and contradictory meanings ranging from patriarchal to feminist. La Llorona continues to be transmitted and adapted to new social and political situations. In order to ascertain how these various meanings are produced, it is necessary to take into account the context of the articulation of the particular variant of the legend.

CHICANA FEMINIST PEDAGOGIES AND EVERYDAY POPULAR CULTURE

As I have explained in the introduction of this book, the meaning of pedagogy expands from classroom practices to teaching and learning in everyday life. Popular culture has an important pedagogical function in all its different manifestations. Of particular importance in this and the next two chapters is to understand that most cultural manifestations and everyday interactions among human beings involve some form of teaching and learning. This process of creating cultural productions is a manifestation of ways in which everyday people construct knowledge. Through the five centuries that the legend of La Llorona has existed, women have been transmitting lessons and knowledge about the meanings they ascribe to the legend.

Understanding these meanings as pedagogical is an effort to recognize Ruth Trinidad Galván's (2001) contention that "everyday ways of learning and teaching that arise around kitchen tables, on church steps, in local stores, and in family courtyards remain untheorized as distinct pedagogical forms" (606) and advance such theorization. Indeed, some critical pedagogues have argued with Trinidad Galván that the kitchen table is not a classroom. The ahistoricism of this statement is emblematic of gender and racist bias in Western imperialism. Education has taken place in many non-classroom sites including pubs, churches, and of course, kitchen tables. Trinidad Galván agrees that the kitchen table is not a classroom per se, but it is a site of teaching and learning and I would add one where meaningful education takes place. Historically, women have had to find places where they can teach, learn, and construct knowledge, and the spaces available and sanctioned to them are those traditionally occupied by women such as kitchen tables or church steps.

The pedagogical transmission of the legend of La Llorona usually occurs in the context of family relations or people "doing" family in informal spaces such as the kitchen table, a parent's lap, or in the car as I recall my first lesson of La Llorona. In this sense, the legend of La Llorona falls under the definition of Womanist pedagogy because it is situated "among groups of people traditionally unheard and spaces continually unexplored" (Trinidad Galván 2001, 607), in ways that "analysis of these spaces opens a different window to our notion of pedagogy and the knowledge created" (607). While the legend of La Llorona eventually was heard in classrooms, and there are scholars who have recognized the need to document many of the different versions, it continues to be transmitted orally within the confines of the family.

LA LLORONA'S AMBIVALENT "ORIGINS"

The legend of La Llorona, transmitted orally from generation to generation, is encountered wherever Mexicans and people of Mexican descent live. The traditional narrative tells the story of a beautiful young woman (she can be mestiza, Creole, and Indian; rich or poor but for the most part of humble origin) sometimes named Luisa or Rita who fell in love with a rich man. They happily lived together and had between one and three children. However, the man's mother demanded that he married within his class, which he did. When she found out about his action, in a moment of jealousy she killed their children. Some versions say that she died a violent death, others that when she died (it is not specified how) and went to heaven, God told her she could not enter until she found her children. That is why she is looking for her children. She returns as a ghost, dressed in white, looking for her children.

Over the years, the legend of La Llorona has become a "boogie man" story to keep children from straying. Children are told that La Llorona is looking for her children and she will take any child she finds. She particularly scares men, and in many versions she has a very cold breath and when she uncovers her face, one sees her skeleton. Once a person (especially a man) sees La Llorona, either he/she dies immediately or when telling the story. More recently, people don't die but do get very scared ("les da susto"), and some end up bed ridden for months.

There is not one "true" version or meaning of La Llorona, but there are similarities and variations of particular themes among the narratives. Shirley Arora (1981), quoting Horcasitas and Butterworth, classifies the narratives as three different prototypes: biographical, encounters/siren, and a combination of the previous two. According to Arora, Horcasitas and Butterworth's first prototype is a reconstruction of various narratives of the biographical prototype. This prototype is similar to the most common narrative, or what Arora calls the Luisa story. Since in many versions her child(ren) drowned or she drowned them, she usually is encountered near bodies of water. Arora believes that "non-folkloric" sources such as plays, movies, et cetera have influenced the oral tradition. According to her, the Luisa story was influenced by an 1893 drama by Francisco Neve (26).

In Thomas Janvier's version in *Legends of México,* La Llorona is considered the most dangerous of ghostly apparitions in México (1910, 134). In this narrative, when La Llorona was alive, she committed terrible sins. As soon as she had a child, she would throw her/him into one of the canals that surrounded México City, and the child would drown. She continued this practice for many years, and at last her conscience began to bother her, but nobody knows if this was due to the priest or saints talking to her. What is certain is that she weeps and wails in the streets as a result of her sins. She wears white, has cold breath, and her face is a skeleton. It is only possible to see her in a dark, deserted street, and it is a death sentence to those who see her. She can be seen at the same time (day or night) in different cities, crying, "Where shall I find my children?" (135–8).

There are many scholarly debates on the origins of the legend of La Llorona. Limón refers to her as a syncretic figure of European and indigenous origin and a relative of the Medea story (1990, 400). Other similarities with European legends include the German legend of *Die Weisee Frau* (Barakat 1987; Kirtley 1960; Lomax Hawes 1968), Lilith of Jewish origin, and the Lamia of Greek folk (Candelaria 1977). Next, I will first explain the Aztec origins, and then I will discuss the aforementioned Western legends that are similar to La Llorona.

Aztec Origins

González Obregón, (1937) in his book *Las Calles de México,* proposes that the legend of La Llorona began at the middle of the sixteenth century, not long after the Spanish conquest. People in México City would be awakened in the middle of the night by the weeping of a woman who without a doubt had deep moral and great physical pain (13). She would wear a white dress and cover her face with a thick veil. She was named La Llorona because nobody knew who she was (14). González Obregón believes that the origins of La Llorona are Aztec and, as do many others, cites Sahagún to maintain this claim. González Obregón also asserts that La Llorona is the sixth prognostication of the doom of the indigenous inhabitants of Mexico (15).[5] León Portilla (1992) states that the sixth prognostication referred to a woman who would cry at night: "*¡Hijitos míos, pues ya tenemos que irnos lejos! Y a veces decía:—Hijitos míos, ¿a dónde os llevaré?*" (4). [Oh my small children we must go far away! And other times she would say:—Oh my children, Where will I take you?" (My translation)]. León Portilla footnotes that this woman refers to Cihuacoatl and is one of the antecedents of La Llorona (4). Janvier believes that the origins of La Llorona are wholly Mexican, and also claims she is related to Cihuacoatl (162). The Aztec elements of the legend include the wailing, water, knife, and general appearance (Barakat 1987). Cecilio Robelo (1951) writes that Cihuacoatl is the mother of human

7. *Connection*

beings. *Cihuatl* means woman, *coatl* snake. She is the snake woman, who when giving birth always had twins. Some traditions believe that the twins she had were Huitzilopochtli and Quetzalcoatl, therefore Cihuacoatl and Coatlicue are confused as the same goddess, as Chavero does (quoted in Robelo). However, in Mexica traditions, Coatlicue is Huitzilopochtli's mother. There is little doubt that La Llorona is related to Cihuacoatl, as this goddess would appear at night with a roaring voice. Her clothes were white, and sometimes she would carry a small crib on her back as if she were carrying a small child (Robelo 1951, 60–62). The water in which the children drown can be a symbol of rebirth, as water in Aztec traditions symbolized rebirth (Heidenreich 2005).

Another relationship to Aztec deities is Cihuateteo or Cihuapipiltin. She was the spirit of the women who had died in childbirth. These spirits would leave their world in the West to come down to earth and bring disease to children. During the days that these spirits appeared, parents would not let their children outdoors. Her image was pale as if her face, arms, and legs had been painted in white. In order to placate these women's spirits, people would make offerings to Cihuateteo of bread shaped into different forms, usually butterflies, lightning, tamales, and esquite (Robelo 1951).

Although some of the early reports of the apparition of La Llorona locate her in México City, she does not belong exclusively to the city (Janvier 1910). There are many Aztec elements in the origin of the legend, but it was quickly diffused to other regions of México and eventually to greater México (including the U.S.). Janvier believes that this diffusion occurred because the Spanish had the custom of strengthening their frontier by placing settlements of loyal Aztecs near such frontiers. These loyal Aztecs took with them their customs and, of course, legends and their beliefs in their Gods (163). González Obregón also writes that it was believed that La Llorona is La Malinche crying after the death of her fallen children: the Mexicans. As is well accepted in popular culture and literature, (e.g., Anaya), the two figures are often believed to be the same. However, Mexican and Chicana feminists have demonstrated that this understanding of La Malinche serves patriarchal ideology and forms part of the trope of treachery that I discuss in chapter 5. In their anthology on Chicana writers, Rebolledo and Rivero (1993) argue that folklore fuse together images and mythology of La Llorona and Malinche to the point that they are considered the same woman. "In general, the image is a negative one, tied up in a vague way, with sexuality and the death of children: the negative mother image" (192). Consolidating the two figures into one assumes that Malinche did betray "her people" and repents. Arora also believes that the identification of La Llorona as Malinche owes more to literary sources than to the oral tradition (27).

European Syncretism

Some of the Western figures that are believed to be related to La Llorona include Medea, Lilith, Lamia, and the White Lady. The distinct relationship between Medea and Llorona is quite clear since the men they loved and trusted betrayed them. Medea fell in love with Jason and helped him on numerous occasions and even killed for him. After long journeys and adventures, Medea and Jason settled down for ten years in Corinth. Jason wearied of Medea and decided to marry Creusa, the daughter of King Creon. In revenge, Medea sent her a nuptial gown, which gave violent flames when she put it on and consumed the palace with Creusa herself and her father. In revenge for this betrayal, Medea kills their children and, as a result, was sentenced to wander along. Afterwards, she fled on a winged chariot. Medea led a wandering life, and eventually found refuge in Asia in the land of Media that took its name after her. There is one tradition that claims that Medea never died, but was carried off to the underworld to be the wife of Achilles.

Lilith is Adam's first wife, according to Hebrew tradition, before Eve. Lilith, unlike Eve, was made of out clay as was Adam. However, the clay that God used was impure and as a result she turned out to be an evil spirit (Patai 1967/1990), or, as I prefer to see her, a strong and defiant woman. Lilith refused to have sexual relations with Adam because he demanded that she lay underneath him. Demanding her equal status, she questioned: "'Why should I lie beneath you,' she asked, 'when I am your equal, since both of us were created from dust'?" (Patai 1967/1990, 223). When Lilith realized that Adam intended to overpower her, she uttered God's name and flew away to the Red Sea (Patai 1967/1990). God sent three angels, Senoy, Sansenoy, and Semangelof, to bring her back to Adam. In the Red Sea, Lilith had "engaged in unbridled promiscuity" (223) and bore many demons. When she was threatened with drowning, she struck a deal with the angels:

> Let me be, for I was created in order to weaken the babes: if a male, I have power over him from the moment of his birth until the eighth day of his life [when he is circumcised and thereby protected], and if a girl, until the twentieth day. (qtd. in Patai 1967/1990, 223)

In Jewish, Christian, and Islamic mythology, she is considered a female demon. Around the middle ages, the Zohar writings ascribed Lilith's two activities: seducing men and killing children. The Talmud describes Lilith as a demonlike hag who terrorizes children and women, especially pregnant women. The King James Version of the Bible describes her as a "screech owl" and other biblical translations as a "night hag."

Her similarity with La Llorona is in that she roams the world seeking out children who "deserve" to be punished. Cordelia Candelaria sees La Llorona as an indigenous "Lilith de las Américas." La Llorona, like Lilith, is portrayed in venomous terms as a disobedient woman who is eternally punished for rebelling against patriarchal norms. She avenges (or atones) her punishment by reclaiming her right to be around women and children whom she prefers to the patriarchs. They are terrorized, however, by her because of the negativity in which she is portrayed—like La Llorona who threatens the doxa (Candelaria, personal communication).

Lamia (gluttonous and lecherous) is based on Greek mythology. She was a beautiful woman and mistress of Zeus, with whom she had various children. When Hera, Zeus' wife found out about the affair, she killed all the children except for Scylla. In revenge, Lamia decided to become a child-killer, and as a result of her evil, she became a monster with the ability to remove her eyes.

Kirtley (1960) believes that La Llorona has similarities to two versions of the German legend *Die Weisse Frau* (the White Lady). In one, in 1340, the Count of Orlamünde died and left a widow, Kunigunde, and two children. The widow wished to remarry. She got word of a remark made by Albrecht the Fair who said that if it were not for "four eyes" he would marry her. Misunderstanding "four eyes" as a reference to her children, she resolved to get rid of them. She thrust a needle through their heads, and said they died of a violent disease. But what Albrecht had meant by four eyes were his aged parents. After the crime, of course, he shunned her altogether. Kunigunde felt remorse and made a journey to see the Pope. As a penance imposed by the Pontif, she crawled on her knees and joined a convent. By the time of her death, she was an abbess.[6] After she died, she appeared to the descendants of Albrecht as an omen of imminent death or other misfortune (158).

The other version is somewhat similar to La Llorona. It is believed that in Cologne at a spot where there used to be a nunnery, a figure wearing a white shroud wanders there at the middle of the night. The legend is that the figure in white is the spirit of a tanner's daughter who became the prey of a knight member of one of Cologne's oldest families. The young nobleman won the woman's love and seduced her. Instead of marrying her when she became pregnant, he mocked her. He carried his scorn to the point of jeering at her and her child as she stood at the window of her home. The young mother became so enraged that when she met the knight in the street she threw the child under the Knight's horse's feet and tore the Knight's sword and stabbed him, mortally wounding him. She was put in prison, where she went mad and hanged herself. Her body was taken to the place where executions took place and was buried without ceremony. Since that time, between 12:00 and 1:00 at night, the White Lady appears at the spot of the double murder and attempts to lure young men with her pale beauty. All who speak with her die within the next few days (158). Kirtley believes that the legend of La Llorona is a syncretic narrative of the German and Aztec elements. He believes that it is probable that members of the Catholic Church carried the legend from central Europe to Spain in the late fifteenth century or early sixteenth century, when it was transmitted to Mexico. In Mexico, Cihuacoatl replaced the White Lady. All of these figures are demonized in Western thought and literature. A superficial analysis might consider the veracity of the demonization, especially if one focuses on infanticide. However, I propose to see these figures as *mujeres rebeldes* who fought against patriarchy. Granted, their tactics might not be the most productive, but they do show the power that women have to undermine patriarchy.

FEMINIST SYMBOLIC MEANINGS OF LA LLORONA

A number of Chicana feminists' interpretations of La Llorona seek to recuperate her as a feminist icon (Anzaldúa 1987; Chabram-Dernesesian 1992; Saldívar-Hull 2000). Contemporary feminist interest in La Llorona has its genesis in the efforts of the 1960s and 1970s to redefine patriarchal images and symbols of women as feminist. For example, Candelaria (1993), who focuses much of her analysis on the patriarchal ideology reproduced in the legend, argues in favor of redefining La Llorona as a feminist symbol. Candelaria proposes that "La Llorona persists in folklore because its meanings are multiple, not one-dimensional, and they have the capacity to expose the very injustices that a superficial reading of the tale seems to prefer" (114). I believe that the various symbolic meanings of La Llorona serve as a template to analyze the pedagogies of La Llorona in oral histories.

Recall that the legend began in México City not long after the Spanish Conquest. Even though the legend is marred by patriarchal meanings, from its inception it has invoked decolonial practices, especially from women. In order to get into the feminist decolonial meanings of the legend, it is necessary to unravel its contradictory meanings in favor of a complex analysis. To accomplish this, I first link the meanings of La Llorona to its colonial origins. Then, I focus on three key elements in the narrative: the loss of children; the scream as the basis for its feminist decolonial understandings; and water that for the Aztecs symbolized re-birth.

The legend of La Llorona began immediately after the Spanish conquest of México, therefore the "timing" of the first narratives of La Llorona is noteworthy. I believe that the social significance, meaning, and pain occasioned by the Conquest were not lost to those who lived it. As soon as the Spanish started to impose a new social order, even those who had sided with them realized that this New World was not a better life than the one they had under Mexica rule (even though there is evidence that it was a very brutal regime). The indigenous peoples of México knew a new life had begun. They also understood that they would be marginalized and oppressed in this new society in similar, if not worst ways, than under the Mexicas. The Indians and emerging mestizo populations thus created cultural icons that responded to, and reflected, the trauma of the new life.

A significant characteristic of colonization is the suppression of the knowledge of the conquered. Similarly, patriarchal societies have also suppressed women's knowledge by defining it as inferior, hence, not legitimate. When groups of people are excluded from the official spaces where knowledge is produced, they find ways to convey their views. Mexican and Chicana women have used music, literature, everyday conversations, myths, and stories to articulate their social, economic, cultural, and political condition. Finding a conduit to express their critique of and resistance to colonization and patriarchy is but one form of communicating alternative ideas. This resistance is different from political action, but it can be effective as well. Ideas are powerful, and so are the sources of their expression such as stories, myths, and legends. Yet, in hegemonic Western thought, ideas manifested in popular culture narratives are normally placed in subordinate positions. However, everyday women can find expression to their criticism of dominant ideology in alternative narratives and in everyday popular culture. La Llorona is one of these stories that help express women's contradictory position in society through a narrative that is transmitted orally from generation to generation.

La Llorona represents the anguish of the indigenous people for the devastation left by the conquest. Chicanas/os would experience a similar anguish centuries later after the U.S. took over Mexico's northern territories (more than half of Mexico's land) as a result of the U.S.-Mexico war in 1848. Once the U.S. had control of what is today known as the Southwest and parts of the West (Utah and Colorado), it imposed new laws that benefited Anglo Americans, language, and culture that resulted in the marginalization of the Mexican population in the U.S. (Almaguer 1994, Acuña 2000, Camarillo, 1979, Gonzalez D. 1999). For women, in particular, La Llorona represents their subordination in patriarchal society. For example, the aforementioned three elements in the narrative are quite symbolic of the effect of colonialism and on the social significance of La Llorona. The third element, water, can symbolize women's transformation from object to subject through a symbolic re-birth.

Symbolic Representation of Past and Future

The loss of children is a powerful cultural symbol of the loss of the past and, thus, future. In this sense, the legend of La Llorona does not necessarily mean the literal death of her children (whether by her own hand or not), but the symbolic loss of the past and future. Colonialism deprives the conquered of their traditional cultures, way of life, rules, and self-determination. Mourning the loss (or at least imposed transformation of a culture) does not mean an idealization of the culture; what it means is that a culture with all its imperfections, but nevertheless owned and honored by its people, is obligated to transform in imposed and unnatural ways. Colonialism imposes political and symbolic systems of knowledge that transform the traditions of the colonized people. Normally, such systems are key elements of subordinate groups' cultural identity. Once such traditions are suppressed, the descendents of the colonized more easily will accept and assimilate the imposed culture and its knowledge base. Yet, subordinate groups historically have found ways to maintain their knowledge and culture in ways that the colonizer might not recognize. Rebolledo and Rivero (1993) suggest that this is a political meaning for La Llorona. The loss of children in the legend conveys their loss to dominant groups and culture. In the case of Chicanas/os, it could be applied to ongoing persistence of unequal power relations manifested in the imperative to assimilate to Anglo-American culture, violence, and prejudice. Subordinate groups have resisted hegemonic cultural practices that objectify them. In creating alternative stories, people find ways to reclaim their subjectivity. The persistence of the legend is one example of the resilience of people of Mexican descent to maintain their traditions, culture, and knowledge, and one way to reclaim their subjectivity.

La Llorona represents a symbolic struggle against patriarchy and economic domination on the part of women, where the loss of children is a way of struggling against patriarchal power.[7] In the early colonial period, sexuality and power are intimately correlated, where reproduction and creation of a new mestizo population signifies the reproduction of workers (Limón 1990). Analogous sexual politics existed during and after the U.S.-Mexico war (Castañeda 1990, Heidenrich 2005, Venegas 2004). Such sexual politics intimately tied to the political economy is analogous to that of slavery in the U.S. As Candelaria observes, "the legend can be interpreted as a 'tender mercy,' a concept from biblical folklore suggesting that within a corrupt system of

death or release fate

authoritarian power; even an act of compassion can be brutal because it, too, partakes of the dominant context of corruption. The tale can thus be read as a political euthanasia, a woman's conscious attempt to save her cherished children from their parents' awful fate" (1993, 114). This argument is comparable to Toni Morrison's novel, *Beloved,* where a mother kills her child to protect her from the suffering of slavery. The legend of La Llorona "eliminates" the children, or they are "eliminated" as a symbolic way of undermining the new patriarchal norms (Candelaria 1993, 114). Indeed, there are versions of La Llorona where she kills her children in order to save them from a life of suffering, or to avoid them falling into the hands of the conquerors. The following version quoted by Lomax Hawes (1968) is telling:

> When the Spanish arrived in Mexico, they were impressed by the beauty of the Indian Children. The Spanish took the children (the most beautiful) and gave them to their wives. Some of the Indian women killed their children in order to keep the Spaniards from taking them. La Llorona is one such woman. She is now searching constantly for her children, whose faces she sees in all children. She kills the children to be united with her own again. (159)

In the mid-nineteenth century in California, not long after the U.S. acquired the territory, indigenous women resorted to infanticide as well. The "Act for the Government and Protection of Indians" passed in the late 1840's legalized indentured servitude of indigenous children. White settlers would kidnap Indian children without impunity, given that indigenous people were barred from testifying against whites. "During this time, indigenous women living in Napa Country sometimes resorted to infanticide" (Heidenreich 2005, 45). La Llorona is not willing to lose her children to the patriarch/colonizer and will do whatever it takes to keep the children away from him. This is the case whether she takes away children the patriarch/colonizer wants, or symbolically removes workers needed for the economic progress of the rulers.

In contemporary U.S. versions and popular culture representations of La Llorona, the death and loss of children are associated with poverty and the struggle of immigrant and working class families with bureaucratic institutions such as INS/ICE. Domino Renee Pérez (2002) documents that as Chicanas/os have become urbanized, so has the legend. Urban versions of La Llorona have appeared in which the children die due to bureaucratic and corporate misdeeds, including environmental pollution. Moreover, recent popular culture depictions such as the PBS series *American Family* depicted La Llorona as an undocumented immigrant woman who loses her baby to immigration officials. In this program, the baby of an undocumented immigrant woman is lost due to bureaucratic mistakes. First, the INS[8] detains the young undocumented immigrant and her baby. The authorities gave the infant to Child Protective Services, but the proper paper work was not completed, nobody knows where the baby is, therefore, it is impossible to find the infant. The viewer is left with the impression that the process of adoption of the infant is in place. If this baby ends up adopted by a white family, the symbolism of losing the children to Anglo-American culture is well represented. Domino Pérez proposes that in contemporary U.S., the legend of La Llorona symbolizes generations of Mexicans who are lost to race, class, and gender oppression. Certainly, the *American Family* series depiction of the loss of a baby symbolically (and tragically) represents such loss.

The Scream: Voicing Resistance

For me, there is no doubt that the death of children is the most difficult and dramatic element of the legend. Nevertheless, the scream is also symbolically significant. Anzaldúa (1987) locates the socio-political interpretation of La Llorona/Cihuacoatl in the wailing, which is the Indian, Mexican, and Chicana women's protest and sign of resistance against colonization. Anzaldúa finds the antecedents of this "political/resistance" wailing from the Aztec women's cries as they send their sons, brothers, and husbands to the "flowery wars" (33). A scream is a bodily reaction to deal with pain both physical and emotional; yet a scream is also an expression of elation and happiness. As women give birth, screaming (among many other techniques such as breathing) is a way to cope with labor pains. As women scream while giving life, they also scream in emotional pain when their children die. The painful and mournful cry of La Llorona, *"Ai mis hijos. Dónde estan?"* can be understood as a symbolic representation of the cries of mothers when they lose their children.[9]

La Llorona's scream also represents the loss of women's voices, their silencing in patriarchal societies. Sarah Amira de la Garza (2004) believes that there is a generalized societal silencing of La Llorona because we do not want to listen to her story, her pain, and most importantly, her secrets ". . . but they're scared you're going to make us hear your story" (70). La Llorona's story is indeed the story of women's oppression and subordination. In the case of La Llorona, crying and screaming is about pain, and this pain is the result of the ways in which women are hurt by sexism and patriarchy, manifested in poverty, domestic violence, and sexual abuse. Moreover, traditional gender roles dictate to women to be passive and obedient to men, to defer to men's desires, wishes, and whims, and take away women's abilities to voice their decisions and desires. In a cultural context under which it is not socially acceptable for women to voice their concerns with their subordinate position in society due to patriarchal structural constraints because it is dangerous to utter counter hegemonic views in a direct way. Women have to find other

ways to be able to express themselves; the legend of La Llorona is one culturally acceptable vehicle.

Sarah Amira de la Garza writes that after she had an abortion, she understood why La Llorona cries. When de la Garza was a graduate student and
found she was pregnant, she agreed to terminate the pregnancy because that
is what her then-boyfriend wanted. De la Garza was in a "disassociative
trance" (74) when she walked into the abortion clinic and had the procedure
done. It wasn't until she was awakened by her own screams that she realized what she had done and that she had "agreed" to terminate a pregnancy,
when she actually wanted to keep the baby: that she had decided to have an
abortion in deference to her boyfriend's desires as "everything depended on
what 'he' wanted" (75). Like La Llorona, "I sobbed. My baby. My baby.
What did I do to my baby? My baby. My baby. I must have been screaming
out loud, because the nurse told me to shut up" (75). The symbolic meaning
of La Llorona here is about how traditional gender roles and various political ideologies over gender and reproductive rights deny women's voices and
agency. Sarah Amira's story of her abortion is about the loss of a child, but
it is also about, at that particular time, her inability to voice her desires and
decisions over her body and future. She found her voice, like La Llorona, in
her screams over her lost baby. In this case, La Llorona is symbolic of the
ways in which different political discourses and ideologies over women's
roles and positions in society can silence women's voices when these beliefs
do not take into account the complexity of the issues and contradictory positions women have over such politics. Abortion and reproductive rights are
perhaps paradigmatic of such contradictions because the different sides (pro-
life, pro-choice, men) proclaim to speak for women but do not listen to the
complex issues that women must confront when they have to make a decision
over an unplanned pregnancy. Indeed, Sara Amira's narrative can easily be
appropriated by anti-abortion rhetoric, but her story is much more complicated. Given all these discourses that speak for women, women need to find a
conduit for the expression of the complex politics over abortion. In the legend
of La Llorona, women are left to scream; yet we must keep in mind that a
scream can sometimes be liberatory and exemplifies such complexities.

In Sandra Cisneros' (1991) short story, "Woman Hollering Creek," the
scream represents a form of female liberation. In this tale of domestic violence and liberation, Cisneros uses La Llorona as the name of a creek that
symbolizes the oppression and eventual liberation of Cleófilas, the main
character. The crossing of a bridge over Women Hollering Creek is quite
symbolic of Cleófilas oppressive life with her abusive husband and her
eventual freedom from him. She must cross the bridge in order to get to her
husband's house and, more importantly, to leave him. Cleófilas is fascinated

by the name of the creek *La Gritona* (the hollering woman). At the end of the story, two Chicanas help Cleófilas leave her husband and return home to Monclova, México to her father and six brothers. One of the Chicanas is named Felice, who, when crossing the creek, lets out a Tarzan-like scream: "But when they drove across the *arroyo,* the driver opened her mouth and let out a yell as loud as any mariachi. Which startled not only Cleófilas, but Juan Pedrito as well" (55). Felice's unlady-like scream symbolizes women's liberation from patriarchal power, or at least a struggle against it. Her name is quite symbolic as well, since it sounds like happiness in Spanish and could also symbolize the satisfaction and empowerment of women from the burden of patriarchal violence.

Renewal and Redemption

La Llorona's representation as form of renewal symbolizes women moving from objects to subject and regaining/finding their voice. Some Chicana feminists, for example Gloria Anzaldúa and Alicia Gaspar de Alba, have redeemed La Llorona as a guardian angel. Before I get to the analysis of such redemption of La Llorona, I examine Helena María Viramontes' (1985) short story, "The Cariboo Café," in which she represents La Llorona as the mothers of politically assassinated and disappeared children. La Llorona, then, symbolizes maternal struggle against patriarchal and social injustice. "The Cariboo Café" is the story of Sonya and Macky, two undocumented children who get lost after Sonya loses the key to their home. A washerwoman, who is also undocumented because she fled the death squads in Central America, takes in Sonya and Macky. She takes the children to eat at the Zero Zero Café, where the racist owner calls the police on her. The washerwoman believes that Macky is her five year-old son Geraldo who was taken by the death squads, accused of being a guerrilla fighter. The washerwoman is transformed into La Llorona when Geraldo disappears.

> The darkness becomes a serpent's tongue, swallowing us whole. It is the night of La Llorona. The women come up from the depths of sorrow to search for their children. I join them, frantic, desperate, and our eyes become scrutinizers, our bodies opiated with the scent of their smiles. Descending from door to door, the wind whips our faces. I hear the wailing of the women and know it to be my own. Geraldo is nowhere to be found. (Viramontes 1985, 68–9)

Once in the U.S, knowing that her son is dead, the washerwoman "adopts" Macky and believes that he is her son Geraldo. She will not lose him again. Like La Llorona, she will take away any child she finds, and prefers to die than to lose her son again. As she moves through this process, the washerwoman/Llorona gains strength and agency. Her act of defiance costs her her life, but she maintains her maternal ties with her son. Viramontes ends the story this way:

> To hell with you all, because you can no longer frighten me. I will fight you for my son until I have no hands left to hold a knife. I will fight you all because you're all farted out of the Devil's ass, and you'll not take us with you. I am laughing, howling at their stupidity. Because they should know by now that I will never let my son go and then I hear something crunching like broken glass against my forehead and I am blinding by the liquid darkness. But I hold onto his hand. That I can feel, you see, I'll never let go. Because we are going home. My son and I. (75)

José David Saldívar (1997) claims that by using and revising the legend of La Llorona as a threat to males, she is a threat to patriarchy,[10] "Viramontes allows us also to hear the deep stirrings of the unhomely wailing woman. Capturing the shared legacy of five hundred years of Spanish conquest and resistance, the legend of La Llorona creeps into the zero zero[11] place of Chicana/o fiction" (105). The washerwoman lives with the guilt of sending Geraldo to the store to get her a mango when the army took him away. She transforms this guilt into action and defiance, including translating la Llorona's wailing into laughter as she refuses to let go of her "son" again.

Gloria Anzaldúa provides a positive representation of La Llorona in her children's book *Prietita and the Ghost Woman*. In this story, La Llorona saves Prietita, a Chicana girl who lives in South Texas near the King Ranch, when she gets lost in the ranch looking for an herb to heal her mother. Prietita enters the King Ranch looking for rue, the herb the curandera needs to heal Prietita's mother. Prietita gets lost and asks different animals for help; all the while she is worried because she is hearing La Llorona weep. Prietita has been told the legend of La Llorona and believes that she will take children away. Nevertheless, even though she is scared of La Llorona, when Prietita sees her she gets close to her and lets her know that she is looking for rue. La Llorona not only points to where the herb is, but also guides Prietita home. When she arrives home, Prietita notices that everyone is looking for her, and she is happy to see her little sister. Anzaldúa redeems La Llorona in the following passage:

> "How did you find your way out of the woods?" asked Doña Lola.
> "A ghost woman in white was my guide."
> "*La Llorona!*" said Prietita's cousin, Teté. "But everyone knows that she takes children away. She doesn't bring them back."
> "Perhaps she is not what others think she is," said Doña Lola. (np)

Indeed, Anzaldúa writes that she wanted to show another side of La Llo-rona, "a powerful, positive side, a side that represents the Indian part and the female part of us" (1995, np). Anzaldúa transverses La Llorona's behavior; instead of taking children away, she is acting more like a guardian angel than a terrifying ghost. Therefore, Anzaldúa provides a whole different interpretation of La Llorona; one where she is powerful and benevolent.[12]

Reclaiming and Re-imagining La Llorona

Limón (1990) sees the legend of La Llorona as a utopian resolution of the imposed patriarchal norms on Mexican women (427). For Limón, women's contradictory positions are resolved in the formal narrative of the legend: the legend begins with the presence of patriarchy and concludes with its exclusion in favor of an implied, utopian, female-centered community of maternity and love (427). Some Chicana feminists, including Norma Alarcón (1989/1990), find this ideal notion of feminism quite dangerous. Limón's assertion that the legend concludes in a utopian community of maternity and love offers a somewhat romantic notion of liberation; more than utopian desire as a decolonial practice the legend represents the symbolic break down of the patriarchal family. The legend puts into question men's superiority over women because in the narrative and folklore, La Llorona is much more dangerous to men than to women (although she is dangerous to women and children too). This is significant given that women are the ones who usually transmit the legend (Limón 1990, Candelaria 1993).

La Llorona can be understood through many different political and ideological lenses; as such the legend defies any form of closure and truthful reading. The legend is not "book-truth, not historically documented narrative truth. This is the kind of truth you make from hearing stories" (de la Garza 2004, 69). Cordelia Candelaria proposes the need to analyze the legend of La Llorona and recapture her as a feminist figure in this way:

> But why try to save the baby-killer of legend? Aren't there better uses of time and political resources than to try to recuperate such a hopeless, worthless case? One very important reason is that the same brush that painted the Weeping Woman portrait in history continues to apply its demeaning brushstrokes of single-minded misogyny to contemporary society It's past time *that* brush got a thorough cleaning and a fresh set of primary paints to color women authentically en route to the twenty-first century. (Candelaria 1993, 113–114, Italic in original)[13]

Similarly, de la Garza concludes "*La Llorona's* power is hidden from us by focusing on fear. Making us want to stay away from wherever she might show up, reminding us with her screams that we all bear secret suffering. That voice of hers is power—terrifying, dark, and beautiful power" (76). The power invoked in la Llorona is that of women transformed from passive to speaking subjects, from Lloronas to Gritonas (Carbonell 1999).

LA LLORONA IN THE SOUTHWEST: FEMINIST CULTURAL STUDIES READINGS OF ORAL HISTORIES

Oral histories, stories, legends, and myths are ways in which everyday people document their views, values, and interpretations of the world. Oral histories of La Llorona from New Mexico and Arizona reflect these colonial relations.[14] The narratives I found in the archives in Arizona and New Mexico epitomize the multiplicity of meanings that can be manifested in the legend of La Llorona, ranging from anti-colonial struggles to the reproduction of patriarchy and capitalism. I selected these stories from oral narratives that I examined from the collections of La Llorona at the Center for Southwest Research Baughman Collection at the University of New Mexico and at the Southwest Folklore Center at the University of Arizona.[15] These oral narratives of La Llorona were documented for the respective universities, usually as classroom projects. Some have the names of the collector and informant; others are anonymous. In most cases, informants tell stories that have been passed from generation-to-generation in various Chicana/o communities; in others the informants have casually heard the stories from neighbors. In the case of one of the narratives I'm analyzing in this chapter, the informant heard the story during an anthropological dig.

In several of the narratives I am examining, La Llorona is a victim, not the perpetrator of the crime of infanticide. When La Llorona's children die due to illness or by accident, and not at her hand, the meaning of the legend changes significantly; in such cases, class and race conflicts are at the center of the story and tragedy. There is no doubt that versions in México, including the Luisa story, have anti-colonial positions, and many accounts are adapted to contemporary socio-political conditions in México. However, in the Southwest, the adaptations of La Llorona speak specifically to conditions of the Chicana/o community after the U.S. took over the territory.[16] These versions are ways in which Chicanas and Chicanos in the Southwest adapted the legend to offer a critique of and resistance to Anglo domination; however, in one of the narratives I am analyzing, the person who sets in motion the events is an "evil Spaniard" and not necessarily an "evil *Gringo*." This particular version makes the connection between different colonizers of the Southwest: the Spanish and the Anglos.[17]

Most of the narratives in these collections are of the biographical and encounter types outlined by Arora. However, there are some versions that differ from these types that I find much more intriguing and interesting for this study. Many of the renditions in these archives follow closely the prototype or Luisa story where she kills the children as revenge for the father's betrayal, or the children die due to her neglect either because she is an incompetent mother or just plain evil. However, there are versions where the children die not at her hand or because of her neglect, but due to poverty, accident, or illness. These versions represent approaches to popular culture to resist colonialism and poverty, even when sometimes endorsing patriarchy. Yet, there is a constant in most of the narratives: the fact that La Llorona, while looking for her children, will take any child she will find. Therefore, parents fear her because she is willing to inflict the pain she has suffered by taking away someone else's child. The fear La Llorona inflicts is a warning against the oppression of women in an effort to create egalitarian societies. As long as there are subjugated members of a society or community due to race/ethnicity, class, and gender inequality, no one will be safe. From a pedagogical standpoint, these narratives include the elements found in the more traditional story that teaches obedience to children and endorses patriarchal power, but they also reflect contestation against multiple forms of oppression.

Following, I will analyze different versions of La Llorona using as a template the symbolic meanings I outlined in the previous section: the scream, loss of children, and renewal/re-birth. I am particularly interested in examining how various versions of the legend show how La Llorona moves from passive victim to an active being. Most of these elements are present in different versions of La Llorona. In the analysis that follows, I highlight the element in that particular narrative that is more salient. By no means should my organization of the analysis be read as if only one element is present in the narrative. There are many overlaps of the elements in the narratives.

Loss of Children

As discussed above, one of the most disturbing aspects of the legend of La Llorona is the act of infanticide. While many of us were told the version in which she kills her offspring as an act of revenge against the father who betrayed her, there are many stories in which the children die due to illness or accident. I am most interested in analyzing the meaning of the loss of children in relation to race, class, and gender inequalities. The following story from the Baughman Collection represents the loss of children in term of class and gender inequalities. This story takes place in Santa Fé, New Mexico:

> A woman lived many years with the husband, couldn't have kids, but finally had a girl. The husband died and she wonders around the street of Santa Fe, because she lost her home. Once looking for food a flash flood washed the child from her hands. She wondered near acequias looking for the child until she died. Since many people hear mournful cries especially during rain. She will grab any kid she finds near acequias. Santa Fe mothers warn their children never to play in ditches, arroyos or acequias or La Llorona will get them. ("Baughman Collection")

In this version, La Llorona is victim, not victimizer. And in this case it is twice: first, her husband, who is obviously the main provider for the family, dies, and then she loses her home and her daughter. This rendition points to the problematic of women's economic dependency within the family and poverty. This account speaks of contemporary problems of poverty within the U.S., mainly homelessness. The story offers a critique of class issues and the effects that capitalism and patriarchy can have on women and children. In her life, La Llorona lived under patriarchal rules; she married, tried to have a child and eventually did, and was supported economically by her husband. But in working class families only supported with one income (usually male), when the main provider loses his/her job, dies, or abandons the family, the material and financial support are also lost. The girl's tragic death is the result of the lack of social resources and interest to assist those in need. The daughter dies washed away from her mother's arms by the water as the mother looks for food in the street because as a single, destitute homeless person, this is the only way she can find sustenance for her family.

This version primarily critiques socio-economic inequality. A first reading seems to suggest that the familiar social arrangement where women are dependent on men for financial support is fine, as long as the support is there. Indeed, one could argue that during her life, and even death, La Llorona does not want to transform the patriarchal family; she wants to fulfill her function as a mother. The tragedy in this narrative is brought about by poverty as La Llorona loses her child during a flood. There is much emphasis placed on poverty and women's dependency as such. If the husband was wealthier, she could have economically survived after his death; but this is not the case in the story. Therefore, I see this story as a critique of dependency and a way to teach women self-reliance. This story reminds me of the narratives of mothers who teach their daughters' self-reliance (see Villenas and Moreno 2001) and the need to change women's position within an unequal socio-economic system and the family.

Eventually, La Llorona figures out that living by the rules dictated by patriarchy and capitalism does not pay off and starts her haunting. By the time she figures it out, it is too late to save herself and child. Thus, she decides to take away any child she can find. The taking of any child serves to keep the community on alert and is a warning about the dire consequences of social inequality. Eventually, the oppressed rise against their oppressors; in this case, La Llorona will inflict the same pain she has endured by threatening to take away any child she finds. Until La Llorona finds peace, no one will be able to find peace as well.

The story also serves as an allegory on the process of proletarianization that Chicanas/os suffered after the incorporation of the Southwest to the U.S., and the multiple losses suffered: land, culture, and language. Symbolically, the loss of La Llorona's daughter represents the loss of Chicana/o children in Anglo society. The process of proletarization that Mexican Americans suffered as the result of the U.S.-México war is symbolized in the destruction of the family: father, child, and eventually mother die. The perpetrators of the "crime" in this story are neither La Llorona nor the father of the child, as both are victims; rather the culprit is capitalism and the unequal distribution of resources. This story is an indictment of a capitalist system and the class, race, and gender inequalities it reproduces.

Clearly, this version has the standard pedagogical strategies that tell children to stay put and avoid dangerous places. In this sense, this version is not that different from the traditional story. However, what makes it different from the other stories is the focus on class issues. Thus, from a pedagogical standpoint, this story teaches children to be obedient and avoid dangerous places; but it is also a narrative that invokes women's self-reliance, which points to the potential for border/transformative pedagogies.

Renewal and Transformation

There is a story from the Chama Valley in New Mexico that I titled "The Evil Spaniard" because the man who betrays the young maiden is referred to as an evil Spaniard. This narrative is also from the Baughman Collection.[8] The narrator believes that it is a very common story from Mexico's central valleys up into the Rio Grande Valley. The story is the following:

> A very widespread story, I'll tell the Chama Valley version of it (it's common though, from the central valleys of Mexico up into the Rio Grande valley) concerns a weeping woman. Now, generally, including the one in Chame [sic] Valley, the woman is a young girl, who is seduced by generally a Spaniard, an evil one at that, and she has a child. The Spaniard went off and left her. She's

living all alone and the child either dies or is killed. The woman cries and generally pines away and dies soon after the child. As legend has it, there is a weeping sound that rolls through town in a white, fury-type ball like a big snowball,
that rolls through town with the weeping sounds coming from it. Also, near the
windows of children or also at a door near their rooms, you can hear a weeping
sound, which is a woman trying to get the child. Now, one further point about
this weeping woman. Don Devero heard it outside his *child's* window. He has a
beautiful little boy and this of course about drove him out of his mind. He and
his wife very carefully guarded the child for seven nights until it went away.
When it went away, it went several houses up the street to a good friend's of his
and haunted their house *child* for a while. There has never been any record of
harm being done to the child. ("Baughman Collection")[19]

The analysis of this narrative focuses on the complex relationship between
patriarchy, colonialism, and decolonialism. Two interrelated yet contradictory
characteristics of this version—the use of patriarchal language to describe La
Llorona and anti-colonialism—are intriguing. Therefore, I focus my analysis
on how these two elements intersect.

The patriarchal elements of this version are first evidenced in how La
Llorona is described. At the beginning of the narrative when La Llorona is
alive and a young woman, she is not named and is shown as a passive woman.
The events of seduction and giving birth "happen to her," she is not an agent
of these events. The only time we have a sense of what she feels is when the
child dies and she "cries and generally pines away." She is transformed from
this passive and depressed young woman to an agent only through death in an
amazing manner: from depressed to a fury-type ball. Now, once she is dead
and returns as a fury-type ball, she shows her anger. But why does she have to
wait to get really angry until her child and she are dead? The narrator makes
it a point to say that she really is not too dangerous as there is no "record of
harm being done to the child," but the representation of La Llorona as a fury-
type ball does imply danger. The word fury does signify violence. Moreover,
while the narrator might recognize that La Llorona as a ghost has some power
and agency, he does not want to grant them to her.

Once she returns to earth as a ghostly fury-type ball, she is objectified,
literally, by the use of the pronoun "it." Even though this use of pronoun
is "grammatically correct," it does have a feel for the objectification of La
Llorona as well as a denial of or fear of her power. This power, we must
recall, is not considered too dangerous as the narrator makes sure to let the
informant know that she has not harmed a child. While I am not advocating
for raw power based on violence, I am intrigued with La Llorona's transformation. What is the purpose of creating a narrative where women are
transformed in such dramatic way from passive to active? I believe that the

narrative camouflages women's desire to transform their social position. Perhaps elements of advocacy for social change are presented in a surreptitiously but that nevertheless urgent.

The anti-colonial implication here is quite powerful given that the perpetrator is a Spaniard, "an evil one at that." The story can be read as an allegory of the Conquest of México (including what is known today as the U.S. Southwest) and of the Anglo domination of the Southwest. The evil Spaniard represents the conqueror that dominates land and women and takes what he needs/wants and then leaves without any remorse. Nothing happens to him; he disappears from the story. Land and women are for the taking of the powerful. At the beginning of the narrative, the young girl/woman is presented as a victim, particularly in life, without any agency, who has no choice but to comply with the Spaniard's wishes. She will continue to fulfill her role as mother even after death, thus she wanders along looking for children she can mother. In the narrative, as in most narratives on La Llorona, her voice is absent. Unlike other versions of La Llorona, she does not fall in love with the Spaniard. She does love her child, as she is devastated and depressed by the death of her child as most mothers would be. Earlier, I mentioned that her agency appears after death; so does her voice, but in the form of weeping. But is La Llorona's weeping an element of the subordination of her gender? Or perhaps, it can also be understood as not weeping but as a scream that signals the beginning of a decolonializing movement.

Even recognizing the decolonial possibilities of this narrative, the patriarchal elements are quite strong and evident, demonstrating the conflicts over meanings and politics as manifested in popular culture. While this narrative has an anti-colonial position, the narrator does not reject patriarchy, but rather reinforces its beliefs. Naming the father of the child La Llorona seeks Don Devero, at the same time that the mother is nameless only serves to affirm patriarchal authority in the story. We must remember that the mother is present, since we are told that Don Devero and his wife watch over their child for seven nights until La Llorona leaves. The narrator makes us believe that it is the power of the head of the family, Don Devero, who saves the child and thus protects the family. Mother/wife presence is neglectful, since family life would have been restored whether she was present or not. There is another pedagogical lesson on "good" and "bad" fatherhood in this narrative. As there are two fathers portrayed, one is the "bad" father (The Evil Spaniard) who abandons his family, and the "good" father, Don Devero, who looks over his child.[20]

In odd ways, this story manifests a form of cultural politics that while it asserts the superiority of the patriarchal family, it also critiques women's contradictory positions within patriarchy and decolonialism. While one patriarch,

Don Devero, is able to get rid of La Llorona, in the narrative structure she has her way given that all she needs to do is move to a different house to continue her haunting. Don Devero is not able to get rid of her altogether; she continues to be a threat. La Llorona has the ability to destabilize the patriarch as her haunting "drove him out of his mind." This unruly and stubborn Llorona, to a certain extent, triumphs over patriarchal power albeit in a limited way. Even though Don Devero and his wife make her go away and are able to restore peace in their home, she does not disappear altogether, she moves a few houses up the street to a friend's house to haunt another child. La Llorona's ability to move to the close friend's house demonstrates her potential to return and disrupt the family's peace. Thus, the restoration of peace and patriarchy is only temporary, leaving patriarchy and the patriarchal family in shaky ground. Although the narrator might seem to allude to the restoration of patriarchal power, in the final analysis, this version of La Llorona has the ability to destabilize such power. Stability will come when social equality is achieved.

The Scream, Disruption, and Power

La Llorona's scream is one of her most compelling and known characteristics. As I discussed above, La Llorona's scream is a sign with multiple interpretations, including protest against inequality and resistance to oppression: breaking women's silence, and bodily reaction toward the physical and emotional pain due to women's subordination. In many narratives of La Llorona, those who hear her scream and see her can become seriously ill. This attribute of La Llorona serves as another example of her ability to threaten and disrupt normal activities, thus, remind people of social inequality. When La Llorona appears to an individual and he/she ends up confined into bed for months, she is disrupting ordinary productive activities of members of the society. Following, I analyze three accounts of encounters with La Llorona that resulted in illness or in a big *susto* (scare).

In a story from Sonoita, Arizona, a woman who, with her husband in 1931,[21] was returning home to Alto, Arizona, tells of the terrifying night they heard La Llorona. At about 8 o'clock, the couple came to a river they needed to cross. There was a big flood, so they couldn't cross. They waited for the water to recede, but instead it started to rain harder. It got dark, and by 11:30 they were still stranded. Suddenly, they heard a cry "(ay ay ay)" coming from the river. "(Ay ay aye e e e e e e e) was the voice we heard again. We heard it the third time and it stayed longer (ay e e e e e e e e e e). We were so nervous that we went over to the Valenzuela's home and stayed there all night. All that next month, August, I stayed in bed. I was so scared that the doctor's [sic] didn't think I would live."

Another encounter occurred to Carlos Valenzuela in 1950 or 1951.[22] The meeting with La Llorona happened in Oracle, Arizona when Valenzuela was by himself in "Campo Benito" near a mine. After supper, he sat down to read the newspaper, got sleepy, and was ready for bed when he heard a cry. At the beginning, he thought it was a wild animal like a coyote, bobcat, or mountain lion. But after 15 minutes, the sound got closer and it resembled the voice of a woman. Eventually, Valenzuela stepped out of his cabin and heard the voice really close. He looked down the wash of the canyon outside the cabin and saw a figure in white. "The woman cried out again. She was in agony or in pain. So he yelled at her. When he yelled at her, he realized, then he realized that it was 'La Llorona' that he was looking at. When he saw what he saw, he turned back to the cabin and went back to the cabin and he just got sick of his stomach and four [sic] about three or four months after that he had to doctor himself—the fright, I mean."

In 1927, in Tucson, a man named Pete (who would become Señora Amalia Moreno y Rios' husband) encountered La Llorona after "visiting a woman" when he was 17 years old.[23] The encounter happened in the following way, "It was about 3 a.m. and he was hurrying so that he could get home before his foster mother discovered he was out. As he came to the corner of Main and W. Fourth in Tucson he heard the wailing women [sic]. He stopped to listen and his hair stood on end. He hurried on and the wailing got closer. He realized that it was coming from four white walls, all that remained of an abandoned house." Years later, Señora Moreno y Rios also comes across La Llorona in the same corner after she had been playing cards with friends and returning home at 11 o'clock at night.

These three narratives symbolize the power of La Llorona to disrupt people's mundane productive activities. In Pete and his wife's case, she serves as a warning about the dangers and social consequences of staying up late at night and "visiting women." Señora Moreno y Rios got a warning against playing cards (maybe gambling) and going home too late for a "respectable" woman. Neither Pete nor Señora Moreno y Rios got sick and bed ridden; presumably once their encounter was over they were able to return to their normal duties. This is not the case for the wife of the couple in the fist narrative who stayed in bed for the month of August, and for Carlos Valenzuela who was sick for about three to four months. In both of these cases, after their respective encounters with La Llorona, the individuals could not attend to their work. La Llorona, then, has the power to interfere with productive activities. It is somewhat apparent that when Pete and his future wife each ran into La Llorona, they were not behaving in appropriate ways for "decent" men and women. When I was growing up and adults referred to men "visiting a woman," it was used a euphemism for using the services of a prostitute or going to a brothel. Because Pete was in a hurry to get home before his foster mother found out he was gone to "visit a woman," I interpret Pete's actions as visiting a brothel. When his wife stayed up late playing cards, she was also not behaving as a proper lady should. This narrative of La Llorona invokes the virgin/whore dichotomy that supports traditional notions of "good" and "bad" womanhood. There is no proof that the individuals in the other narratives are engaging in inappropriate activities. For example, we do not know why the first couple was going home and what Carlos Valenzuela was doing in his cabin. As the wife in the first couple stays in bed and Carlos Valenzuela is not able to work, the activities that are probably disrupted are housework and mining. Both forms of work are essential for economic development but are normally devalued and not paid (housework) or paid a very low wage (mining).

In another story documented bilingually in Spanish and English, an 11-year-old girl narrates her encounter with La Llorona in 1948.[24] One night, when the girl was visiting with her mother, a friend named Tirza, and her husband, Don Justo, they heard a very long and horrible cry that was very sad. As the girl heard the cry, she told her mother "Le estan pegando a alguna mujer" (They are hitting a woman). Further, the girl adds, "Next day grandmother told me what it was, so I didn't feel afraid. Es la única vez que la oí (It's the only time I heard her). There's an arroyo—we heard the sound from there. My mother knew about it, but she didn't want to tell me. They all said it was La Llorona. It cried about four times, but it hasn't been heard latterly. Antes molestaba a los vecinos case [sic] todas las noches." (She used to bother the neighbors almost every night.)

Is this narrative really about hearing La Llorona or about a mother and grandmother protecting a young girl about the knowledge of domestic violence? The young narrator says that after hearing La Llorona, she did not want to stay with Tirza again, and that the cry she heard used to bother the neighbors. Many elements in this narrative are somewhat consistent with the possibility that a woman is being abused near Tirza's house. Everyone hears the cries, they happen often, and they used to bother the neighbors almost every night; the cries, however, disappear. The story does not explain why the crying ended; therefore, we can only speculate on why the crying ended. This narrative of La Llorona represents the scream or cry as a response to pain. It also speaks about the silence that surrounds domestic violence, as mother and grandmother explain the screams as being La Llorona and not a real woman being abused—although the girl knew about it already. Interestingly, the girl's caretakers believe that a ghostly figure is less frightening than the reality of women being abused in their homes.

La Llorona's scream also has a decolonial meaning. In the narrative that I quote at the beginning of this chapter, La Llorona is represented as Mother

Earth who has the ability to foretell disasters for a community or a nation, but usually not of a personal nature. The narrative explains that, "There are stories that her wailings were heard for weeks throughout the villages of Mexico before the landing of Cortes." And further it adds, "There is rarely an earthquake that the old women do not say, oh yes, I knew it was coming, I heard La Llorona the other night." This representation of La Llorona's scream is quite different from the other narratives I have analyzed thus far. In this case, the crying is an omen, notifying the people that something terrible is about to happen. Thus, La Llorona is not reacting to colonization and patriarchy; resisting traditional gender roles; or acting in a vengeful manner. Rather, she is attempting to prevent colonization and is helping the public survive a natural disaster. In both cases, she is trying to do right and is proactive, not reactive; she is not snatching someone else's child or causing adults an illness that has them bedridden.

PEDAGOGICAL IMPLICATIONS

La Llorona, as I have demonstrated in this chapter, is a complicated legend. The pedagogies I am highlighting in this chapter show that there is not a single meaning to the legend. Rather, La Llorona illustrates the complexities of life. The reality is that neither people nor representations of mythical figures are one-dimensional. La Llorona is not only a terrifying dangerous ghost that represents evil, and neither is she an innocent victim of circumstances. What she represents are ways in which people and society respond to injustice by evoking the same issue that might terrify us in the first place. For example, when La Llorona loses her children either by her own hand or by circumstances of life, she seeks to take someone else's child. In this case, she is subjecting to others the pain she has suffered. Social injustice creates this type of circumstance; as long as there is no social justice, there will be no harmony in the social order.

Critical educators are concerned with understanding how popular culture is implicated in the formation of subjectivities and desires. Most societies have used myths in order to "socialize" their young into appropriate behaviors. The legend of La Llorona does precisely that, but in a complex way. The traditional patriarchal interpretations of La Llorona offer a warning to women about the dire consequences for transgressing sexual mores. However, women have produced alternative meanings to this strict (somewhat "didactic") function of the legend. Examining the accounts produced by women shows how they are constructing alternative Chicana identities and subjectivities. The narratives of La Llorona intercede in the struggles over the meanings of Chicana womanhood in ways that are empowering to *las mujeres*.

The analysis of the multiple meanings and articulations of La Llorona attest to the reality that Chicana/o identity is, like all identities, constantly negotiated and contested. This is something that is lost in so many educational practices that rely on old-fashioned and tired stereotypes of Mexicans. Therefore, one of the strategies that can be followed with this analysis is to bring La Llorona into the classroom (or the museum) and explore the multiplicity of versions that exist. Through analysis of the many stories of La Llorona, students can learn how cultural productions, including popular culture, respond to the changing conditions of a community. Studying how the legend changed after the U.S. annexed México's northern territories provides not only an analysis of historical events, but also an understanding of how the people who lived through those events adapted to a new social order. By doing some of these exercises, educators would be hard pressed to continue relying on stereotypical representations of Mexican Americans.

The ways in which the legend of La Llorona is transmitted from generation to generation forms part of this pedagogical practice as well. The cultural pedagogical politics involved in the formation of the legend are linked to how communities respond to their material conditions.

By focusing on the multiplicity not only of possible readings, but also the creation of those multiple meanings through oral traditions, it is possible to analyze how these conflicting meanings attempt to counter dominant forms of economic and gender inequalities. This focus also avoids a facile analysis that promotes one correct ideological reading over another. This pedagogical practice, then, understands cultural productions as sites where forms of domination are, or can be, contested and recreated in ways that allow for the construction of alternative identities and subjectivities.

NOTES

1. I am maintaining the quotes of oral histories as I found them in the archives. I am not correcting grammar, spelling, syntax or even inconsistencies in order to maintain everyday forms of speech and expressions present in oral language. I realize that because these oral histories are archived in written form, they already have been translated from the oral to the written word. There is evidence that some narratives have been corrected after they were transcribed.

2. In most families, women tell the stories, which is the case in my extended family. Coming from a mixed Mexican and Anglo-German family, with a Mexican father and an "American" mother, the role of transmitter of Mexican culture and values rested on my father who had the cultural knowledge to do so. This was particularly the case when my siblings and I were very young children in the late 50s and early

60s; my mother was learning Spanish and adapting to Mexican culture, as we lived in Mexico. I do recall my paternal grandmother and my aunts telling many stories, including the legend of La Llorona.

3. There is a belief that humans' reproductive "instinct" is to ensure our "immortality"—that is, our genes will live forever in our offspring and their descendents—then, killing children is a way to destroy that immortality. La Llorona can deny the father of her children such immortality in the act of infanticide.

4. I am not trying to justify infanticide. Indeed, I will put myself in the camp of those who feel scorn for Susan Smith because not only did she kill her two little boys, but also used racial politics to try to frame a black man. On the other hand, Andrea Yates' desire to be the perfect mother by emulating an exaggerated notion of super mom where she was a stay-at-home mom, home schooled her children, and did many things contemporary mothers do not do anymore (like baking birthday cakes), did not have a moment of respite from her motherly duties. Such idealization of motherhood, coupled with clinical depression, ended up in disaster. Please note that the issue with Yates is not so much her efforts to become the perfect mother—many of us try our best, but that this striving towards perfection in combination with a diagnosed mental illness, took her over the deep end. Moreover, I do believe that Yates is ill as reports in the news media state that she is refusing to eat and drink (see, "Andrea Yates returned to prison after hospital stay," *The Associated Press*, July 17, 2004; Pam Easton "Andrea Yates' husband files for divorce," *The Associated Press*, August 2, 2004). In the years that I have been researching La Llorona, I became a mother of a now twelve-year-old boy. Once I became a mother, I started to feel much more anxious about writing about a story of infanticide and death of children. Indeed, one night when I was writing a draft of this chapter, I twice checked to see that my son, who was asleep, was fine.

5. According to León Portilla, the other prognostications are: 1) A great column of fire in the night that lasted one year; 2) A fire in Huitzilopchiti's temple that nobody started; 3) a lightning bolt that struck Xiuhtecuhti, a temple made of straw, when nobody heard thunder, and it also started a fire; 4) a fire divided into three parts (it seems it was a comet) and fell when the sun was out; 5) The water in a lake boiled and destroyed the houses next to the lake; 6) The weeping woman; 7) Moctezuma had a bad omen, in a vision he saw some warriors (the Spaniards) riding in some "deer"; and 8) Often times deformed people, one body two heads, were brought to Moctezuma to the magic house. Once he would see them, they would disappear. (Miguel León Portilla. *La Visión de los Vencidos: Relaciones indígenas de la Conquista*. [México, D.F.: Universidad Autónoma de México, Décimotercera edición,]1992, pp. 2–5).

6. An abbess is a superior of a convent.

7. I propose that La Llorona is a struggle against patriarchy because I am ascribing feminist symbolism to two of its elements: the loss of children and her screaming. I contend that by looking at the multiple and contradictory meanings, we can excavate such feminist meanings, even though I am cognizant that a first and traditional meaning would argue that La Llorona reinforces patriarchy. Certainly, many of the messages given to women about sexuality do reproduce traditional gender roles and

thus patriarchal meanings. In order to understand the complexity and contradictory meanings, we should understand the legend as third space feminism where we can find both meanings operating at the same time.

8. The program was produced before the change from INS to ICE.

9. I am thinking here very specifically of Russian mothers crying in the funerals of the children who died during the school hostage in Belam in September 2004. Iraqi mothers also express mournful cries during funerals of their sons and daughters. While these are two different circumstances and cultural contexts, there seems to be an almost universal belief that children should bury their parents, and not the other way around.

10. A point of clarification is necessary. Of course, it is not the same to eradicate the ideology of patriarchy than eliminating men. However, we should not undermine the symbolism behind the "fact" that apparitions of La Llorona are much more dangerous for men than for women and children. This creates a double-edged sword for women and any feminist analysis, for that matter. On the one hand, it is important to take this into account in conjunction with the reality that women are the ones who usually tell the story. On the other hand, historically, women have been persecuted when it is believed that they have special or supernatural power, such as witches. Therefore, it should not be lost that her threat to men can also be used as a tool of patriarchy.

11. The zero zero place is the name of the Café in Viramontes' story. Saldívar is using a word play to underscore his point.

12. In preparation to the analysis of *Prietita and the Ghost Woman,* I asked my son to read the story with me. At the beginning, he was getting a bit scared, worried that La Llorona will harm Prietita. After we finished reading, I asked him what he thought of this version of La Llorona. In the simple and straightforward manner of a child, he told me it was very different and not scary as the story *he imagines* when he sees Clara Loma's artwork on La Llorona.

13. Although, Candelaria's usage of authenticity differs from my arguments, I find the rest of the quote compelling and useful for my argument.

14. There are similar versions of the legend in other parts of the Southwest and West. The richness of the narratives in New Mexico and Arizona was enough for my analysis and argument in this book.

15. As I start this analysis, I do want to take into account the problematic of "translation" of oral text to written texts. The texts that I am analyzing here, although documented as oral narratives, were selected from narratives archived in written form. Thus, there is much lost in this translation in terms of voice intonation, pauses, modes of speech, et cetera. Moreover, there is evidence that some of these narratives have been altered (as is the case of the "Evil Spaniard"), therefore, they are not "faithful" to the "original" narratives. Given this caveat, I proceed with caution. Nevertheless, for the purposes of this analysis, these narratives suffice because I am focusing on variations and multiple meanings.

16. This does not mean only U.S. Southwest versions of La Llorona are anti-colonial, or that these versions idealize society under Mexican or Spanish rule. What

I am arguing here is that every time there is a new colonizer or historical intervention, cultural productions, including popular culture, adapt to the new situation and particular forms of resistance that respond to that historical contingency are produced. And because I am analyzing Chicanas' re-construction of the legend, I am focusing on Southwest stories.

17. While the colonizing behaviors of Spain and the U.S. are significant, it is important to take into consideration that for many American Indians, the Mexican period was also problematic and viewed Mexicans as invaders of their lands as well.

18. Fritzi H. Reay collected this story, and the informant was Jack L. Frain from Albuquerque. The story was recorded in 1967, but the informant heard it in 1966.

19. The version I photocopied from the Baughman Collection has several alterations. In one case, the word "child's" is inserted by hand. In another, the word house is crossed out by hand and the word "child" handwritten on top. One typo is corrected by hand.

20. I owe this point to an observation by Mónica Rusel y Rodríguez, who brought this to my attention during a presentation at the 2005 NACCS conference in Miami, Fl.

21. This narrative is archived in the Southwest Folklore Center of the University of Arizona in 1948. The mother of the collector Angel Laguna told him about her encounters with La Llorona.

22. Carlos Valenzuela told this story to collector Arvella Elias. The narrative is part of the Southwest Folklore Center of the University of Arizona.

23. This narrative is from the Southwest Folklore Center collection of the University of Arizona. It is not clear who was the informant, the name Desmond Powell appears on the left hand side of the page.

24. This narrative is also from the Southwest Folklore Center, University of Arizona. Spanish translation into English is mine.

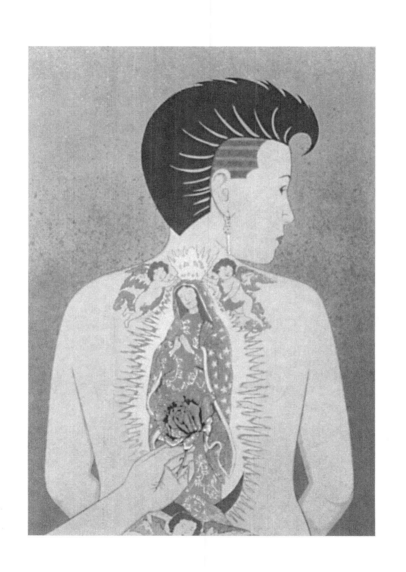

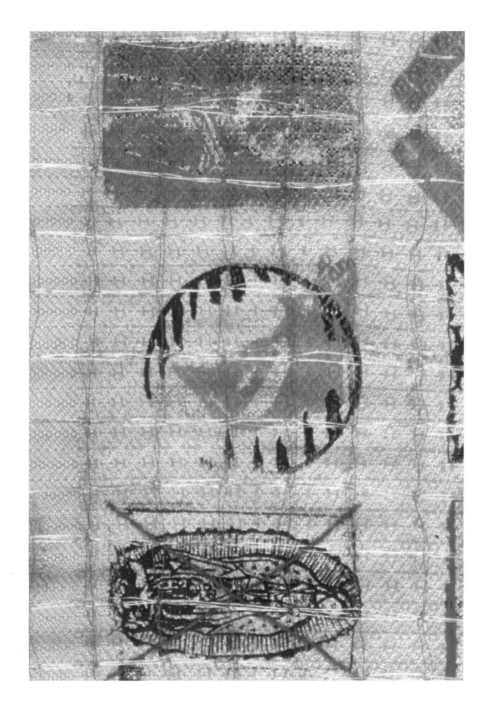

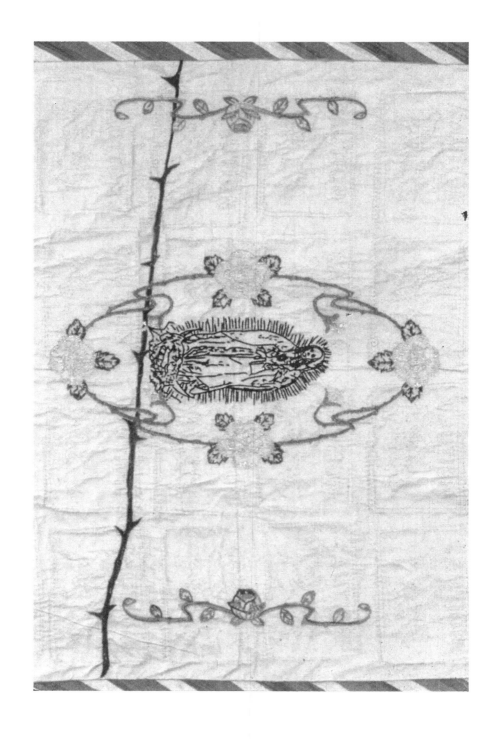

Chapter 4

The Virgin of Guadalupe

Spirituality, Desire, Consumption, and Transformation

"*La gente Chicana tiene tres madres.* All three are mediators: *Guadalupe,* the virgin mother who has not abandoned us, *la Chingada (Malinche),* the raped mother whom we have abandoned, and *La Llorona,* the mother who seeks her lost children and is a combination of the other two." (Gloria Anzaldúa 1987, 30)

When our Mother is seen only as the one-dimensional Mary of modern times, instead of the great dual force of life and death, She is regarded to the same second-class status of most women in the world. She is without desires of Her own, selfless and sexless except for her womb. She is the cook, the mistress, bearer and caretaker of children and men. Men call upon Her and carry Her banner to lead them out to war. They show Her off, take Her love and magic to form a formidable fortress, a team of cannons to protect them against their enemies. But for a long, long time the wars that women have been left to wage on behalf of men, on behalf of the human race, have started much sooner, in the home, in front of the hearth, in the womb. We do what we must to protect and provide for our young, our families, our tribes. Because of our humility, we call upon Her privately, quietly in prayer, from our kitchens and bedrooms, as if She had more important matters to tend to besides those of a mother, of all mothers, besides those of any ordinary woman—when no woman born who knows herself could ever be ordinary. (Castillo 1996, 78)

La Virgen de Guadalupe is a significant nationalist, cultural, and religious figure among Mexicans and Chicanos. While the patriarchal Catholic meaning maintains its hegemonic power to construct notions of womanhood, some Chicana and *mexicana* feminists engage in a process of self-renewal, shedding away patriarchal notions of femininity. Chicana feminists Gloria Anzaldúa and Ana Castillo articulate this process of renewal of not only the Chicana woman herself, but also of the images of traditional femininity that

have distorted the meanings and lives of our three mothers. In this chapter,
I examine this process of renewal through the re-imagining of La Virgen de
Guadalupe.

In 1531, ten years after the fall of Tenochtitlan (today Mexico City), a dark-
skinned Nahuatl speaking Lady appeared to the Indian Juan Diego, a *macehual,*
and member of the humbler people. She is believed to be an apparition of the
Virgin Mary, mother of God, who became known as La Virgen de Guadalupe
(The Virgin of Guadalupe). The timing of the event, the language she spoke,
and the race of the Virgin are all significant because they signal recognition
of the subjectivity of the indigenous and mestiza/o inhabitants of México. The
presence of the Christian Virgin speaking in Nahuatl blends Aztec religious
practices with Catholicism. La Virgen de Guadalupe is one of the most revered
Catholic religious and nationalist symbols in México. The image of the Virgin is housed in the Básilica de Guadalupe in México City, where every year
millions of people make pilgrimages to honor her. La Virgen de Guadalupe's
power emanates from the circumstances surrounding her appearance and her
physical attributes. From the outset, she has all of the elements necessary to
make her a Mexican national symbol. She is the dark-skinned virgin who manifested herself to a peasant. She symbolizes solidarity with Indians and mestizos.
She is associated with Aztec deities, such as Tonántzin, "Our Mother," who
was worshiped in Tepeyac; since the mid-sixteenth century, indigenous inhabitants of central Mexico continued their veneration and looked for Our Lady of
Guadalupe in Tepeyac (León-Portilla 2000).

Today, her image is found in countless artifacts of popular culture: tee
shirts, refrigerator magnets, key chains, long distance phone calling cards,
and almost any kind of knick knack. Her image has appeared on banners
used in nationalist liberation struggles, including Mexican independence
from Spain, the Mexican Revolution, the Chicano movement, and the United
Farm Workers (UFW). In the mid-twentieth century, her iconography became
ubiquitous in the Mexican American barrios in the U.S. The rise of the Virgin
as an icon is tied to the emergence of the Chicano nationalist movement and
its legacy. Guadalupe has been represented in religious art, murals, folk art,
and Chicana and Chicano art. She even lives in cyberspace where there are
literally hundreds of web pages devoted to Guadalupe. For centuries, she has
been a transnational figure; her image has crossed borders since the seventeenth and eighteenth centuries, and people venerate her in Latin America,
the U.S., and Europe.

Traditionally, La Virgen de Guadalupe is interpreted through patriarchal
ideology that views her as symbolic of feminine ideals such as passivity,
obedience, and self-suffering. However, there are multiple elements in her
ethnicity, symbolism, and iconography that make her (or have the potential

to make her) a woman-centric and feminist figure. Indeed, Chicana feminists who reclaim her as a decolonial figure offer alternatives to the patriarchal representations of Guadalupe by enacting politics of memory (Blake 2008). These politics of memory perform border/transformative pedagogies and Chicana feminist epistemologies in that Chicana artist and cultural workers use their creative energies to transform the meaning of Guadalupe and produce radical subjectivities that challenge mainstream patriarchal (Colonial, Anglo and Chicano male) epistemologies. While there is a significant difference between Chicana feminist reinterpretations of La Virgen de Guadalupe and the mainstream Church sanctioned one; I do believe that even in the most traditional interpretation, Guadalupe transcends stereotypical notions of appropriate femininity. For example, Guadalupe is a protector—a role traditionally assigned to men (Rodríguez 1993). Moreover, respectively Rodríguez (1993) and Blake (2008) document that everyday women also offer different meanings of La Virgen of Guadalupe. Additionally, Blake proposes that working class and semi-professional women were able to construct alternative meanings because the meanings of Guadalupe oscillate between liberation and tradition. That is, the instability and ambiguous meanings of Guadalupe open a semiotic space that allowed women to invoke their own significations outside the official Church one, but which are different from Chicana feminists.

The apparition of La Virgen de Guadalupe is associated with the Spanish conquest of México, which in turn, devastated the indigenous population by taking away land, culture, and most of their material possessions. Colonization also tried to take away the dignity and subjectivity of the colonized peoples. It is considered one of the most traumatic events in Western history, with five to eight million dead due to genocide and disease as a direct result of Cortés' conquest of México itself (Acuña-Soto, Stahle, Cleaveland, and Therell 2002). This accounts to a one third reduction of the native population (Matovina 2005, 12).

According to Wolf, the appearance of Guadalupe to a humble Indian validates the rights of Indians as Subjects. "Guadalupe embodies a longing to return to the pristine state in which hunger and unsatisfactory social relations are minimized" (Wolf 1958, 36). La Virgen de Guadalupe validates the Indian rights of legal defense, orderly government, to citizenship, to supernatural salvation, but also to salvation from exploitation (Wolf 1958, 37). The symbolism of La Virgen as both a spiritual and nationalistic figure shows that the conquered Indians are complete humans (flesh and soul) who deserve to live a decent and productive life, and whose souls can be saved.

In this sense, La Virgen is a powerful symbol of the rights of the oppressed and a hope for a better future (Trujillo 1998). The Virgen of Guadalupe's association with life symbolizes the possibility that the oppressed can triumph

over the powerful. The hope that Guadalupe gives is not only in the after
life, but is a political hope in the here and now that the disenfranchised will
prevail over social inequality. Chicanas have reclaimed this meaning of La
Virgen de Guadalupe to claim their rights as women, and in so doing have
produced Chicana subjectivity that seeks to transform unequal social relations
and material conditions.[1]

Moreover, when Chicana feminist artists, cultural workers, and intellectuals focus on Guadalupe's strength and reconstitute her from the traditional
passive being to an active subject, they are reinscribing her beyond patriarchal meanings. Border/transformative pedagogies draw from Chicana/o
cultural productions that understand Chicana/o subjectivity in its multiple
manifestations avoiding the reification of essentialist notions of identity
(Elenes 2006). Border/transformative pedagogies include cultural politics
that incorporate as social practices the constructions of knowledge capable
of analyzing conflicts over meanings and offer a critical space to do so. An
example of this is Ester Hernández's (1975) representation of Guadalupe as
a Karate figure in *La Virgen de Guadalupe Defendiendo los Derechos de los
Xicanos*.[2] Iconographically, the image of the Virgin is symbolic of femininity,
a gynocentric figure. The manner in which the mandorla frames Guadalupe,
how she is placed at its exact center and the rays that emanate from her, visually form a vagina (Pérez, L 2007, Trujillo 1998), and as the mandorla rounds
up at the top and gets enclosed, it forms a perfect image of female power and
sexuality. From her inception, one can witness the subversion and rebellion
through her iconography.

Chicana feminists' most powerful source to claim Guadalupe as a feminist symbol is that she is associated as Tonántzin (Castillo 1996, Trujillo
1998). As Tonántzin, Guadalupe is a Goddess in her own right; she is not the
Christian mother of God, she is God/Mother (Castillo 1996). Some Chicana
feminists believe in her spiritual power, which is significant in the transformation of Guadalupe from the meek mother of God to a goddess in her own
right (Trujillo 1998). The pedagogical strategies invoked by Chicanas transform superficial readings of Guadalupe that view her as a model of women's
passivity and traditional gender roles to a model of strength and activity(ims)
that constructs a radical subjectivity.

In this chapter, I am using transnational feminist cultural studies theory
to analyze the representation of La Virgen de Guadalupe as a form of global
consumption and Chicanas' reinscription of the traditional patriarchal meanings in their pedagogical and epistemological considerations from three
perspectives. First, I examine how representations of the Virgin's image
become the object of commercialization and consumerism characteristic of
a global economy. I then contrast this consumption with the Chicana artists'

decolonial representations of Guadalupe. Specifically, I examine the artwork of Ester Hernández, Alma López, Yolanda López, and Consuelo Jiménez Underwood as examples of border/transformative pedagogies. I selected these artists because their art "speaks" the language of border/transformative pedagogies. In their own ways, they exemplify how the conflicts over meaning address contemporary feminist politics, pedagogies, epistemologies, and subjectivities. Through their respective artwork, these feminist artists are transforming the meaning of Chicana/o culture by incorporating the multiplicity of Chicana subject positions such as artists, workers, working class, and queer within spiritual and feminist sensibilities. And third, I examine Chicanas' reimagining of Guadalupe as feminists spiritualities. First, I offer a historical account of the apparition of La Virgen de Guadalupe.

Historical Accounts of the Apparition of the Virgin of Guadalupe

The narratives about the apparition of the Virgin of Guadalupe sanctioned by the Church were not disseminated until the seventeenth century. Given that these accounts and agreement that she performed miracles did not become acceptable until the seventeenth century, there is much speculation about her celestial origin (Matovina 2005). It should not be a surprise that Guadalupe has ambiguous meanings given that a century lapsed between Juan Diego's vision, the miracle of growing flowers, and the appearance of her image in the *tilma*. Nevertheless, the first description of the apparition is documented in the *Nican Mopohua (Aqui se Narra)* [Here it is Told], written by Antonio Valeriano in Nahuatl and in paper made of the pulp of maguey between 1540–1545 (following Aztec practices).[3] Valeriano was of Indian noble class and knew classic Nahuatl. He was educated in the *Colegio de Santa Cruz de Tlatelolco* under Fray Bernardino de Sahagún. Valeriano knew Juan Diego; it is believed that it was Juan Diego himself who gave him his first-person account of the apparition of the Virgin of Guadalupe and the miracles she performed. The *Nican Mopohua* is considered the authoritative document that describes what happened in December 1531. There are also four "evangelists" that document the development of the devotion of Guadalupe. In 1648, Father Miguel Sánchez wrote *Imagen de la Virgen María, Madre de Díos de Guadalupe, Celebrada en la Historia con la Profesía del Capítulo doce del Apocalipsis*. The second evangelist was Lasso de la Vega who published in 1649 the *Hue Tlamahuizaltica,* which is the *Nican Mopohua* (Here it is told) written in Nahuatl.[4] In 1666, Luis Bezerra Tanco wrote *Origen Milagroso,* which was posthumously published by his friend Antonio de Gama with the title of *Felicidad Mexicana.* And the fourth evangelist is Francisco de Florencia, who in 1688 published *La Estrella del Norte,* which expounded

Creole Theology. *La Estrella del Norte* is considered the first translation to Spanish of the *Nican Mopohua*. The development of the worship of Guadalupe and modern understanding of Guadalupe are based on the writings of these four evangelists.

Early opposition to the veneration of Guadalupe appeared in an *Información* that Fray Alfonso de Montúfar ordered in 1556 (Florescano 1994, Matovina 2005). Fray Francisco Bustamante used this *Información* in a sermon, in which he attacked the worship to the *image* of the Virgin of Guadalupe:

> It seemed to him that the devotion that this city had taken in a hermitage and home of Our Lady that they have entitled of Guadalupe is a great harm to the natives because it leads them to believe that the image *painted by the Indian Marcos* perform miracles . . . and to tell [the Indians] that an image that was painted by an Indian perform miracles, would be great confusion and undo good that had been planted there. (Bustamante qtd. in Florescano, 1994, p. 132. My emphasis)

Miguel Sánchez's *Imagen de la Virgen María, Madre de Díos de Guadalupe* was based on oral accounts of old men about the apparition. According to this account, the Virgin Mary appeared in Tepeyac to the Indian Juan Diego early December 1531. Juan Diego heard sweet music and his name called. He then saw a lady who, speaking in Nahuatl, ordered him to go toward her and asked him where he was going. She revealed herself to Juan Diego and asked him to give her message to the bishop. Her request was to have a temple built where she appeared so she could protect her people, and they could venerate her. Juan Diego obliged and paid a visit to Fray Juan de Zumárraga, the bishop of Mexico, who indifferently told him to come another day. On his way back home, when the Virgin appears to him a second time he informs her of the bishop's behavior. Juan Diego begged the Virgin to choose another person with more credibility to give her message to the Church authorities. But the Virgin assured him that he is the one who should and will convey the message to the bishop. On the third appearance, Juan Diego informed her that the bishop had asked for a sign. The Virgin promised to give the sign the next day. But the next day, Juan Diego's uncle became severely ill, and he had to look for a priest to perform the last rites. Juan Diego did not want to get distracted by the Virgin and tried to avoid her to no avail. The Virgin appeared to Juan Diego and assured him that his uncle was fine and that he should not be afraid since she would protect him. The Virgin then proceeded to ask him to climb up the hill to the place where he had seen her and cut and pick up the roses and flowers he would find there. Without questioning the "odd" demand, since it was December and the nature of the terrain (stone) was not conducive for flowers to grow, with haste he went and found the flowers, which he picked and put in his cloak. Juan Diego proceeded to show the sign to the bishop. As he was waiting to see the bishop, his assistants, who were not letting him in, noted his patience and that he had something in his cloak. Once they realized that what he had were flowers and that it was not possible to take the flowers out of the cloak, they informed the bishop. When Juan Diego was before the bishop, he informed him of everything that had happened, and the miracle occurred:

> He reveal the clean blanked to present the gift of heaven to the fortunate bishop; he anxious to receive it, saw on the blanket a holy forest, a miraculous spring, a small garden of roses, lilies, carnations, irises, broom, jasmine, and violets, and all of them, falling from the blanket, left painted on it the VIRGIN MARY, Mother of God, in her holy image that today is preserved, guarded, and venerated in the sanctuary of GUADALUPE in Mexico City. (Sánchez, 1648 qtd. in Florescano, 1994, 141)

As early as the sixteenth century, the Catholic establishment identified her with Tonántzin and viewed her veneration as idolatry. The transformation of Tonántzin as a Catholic symbol and the ideal icon of femininity did not occur until the seventeenth century. However, since the mid-sixteenth century, Mexicans have been devoted to La Virgen de Guadalupe. This spiritual connection marks the beginning of her symbol as a national and spiritual icon. A practice that is not difficult to understand after the Spanish conquest of Mexico, as "She was a powerful mother and intercessor, a brown-skinned woman like them who provided continuity with an ancient Nahuatl image and pilgrimage site and came to symbolize the Indigenous peoples' dignity and right to self-determination" (Matovina 2005, 12).

One of the ways in which many Chicanas reclaim their indigenous roots and spirituality is through their reverence of the Virgen de Guadalupe. This is part of a spiritual mestizaje that combines Catholic imagery and indigenous practices. The spirituality associated with La Virgen de Guadalupe understands that Guadalupe and various Nahua female deities such as Tonantzin, Coatlicue and Tlazeototl are interrelated. Tonantzin literally means "Our Mother." *To* means ours, *nanti,* means mother, and *tzin* is a term of respect (Blake 2008, Robelo 1951). Tonántzin is an antonym for Centeotl, the Goddess of Maize, whose celebration occurred near the winter solstice. Tlazolteotl was the goddess of fertility and sex. She is considered the Venus of Nahua mythology. She had the power to make people become lustful, yet she had the power to forgive such sins if these were confessed to the priests. Coatlicue was the mother of Huitzilopochtli and Coyolxauhqui, *La Hija Rebelde* (the rebel daughter)[5] (Cisneros 1996; Robelo 1951).

Cihuacóatl, the serpent woman, Coatlicue, serpent skirt, and Tonántzin are thought to form a whole based on Aztec duality. Cihuacóatl, the mother of humans, was also known as Tonántzin. She would carry a crib in her back or sometimes leave it at the tianguis. When women would look into the crib, they would see a knife inside (See chapter 3 for an explanation of the association between Cihuacóatl and La Llorona). Chavero makes Cihuacóatl, Chimalma (believed to be Quetzalcoatl's mother and confused with Coatlicue), and Coatlicue one goddess; however, Robelo believes that Aztecs confused Cihuacóatl with Coatlicue. Coatlicue is the mother of Huitzilopochtli, and she had a human skull or serpent as a head and a skirt of serpents (Campbell 1982; Anzaldúa 1987, Robelo 1951). Some believed that Cihuacóatl had given birth to twins, Quetzlalcoatl and Huitzilopochtli. To understand these associations, it is important to remember that Aztec philosophy was based on dualism, sometimes even contradictory ones. There are those who believe that Cihuacóatl and Tonántzin are associated and that they represent different sides of a duality. According to Anzaldúa (1987), the Mexica-Aztecs male domination split the female self from the female deities. With such a split completed, Tonántzin becomes the good mother and Coalticue, Chimalma and Cihuacóatl, the dark side.

For Chicana feminist writer Sandra Cisneros, the interrelationship of these figures helps her understand the multifaceted aspects of La Virgen de Guadalupe. Cisneros, who in her youth was angry at the unattainable expectations for women represented in the traditional virgin, also believes that La Virgen was ". . . damn dangerous, an ideal so lofty and unrealistic it was laughable. Did boys have to aspire to be Jesus? I never saw evidence of it" (48). By rediscovering the antecedents of Guadalupe in pre-Columbian deities, she was able to associate Guadalupe with sexuality and women's freedom. Cisneros further writes, "Perhaps it's the Tlzolteotl-Lupe in me whose *malcriada* spirit inspires me to leap into the swimming pool naked or dance on a table with a skirt on my head. Maybe it's my Coatlicue-Lupe attitude that makes it possible for my mother to tell me, *No wonder men can't stand you.* Who knows? What I do know is this; I am obsessed with becoming a woman comfortable in her skin" (50). Cherie Moraga (1996), however, prefers to pray to *La Hija Rebelde,* rather than to Coatlicue, who she views as a male-identified mother. Nevertheless, Moraga's spirituality is part of her drive to write and to search for the whole woman who is "A free citizen of Aztlán and the world" (70).

The mother figure represented in La Virgen de Guadalupe is part of a decolonial spirituality. For Castillo (1996), conquered indigenous peoples may have turned to the mother to bring comfort, assurance, and hope after the Spanish conquest. The male gods "became silent," and La Virgen represents the archetype of the mother figure "that appears and speaks with such melodic tenderness that it was compared to the singing of birds, flor y canto[6]—that is, beauty and truth. It sounded like music never heard before" (xvii). La Virgen de Guadalupe was adopted by indigenous and mestizas/os as a spiritual figure through which they could reclaim their humanity. Ana Castillo understands La Virgen de Guadalupe as "mythistory" which shares similar characteristics with Chicana feminist spirituality,

> Myths are the stories that explain a people's beliefs about their purpose for liv-ing and their reason for dying. The stories are often told through allegory and parable to facilitate a cultural understanding of what is by its nature perhaps too complex for the general populace to grasp. The Mexican indigenous account of the apparitions of the Mother Goddess is rich with Nahua symbolism and meaning. To ignore the meaning the account of Her apparition may have had the Nahua people, merely ten yeas after the violent conquest and destruction of their world, and despite their recent (imposed) conversion to Catholicism, would be a travesty. (Castillo 1996, xviii)

Jeanette Rodríguez (1996) also sees that La Virgen de Guadalupe repre-sents the power of memory, which stands for justice and solidarity with the oppressed. She quotes Acuña-Siller who uses the image of the *yollo* (heart), which is what moves individuals to action. If the devotion to La Virgen de Guadalupe is not accompanied with solidarity with the poor, then the devo-tion is not "authentically Guadalupana" (30). As we can see, Chicana feminist spirituality is multifaceted, and its sources of inspiration are varied. Yet, these are spiritual practices that are connected with the quest for social and gender justice and for women to express their agency as complete beings. La Virgen de Guadalupe is more than a spiritual, religious, and national symbol. She is an expression of Mexican and Chicana/o ethnicity.

Transnational Feminist Cultural Studies and Deconstruction

La Virgen de Guadalupe is, as well, an example of transnationalism and globalization. A transnational feminist cultural studies perspective offers theoretical tools to understand La Virgen of Guadalupe in its multiple mean-ings and representations; from an object of global consumption to a Chicana feminist decolonial strategy.

Transnationalism studies how globalization impacts the movements of peo-ple, goods, services, ideas, and cultural productions across national boundar-ies. A significant body of transnational scholarship focuses on migration of labor (Guevarra 2010, Spivak 1996) and on the labor conditions of "Third World women" working in factories producing goods for global consumption

(Mohanty 2003, Fernández-Kelly 1983, Ngai 2005, Ong 1987, Louie 2001). Studies of migration and exploitation of labor are not new. What is distinctive of transnational theorization is the focus on conditions of globalization at the end of the 20th and the beginning of the twenty-first century such as global capitalism, consumerism, and the globalization of communication systems (Mahler 1998) that facilitate links among communities that are separated not only geographically, but also culturally. Transnational scholarship offers a paradigmatic shift that does not privilege Western theories and capitalism as "monopolies of exploitation and repression, while localities are stereotyped as static" (Mahler 1998, 64).

The terms transnationalism and globalization are sometimes used interchangeably, yet as Grewal (2005) proposes, the word "transnational" is more humble than "globalization." The word "global" serves as a universal register or regime of truth that travels transnationally within powerful knowledge connectivities (Grewal 2005). Transnationalism has also been used to assess the impact of diasporic and immigrant communities in the developed nations such as the United States (McCann & Kim 2003). As Gayatri Spivak (1996) explains, global financial policies (e.g., IMF) serve to suppress decolonization movements. Therefore, globalization has political and economic impact on communities that do not have the power to compete globally (Téllez 2005). Transnational feminist scholarship focuses on the critique of exploitation of women in a globalized economy (see Mohanty 2003). However, transnationalism also enables the movement of alternative ideologies that try to counter the effects of globalization. Nancy Naples (2002) argues that the concentration on the economic dimension of globalization neglects an analysis of how it affects the everyday life of women. Thus, analyses of transnationalism and globalization must focus on political, economic, and cultural practices as they move around the globe in multiple directions. As Kaplan and Grewal (2004) argue, "the situation today requires a feminist analysis that refuses to choose among economic, cultural, and political concerns" (358). One aspect of the "New Cultural Politics" (Grewal 2005) of globalization is that individuals and collectivities become citizen-consumers[7] and citizen-workers. Indeed, populations gain notoriety through their ability to consume. Capitalist interests pay attention to particular groups (e.g., teenagers or Latinas) when they acquire purchasing power as a group.

Transnational scholarship offers tools to study the dynamics of globalization from a multidirectional and anti-binary perspective. That is, transnational scholarship does not only focus on how power emanates from structural capitalism, but also looks at how different communities struggle against such global forces. Naples (2002) proposes that the complex process of globalization has two faces: (1) it includes the oppressive consequences of global capitalism and militarism; and (2) it reflects possibilities for resisting imperialism to achieve equality and justice around the globe. Moreover, feminist scholars recognize that not all transnational movements are oppressive, as some can also be liberating. Some scholars use the concepts of transnationalism from "above" and "below" (see Guarnizo & Smith 1998) to show the differences between structural modes of globalization (e.g., global capitalism) and grassroots, decolonizing, feminist, and anti-racist movements. Manisha Desai (2002) proposes that just as capital is fluid and exists in multiple sites that result in "scatter hegemonies" (Grewal and Kaplan 1994), so is women's agency, which is evident in multiple spaces of resistance within transnational networks.

The movement of people, goods, and services obviously includes cultural movements and transformations. When people, culture, goods and services transcend borders, groups and individual identities are also transformed. A key aspect of transnational scholarship is that it offers a flexible theoretical framework to understand contemporary global structures and social relations from multiple perspectives, including a critique of global capitalism, the significance of communication technologies, decolonization, and the expansion of social networks (Guarnizo & Smith 1998). For example, satellite technology makes it possible for people to watch television from their country of origin no matter in what part of the globe they are. Thus, Central and South Americans can watch television from Nicaragua or Colombia if they can afford a satellite connection. Such flexible framework does not privilege one perspective or single issue but recognizes how cultural and economic issues are interrelated with the construction of identities. Studying the movement of people, goods, and services necessitates an understanding of how culture and cultural productions are affected by and affect globalization and consumption. I apply the perspective of transnational cultural studies to analyze La Virgen de Guadalupe as a transnational image.

Transnational feminist critics and scholars resist Western hegemony, including the critique of totalizing master narratives and essentialized subject positions (Sampaio 2004, 198). Transnational feminism engages in the form of oppositional and differentiated mode of consciousness proposed by Chela Sandoval (2000).[8] Sandoval understands subjectivity as decentralized and strategic, and through which women express their agency in various forms of political activity (Sampaio 2004). Subjectivity and identity are complex and always in flux, yet as many "Third World" and feminists of color propose, this complexity does not mean that they do not exist. Rather, going beyond the oversimplified binary that understands identities as either essentialist or non-essentialist, feminists of color recognize that identities are not fixed once and for all, but at the same time are constructed from the multiple dimensions of race, class, gender, and sexuality, among many others. That is, they enact borderland subjectivities. This, as I have elaborated in this book, is one of the central characteristics of border/transformative pedagogies, as well. As Sampaio writes, "Transnational feminism's engagement with the differential and oppositional consciousness examined in third world women's feminist work (both inside and outside the United States), and the critiques of hegemonic feminism found in postcolonial feminist writings, have contributed to the development of a new discourse about women's political location and activism in the new global matrix" (Sampaio 2004, 199). Agency is based on identities developed from feminist and anti-racist movements that move in multiple directions that are mixed and created through contradictions, tensions, and struggles (Grewal 2005). Naples (2002) proposes that feminist scholars offer insights into contradictions associated with globalization exploring how race, class, gender, and sexuality are marked through differences in market relations.

Transnational feminism also studies how bridges are constructed in Western societies (including the U.S.) among new immigrants and older communities of struggle (e.g., Native Americans, African Americans, Latinas/os), taking into account how race, class, gender, and sexuality connect with social, political, and economic issues (Mufti & Shohat 1997). Indeed, Mufti & Shohat propose that "Multicultural and transnational feminism(s) inscribes the notion of race and (neo)colonialism into the debates about feminism, while simultaneously inscribing gender and sexuality into the debates about nation and race in the era of globalization" (5). Similarly, Mohanty (2003) argues that such movements are necessary in the process of decolonization. Some of the cognitive elements in the construction of oppositional selves such as history, memory, emotion, and affectional ties can lead to the development of alternative feminist epistemologies when they are associated with collective practice (Alexander & Mohanty 1997, qtd in Mohanty 2003), which in turn form part of decolonialism. I argue that some of the feminist meanings ascribed to La Virgen de Guadalupe offer alternatives to dominant epistemologies. For example, Laura Gutiérrez (2006) proposes that Chicana feminists' cultural productions depicting La Virgen de Guadalupe are sites of transnational multiple meanings where the sacred is transformed and acquires sexual agency. Before I move to the analysis of these spiritual and decolonial processes, I turn to an examination of the commodification of La Virgen de Guadalupe.

Consuming Spirituality

Since the second half of the twentith century, we have witnessed the increase in the production and commercialization of objects representing La Virgen de Guadalupe. Today, Guadalupe's image can be found in all sorts of objects such as belt buckles, lamps, light switches, watches, or Christmas ornaments. The type, form, and consumption of these objects are quite varied. The diversity and assortment of products depicting La Virgen de Guadalupe demonstrate the level of commodification[9] through which she has gone. The figure of the Virgen of Guadalupe is ubiquitous in Mexico and Mexican barrios in the United States. Historically, the Virgin has been depicted in religious art and objects sanctioned by the Church. Since the 1960s, Mexican and Chicana artists have symbolized La Virgen through their art, much of it secular in nature and which reconceptualizes the meaning of La Virgen (Pérez, L 2007). Contemporary objects depicting Guadalupe are a diverse assortment of everyday items that can be quite different from religious and artistic expressions. These objects are a mix of commercial interests with ethnic and national pride, religious perspectives,[10] and spirituality.

The selling of products based on La Virgen de Guadalupe to a variety of communities recognizes people of Mexican descent as a market. Such marketing, while a welcome recognition of a Mexican/Chicana cultural and religious icon, raises questions about the relationship between culture and commercialization. When a figure such as La Virgen de Guadalupe becomes a commodity, it runs the risk of losing its spiritual and decolonial value; much in the same way that the image of El Ché has gone through. At the same time, this process of commodification is quite contradictory. That is, while there are dangers in the process of commodification, these are items that are either produced by the Mexican and Chicana/o community (although not always) or are marketed to a population that usually does not have its culture recognized by mainstream society. One could assume that some members of the Chicana/o and Mexican community can find it empowering and exciting to see products depicting La Virgen de Guadalupe, as I often times do. Thus, the commodification of La Virgen can be understood from many different perspectives. At some level, one could argue that the marketing and commodification of La Virgen de Guadalupe signals some form of power or recognition of the Chicana/o community in the U.S. However, being recognized as a market is not the same as having access to political power. Commodification runs the risk of depoliticizing alternative cultural productions.

Marketing promotes an essentialized and static definition of identity (whether of race, class, gender, or sexuality) and in doing so idealizes the consumer by an arbitrary created standard. Advertisers create an ideal consumer based on a narrow definition of such a community and gear their messages in order to reach the largest audience possible. The differences that exist among ethnic communities, for example, are ignored; thus, advertisers deliver their message to a perceived or idealized common denominator. The rapid growth of the population of Mexican descent, and its subsequent "buy-ing" power, makes this community a "market that is worthy of advertising." The focus on the buying power of the Mexican community can idealize it as affluent. When the marketing industry propagates these myths of affluence it ends up presenting a picture that obscures poverty, marginality, unemploy-ment, and racism. Marketing discourses are not without political and eco-nomic repercussions (Dávila 2001).

Globalization affects how ethnic communities are constituted as a market and a political force. Marketing is involved in the construction of public iden-tities where individuals are considered consumers first and foremost (Dávila 2001). And ethnic communities are now included within these consuming identities because of the growth of specialized ethnic marketing (Dávila 2001). However, such promotion is rooted in prevailing ideas of culture and consumption. The promotion of different ethnic cultures usually is based on hegemonic practices derived from hierarchies of race, ethnicity, language, and nationality which tend to reify cultural practices. Usually, such reifica-tion is done by invoking essentialist notions of cultural authenticity based on stereotypes. Alternative and contradictory cultural practices which, ironi-cally, one could argue are more "authentic" are dismissed. For example, the controversy that Alma López's digital art *Our Lady* caused in 2001 when it was exhibited in the Museum of International Folk Art (MOIFA) in Santa Fe, New Mexico signals to the debates over cultural authenticity and who has the power to decide what is authentic and what is not. The Catholic Bishop and some Chicano nationalists objected to this image because it sexualized and re-interpreted the meaning of the Virgin. As I will elaborate in more detail below, a significant aspect of their objections centered on the process of sexu-alizing La Virgen and on reinterpreting her meaning in feminist ways. The debates over the authentic meaning of La Virgen de Guadalupe enact various pedagogical discourses; Alma López's re-inscription is clearly an example of how border/pedagogical discourses are presented in her artwork by cross-ing the boundaries of ideal femininity from passive women's sexuality and objectification to a construction of a feminist subject that celebrates female desire, sexuality, and spirituality. The pedagogies of consumption that claim authentic ethnic subjects are quite different and tend to serve the interest of capital and colonialism.

Marketing pays attention to ethnic communities because they will buy products, not because it might be the right thing to do.[11] The variety of products featuring La Virgen de Guadalupe can be read as examples of the reification of culture and reducing individuals to consumers. This does not deny that people find appeal and pride in seeing such products (while others do not). In other words, that La Virgen de Guadalupe is commodified does not mean that she has lost her religious, nationalist, or ethnic meaning (albeit the danger that this occurs is very real). For example, as cultural critic Toby Miller (2007) proposes, "the oppressed become producers of new fashions, inscribing alienation, difference, and powerlessness on their bodies" (3). That is, I do recognize that the types of objects we consume are a manifestation of not only taste, but also of our cultural identity.

Products representing La Virgen are so varied that they are segmented by class. The constitution of a segment of the Mexican community as middle class has created a "new" market for objects representing La Virgen de Guadalupe geared to the middle class. For example, Armani sells statuettes of La Virgen de Guadalupe that cost $475.00 via the Internet. The department store Dillard's sold a beautiful Christmas tree ornament with the image of La Virgen during the 2004 Christmas season. (A friend of mine gave me that ornament as a Christmas present.) The department store Mervyn's (years before it went bankrupt) promoted watches with the image of La Virgen in their Sunday paper advertising. And recently, Wal-Mart was selling garden statues about three feet tall for $49.50, and yes, made in China. Mainstream markets and department stores have found a niche on an ethnic market. Of course, there are also everyday items such as key chains, tee shirts, car decals, and phone cards that represent La Virgen which are geared toward the working class.

Acquiring these items, whether by middle or working class individuals, can be read as a manifestation of ethnic pride, a pride that I express in some of the objects with the Virgin's image that I possess. As I am writing these words, I am surrounded by various objects that are precious to me that decorate my home: sofa cushions, an apron, a roof tile, countless pictures, including the Catholic Church sanctioned one that I bought at La Basilica de Guadalupe in Mexico City, and popular artwork. In my home, I mix pedagogies of consumption with border/transformative pedagogies in that I have created a home space where a multiplicity of meanings of La Virgen de Guadalupe is on display. I have personally purchased many of these items both in México and the U.S.; many of these were acquired at MALCS and NACCS conferences. My closest friends and family members have given me many birthday, Christmas, and thank you gifts featuring La Virgen. I love all of these objects, and they do reflect how I perform my ethnicity and spirituality. While it is true that ethnicity is commodified; these objects do bring me pleasure. Yet, as examples of border/transformative pedagogies, these objects represent contradictory meanings and are situated at the border between the reproduction of global capitalism and its critique.

The consumptions of objects are somewhat different from artistic works because the latter better represent border/transformative pedagogies, even though everyday objects can do so. I believe this is the case because the Chicana artists that I will analyze in the next section are reconstituting a radical Chicana subjectivity that is not always that apparent in everyday productions. What I mean by this is that some people, like myself, can offer a radical meaning to everyday objects (e.g., using an apron with the image of La Virgen as decoration and not for cleaning), but the subjectivity invoked in Chicana feminist cultural workers reinterpretation of La Virgen is more readily available. In this sense, I am not trying to make a modernist argument that high art has more radical potential than popular culture, but that the radical reframing in artistic productions by Chicana artists are more evident in their radical and subversive possibilities.

RECLAIMING TONANTZIN: CHICANA FEMINISTS' REINTERPRETATION OF LA VIRGEN

In this section, I illustrate the border/transformative pedagogies and epistemologies in which Chicana feminist visual artists engage in their process of cultural transformation and redefinition of La Virgen de Guadalupe. The conflict over the meanings of La Virgen and subsequent debates among traditionalists and Chicana feminists signal to the changing meaning associated with La Virgen from a model of ideal femininity such as passivity, obedience, self-suffering, and asexual, to depicting her as an active and sexual being. Maintaining the classic or patriarchal meaning of La Virgen de Guadalupe as meek and passive, as Chicana feminist writer Carla Trujillo (1998) reminds us, is to continue the oppression of Chicanas. Therefore, Chicana feminist cultural workers who represent alternative meanings of La Virgen de Guadalupe tend do so in the service of their needs, desires, and liberation.

The artistic productions of Ester Hernández, Yolanda López, Consuelo Jiménez Underwood, and Alma Lopez produce deconstructive meanings of La Virgen de Guadalupe and reconstruct her as a symbol of Chicana feminism and struggle for social justice. That is, these Chicana feminist visual artists transform the meaning of La Virgen de Guadalupe by producing a new ideology composed of shifting and contradictory layers of signification. Through the voicing of innovative visual narratives, as Chicana feminist artist and critic Amalia Mesa-Bains (1991) asserts, they produce "multiple text composed of shifting layers of meaning" (131). As border/transformative pedagogies, these artistic productions address the ways in which Chicanas have been oppressed and seek to restore women's rights as workers, as immigrants, and to their sexuality.

In the analysis further down, I show how through alternative forms of cultural productions Chicana artists depict La Virgen as a subject, instead of an object, by which we can recognize Chicana multiple subjectivity. Chicana artists reclaim, reconfigure, and deconstruct the representation of Guadalupe as the patriarchal ideal of femininity. By doing this, Chicana artists are constructing a cultural identity that claims a historical space within the Chicano community that shows the need to alter the social structures that oppress, subordinate, and produce unequal social conditions for women. Amalia Mesa-Bains (1991) asserts that Chicana artists construct their cultural identity using the female lenses of narrative, domestic space, social critique, and ceremony. The visual representations of La Virgen de Guadalupe can be understood as feminist counternarratives through which Chicana artists affirm their position in society by centering the emancipation of women (Mesa-Bains 1991). The domestic space and female body are reclaimed as sites for social critique of women's subordination showing the contradictory experiences of women's roles such as wives and mothers (Pérez, L 2007). Mesa-Bains calls these reclaimed spaces in the home, such as the kitchen, altars *domesticana* because they are affirmation of women's resistance and reappropriation of the domestic space. Mesa-Bains asserts that "she [the Chicana artist] employs the material of the domestic as she contests the power relations located within it" (2003, 302). By contesting how Chicanas are marginalized from community structures (e.g., Church, schools), Chicana artists are offering a social critique that constructs a new ideology (Mesa-Bains 1991).

Gloria Anzaldúa (1998) proposes, as well, that Chicana artists attempt to find the lost history, language, identity, and pride by "digging into our cultural roots and making art out of our findings" (163). Anzaldúa suggests that the feminist transformation of La Virgen de Guadalupe into a feminist figure is a process that must be done in order to alter colonial cultural practices into decolonial ones. She explains her view in the following way, which is worth to quote at length,

> Through the centuries a culture touches and influences another, passing its metaphors and its gods before it dies. (Metaphors *are* gods.) The new culture adopts, modifies, and enriches these images, and it, in turn, passes them on changed. The process is repeated until the original meanings of images are pushed into the unconscious. What surfaces are images more significant to the prevailing culture and era. The artist on some level, however, still connects to that unconscious reservoir of meaning, connects to that *nepantla* state of transition between time periods, and the border between cultures. (Anzaldúa, 1998, p. 164–65)

Chicana feminist visual narratives of La Virgen de Guadalupe offer a process of deconstruction of the Catholic and traditional meanings by refashioning them into women-centric feminist significations. In doing so, Chicana artists are enacting border/transformative pedagogies.

Activism, Struggle, and Agency

The work of Ester Hernández, Yolanda López, and Consuelo Jiménez Underwood respectively show Chicanas' struggle against oppressive forces. Themes that are evident in their artwork are depictions of the Virgin of Guadalupe symbolizing the struggle for women's, workers', and immigrants' rights. Ester Hernández is a Chicana artist from San Francisco and a graduate of UC, Berkeley. Her artistic portrayals of women, including La Virgen de Guadalupe, "reflect political, social, ecological, and spiritual themes" (http://www.esterhernandez.com/Bio_1.htm). She is one of the first Chicana artists to explore alternative representations of Guadalupe. Her famous 1974 linocut, *La Virgen de Guadalupe Defendiendo los Derechos de los Xicanos* (see Figure 1), is a powerful feminist representation of Guadalupe. Guadalupe is dressed in Karate attire and is in an active Karate move, with her legs almost forming a 90 degree angle. Her left leg comes out of the mandorla. The typical starred mantle is almost falling from her head. The angel sustaining the half moon is also in a very active pose. Hernández explains that the figure "represents woman becoming an active participant, breaking out of some traditional images—the colonial mentality, while maintaining her culture, informing, teaching, and learning from her people; taking a militant stand on all fronts, on behalf of La Raza: La Chicana at the forefront of the arts, in schools, as writers" (qtd. in Quirarte, 1992, p. 21). Hernández situates her artwork as a pedagogical practice that emanates from the people. While La Virgen historically has been associated with the plight of the oppressed, Hernández takes this symbol much further as Guadalupe is in an active pose taking charge. Thus, she endorses an activist border/transformative pedagogy which encourages women to fight for and defend their rights.

Social inequality is represented in Yolanda López's visual productions of Guadalupe. López was born in San Diego, California in 1942; yet found her "voice and discovered her gallery in the streets of San Francisco's Latino district" (http://www.speakoutnow.org/People/YolandaLopez.html). In addition to being one of the most widely recognized Chicana artists, López has a history of activism. She was part of the Third World Strike in San Francisco State University in 1968 and worked as a community artist with the group Los Seis de la Raza in the Mission District (http://mati.eas.asu.edu:8421/ChicanArte/html_pages/YLopezIssOutl.html). Her series on La Virgen de Guadalupe dates to 1978 and re-portrays Guadalupe as an ordinary woman (Trujillo 1988; Yarbro-Bejarano 1993). López recreates Guadalupe by transforming the stoic, passive figure into a dynamic image. Chicana feminist cultural studies critic Angie Chabram-Dernersesian (1993) argues that through this reconfiguration, López "reimages Guadalupe for contemporary Chicanas/Mexicanas seeking liberation from oppressive male-oriented images of Chicana women and from the debilitating influences of social institutions and beliefs" (42–3). López's reinterpretations of Guadalupe are some of the most significant feminist and provocative explorations of her.[12]

In most of her representations of Guadalupe, López substitutes the original image with everyday Chicanas. Thus, she is reclaiming Guadalupe for Chicanas in their everyday life and activities. "López's Guadalupes are mobile, hardworking, assertive, working-class images of the abuela [grandmother] as a strong, solid nurturer, mother as a family-supporting seamstress, and daughter as a contemporary artist and powerful runner" (http://magti.eas .asu.edu:8421/ChicanArte/html_pages/YLopezIssOutl.html).

In one of these representations, *Portrait of the Artist as the Virgen de Guadalupe* (1978), she substitutes the Virgen for a self-portrait. Guadalupe's traditional "gown" is cut short, especially on the front, giving it a modernized outlook. López grabs a snake in one hand and carries the starred mantle as a cape on the other. She is wearing running shoes, and she is moving toward the viewer. As she moves, she steps over the angel that sustains the figure, and one of her legs gives the impression that she is kicking back the crescent moon. Her muscular legs are showing, demonstrating strength. Even the traditional mandorla gives the impression of movement. López is thus symbolically leaving behind the patriarchal constructions of Guadalupe. Indeed, according to Gaspar de Alba, (1998), López described the angel as a "middle-aged agent of patriarchy" (141). López disassociates Guadalupe with Catholicism and reasserts Guadalupe's power for herself and the communities of Chicanas.[13] She believes that real, in-the-flesh women also deserve the power and respect that Guadalupe receives (http://magti.eas.asu.edu:8421/ ChicanArte/html_pages/YLopezIssOutl.html).

Mesa-Bains asserts that the art in the Guadalupe series, "does not simply reflect an existing ideology; it actively constructs a new one. It attests to the critique of traditional Mexican women's roles and religious oppression in a self-fashioning of new identities" (137). In *The Portrait of the Artist as the Virgen de Guadalupe,* as she grabs onto the mantle, López maintains traces of Guadalupe. By running with the snake, López is providing a semiotic space for Nahua epistemologies. The snake has different meanings in different cultural/epistemological traditions. In Mesoamerican belief systems, serpents were associated with wisdom, consciousness, death, and regeneration (Blake 2008, Lara 2008b). Moreover, in Mesoamerican cultures, the snake, or Coatl, was the object of universal veneration (Robelo 1951). Quetzalcoatl, the plumed serpent, is considered to be the link between the earth and the sky (Lara 2008b). Anzaldúa (1987) writes that the Olmecas associated the serpent's mouth with womanhood. "They considered it the most sacred place on earth, a place of refuge, the creative womb from which all things were born and to which all things returned" (34). López's depiction of the snake is a deconstructive move away from the Judeo-Christian meaning[14] of the snake in favor of the Mesoamerican one.

The commitment toward the struggles of working class Chicanas is represented in López's *Our Lady of Guadalupe: Margaret F. Stewart* (1978). Here, Guadalupe is re-created as a garment worker. Guadalupe is sitting in front of a sewing machine, the rays behind her. Guadalupe is sewing her own mantle, which flows from the sewing machine to the floor. There we see the crescent moon almost covered and the angel, whose wings have the colors of the Mexican flag, looks pensive, sustaining himself in the crescent moon, instead of his whole image. On the lower left corner are roses on the floor partially covered by the mantle. Guadalupe is a modern day Chicana with short hair and reading eyeglasses. In reality, she is Yolanda López's mother, who supported the family for over 30 years by working as a seamstress. Visually, she is at the center of the frame, yet her face is partly covered by a lamp.

Pedagogically, the viewer is invited to learn about the struggle of garment workers. Guadalupe's eyes are looking up and look tired from so much work. The lamp covering the mouth symbolizes the silencing of women. In spite of such silencing, women historically have fought for their rights as workers. For example, there is a long history of union organizing among Latina garment workers (see Ruiz 1998, Mendez 2002). Moreover, as sociologist María Soldatenko (1999) has documented, garment work by Third World women, particularly Latinas in the U.S., is prone to labor exploitation. "Working conditions in sweat shops are unhealthy. In some shops there is no ventilation; in others there are drafts. Many of the shops are infested with rats and cockroaches" (Soldatenko 1999, 323). Moreover, exposure to dyes and fabric can affect workers' health; contact to cotton dust can result in lung damage (Soldatenko 1999). Pedagogically and epistemologically, López is using Guadalupe symbolically to articulate the plight of Chicanas who need to work in order to economically subsist. The imaginary of seemingly endless job, conveys a political message of the struggle of working-class women to survive.

The struggle of working class Chicanas and Latinas is linked to immigrant rights. This is a theme that is prominent in Consuelo Jiménez Underwood's cultural productions. Borders occupy an important symbolic space in Consuelo Jiménez Underwood's artwork, through which she expresses a borderland sensibility that articulates the tension between the U.S. and Mexico and amid mainstream America and Chicana/o cultures. Jiménez Underwood seeks to construct a Chicana cultural identity from her personal memory that blends her indigenous and Mexican backgrounds. She is the daughter of a Mexican father of Huichol origins and a second generation Chicana. She recently retired as a professor at San Jose State University to dedicate herself to her art and political struggle (personal conversation February 2010). She situates her work against a political landscape that is oppressive to the Other, to those who are different from the U.S. normative articulation of race, class, ethnicity, and gender. She is trying to reaffirm a political identity that questions social conventions. The political nature of her work is manifested not only in the form, but also in the medium chosen: textiles. Through textiles, she is trying to recuperate a traditional indigenous female identity. The construction of Chicana cultural identity has also led her to explore and deconstruct La Virgen de Guadalupe. Jiménez Underwood asserts that "In general, each of the Virgen portraits incorporates a large range of formalistic approaches to the material and the media. But the imagery is consistent as well as the message . . . "Get off our backs!!" (Personal correspondence, October 22, 1995).

Like Ester Hernández and Yolanda López, Jiménez Underwood's work invokes committed pedagogical politics that serve as indictments against social inequality. Even the form she chose, textiles, is a political move, since this is not an accepted medium. She explains her work this way, "My work is about our struggle to consciously discern the underlying messages presented through images that bombard us every day. We too easily become numb to the greed and deceit that continue to affect our interaction with this beautiful and sacred land" (Jiménez Underwood 1995, 19).

The Sacred Jump (1994) (see figure 2) is woven and silk-screened silk threads and gold wire, 216 x 98 cms. A series of different icons are symmetrically lined up forming four columns that each have six images. On the top, there is a repetition of a salmon jumping a hoop or circle that looks like an aura. Below are images of tire marks, the "caution" sign found in Southern California highways, similar to the deer crossing sign, of an undocumented family crossing the freeway. There are a couple of images of La Virgen de Guadalupe. One is crossed out with a red cross, and the other has a yellow "V" simulating an ear of corn on her feet that seems to sustain her. Immediately below the crossed out Virgen is an image of a Mesoamerican deity, perhaps Tontantzin or Coatlicue. She sewed gold-colored silk thread simulating barbed wire on top of all of the icons. According to Jiménez Underwood, "the selection and arrangement of the imagery—the salmon struggling to come home, real colonial prints, a 'welcome' sign—is inspired by both anger and awe" (1995, 19). In *The Sacred Jump,* Jiménez Underwood depicts the struggle of undocumented immigrants making their journey to the United States and the dangers they encounter. She incorporates "the cynical welcome sign" of an "illegal alien" family crossing the highway found on Southern California freeways as a reminder of the discrimination that Mexicans and Chicanos suffer at the hands of immigration officers.

Central to the piece is the image of the Virgen of Guadalupe; this is a subtle image that is recognized by the traditional iconographic elements. However, this is the crossed out figure. Jiménez Underwood, in her effort to "get her off our backs," utilizes Derrida's sign of deferral to deconstruct the Virgin. She recognizes the polyvalent characteristic of La Virgen de Guadalupe. By marking her, she makes visible how she can symbolize the oppression of Mexicans and Chicanas/os. Yet, she is deconstructing the oppressive construction. In Jiménez Underwood's artwork, we see La Virgen de Guadalupe represented within the multiplicity of meanings that can be attributed to her: as a symbol of liberation, hope, and protection of the oppressed, while deconstructing her as passive and meek. By crossing her out, Jiménez Underwood refuses to give Guadalupe a static meaning, especially the meaning assigned by patriarchy and the Catholic Church. Underneath this crossed out Virgen is the image of Tontantzin or Coalticue; thus, she is reclaiming her indigenous identity. In associating Guadalupe with her Mesomerican identity, Jiménez Underwood enacts a decolonial reading.

Jiménez Underwood links the contemporary plight of Mexican migrants to the U.S. with the histories of the colonization of México by Spain in the sixteenth century and the U.S. Southwestern region in the nineteenth century. The colonial prints, the sign of the undocumented family crossing the freeway, and the image of barbed wired sewed over the icons, connect this long and complex history of colonization. The salmon jumping over the aura also brings together these different forms of colonization. Salmon swim upstream to return home and spawn. Mexican migrants must also engage in a dangerous, and often times deadly journey to the U.S. as a result of neo-liberal global capitalism that make it very difficult for people in developing societies to compete economically. Increased migration is a consequence of current globalizing economic policies. While the salmon is struggling to *come* home, so are the undocumented workers struggling to *find* a home. There is a paradoxical position of presence and absence being worked out in her work. The presence of La Virgen is undeniable, but because Jiménez Underwood is continuously deconstructing her meaning from its colonialist connotation—and in doing so offering a strong critique of colonialism—there is an absence of a traditional Guadalupe. That is, there seems to be a movement or process of looking back to the pre-colonial past in an effort to reconstruct Mesoamerican philosophies within contemporary sensibilities and struggles.

The *Virgen de los Caminos* (1994) [Drawn, sewn, embroidered, cotton, linen, silk] (see Figure 3) frames the Virgen with a sewn frame and embroidered roses. There are three stems of roses that cut across the piece, almost dividing it into three parts. At the center is the Virgen, with wires that cut just beneath her feet. In most of Jiménez Underwood's art work, the Virgin appears in a very subtle way; sometimes the viewer has to be familiar with the image in order to recognize her. *La Virgen de los Caminos* is somewhat different because here, La Virgen is displayed prominently. The traditional iconography of Guadalupe is maintained intact, except her face: it is the traditional Mexican skull. In Nahua cultures, the skull represented life, not death. Again, Jiménez Underwood is deconstructing Guadalupe. Guadalupe is historically associated with life, and as in *The Sacred Jump,* Jiménez Underwood reframes her within Mesoamerican epistemologies. The replacement of Guadalupe's face with a skull, can lead us to associate her with Coatlicue.

Borders are very present in this piece. For art critic Constance Cortez (2007), Jiménez Underwood "employs both barbed wire and silk in her art, weaving topographies that recreate conflict and contradictions born of historic circumstances" (36). As I explain in chapters 1 and 2, the history of the México-U.S. border continues to inform the tensions between these two nations and its respective citizens. This is a painful history; as such, it forms part of the "common historical memories" (Ruesga Bono, nd) of people of Mexican descent on both sides of the border. *La Virgen de los Camino,* refers to this history. Many migrants, before they embark on their journey, pray to La Virgen de Guadalupe to protect them. *La Virgen de los Caminos* points out to this need for protection; but also shows that in-spite of the protection, there is danger, and the journey can be deadly.

Jiménez Underwood is offering decolonial representations of La Virgen de Guadalupe by connecting borders as geographical spaces and boundaries that are meant to separate different groups of peoples. She alludes, as in *The Sacred Jump,* to the socio-economic circumstances that obligate Mexicans to seek employment as undocumented workers in the United States and the struggle to cross such borders, For Jiménez Underwood, preserving the past is necessary to maintain "common historical memories" (Ruesga Bono, nd). *La Virgen de los Caminos* is a reminder, as well, of the difficult and often times deadly consequences of crossing the border.

Sexuality, Desires, and Spirituality

The ability to express women's sexuality is essential for Chicana feminist politics. As the control of women's sexuality is a key aspect of the patriarchal meanings of Guadalupe, Chicana artists seeking to break with virginal and heterosexist definitions of sexuality produce artwork that claims a radical subject position that reclaims sexuality, desire, and spirituality. Alma Lopez identifies as a visual storyteller; she is a digital artist and activist (www .almalopez.net). She is originally from Mexico but grew up in California. She received her BA from the University of California, Santa Barbara and an MFA from the University of California, Irvine. Her work has been featured in a variety of outlets, including covers for Chicana/o studies books. In her cultural productions, Lopez addresses issues that affect the Chicana/o and Mexican communities in the U.S. such as immigration, racism, queer identity, and colonization (Herrera-Sobek, Latorre & Lopez 2007). Her art decontextualizes traditional Mexican iconography from their patriarchal meanings. Pedagogically, in her artwork she transcends and transfigures traditional Mexican icons such as La Virgen de Guadalupe into feminist representations. She produces decolonial art founded on Chicana feminist politics that centers, honors, and celebrates Chicanas' sexuality, desires, and spirituality.

Our Lady is a small (17.5 x 14) digital print created in 1999 (www .almalopez.net). *Our Lady* features two of Alma Lopez's friends: performance artist Raquel Salinas as the Virgen dressed in roses; and Raquel Guerrero, a cultural activist, as a nude butterfly angel. Lopez was inspired by Sandra Cisneros' essay "Guadalupe Sex Goddess" published in Ana Castillo's anthology *Goddess of the Americas,* in which Cisneros wonders what Guadalupe is wearing under her garments. Raquel Salinas's one-person performance "Heat Your Own" also inspired *Our Lady* (Lopez 2002). *Our Lady* features Raquel Salinas posing as La Virgen, showing her undergarments made of flowers. Instead of the traditional star mantle, she is wearing Coyolxauhqui's robe. The background is made out of the fabric of the gown that La Virgen de Guadalupe wears in the traditional image. The mandorla is lighted on the back, giving it a yellow glow. Coyolxauhqui's robe is open and exposes Guadalupe's undergarments. Lopez says that after reading Cisnero's essay, she also wondered what Guadalupe would be wearing under the robe; she realized that it had to be roses (www.almalopez.net). Hence, Guadalupe is showing the rose undergarments. Guadalupe's hands are on her hips, gazing at the viewer; unlike the traditional image in which she is facing down, eyes closed, and her hands in prayer position. Her head is not covered, with her long black hair showing. She is standing on the crescent moon. The angel that sustains the moon is displaying her breasts prominently and is in front of a Viceroy butterfly. Roses frame the Virgin and the angel, and the traditional star mantle is at the bottom of the picture along with some rays.

By replacing the traditional mantle with Coyolxauhqui's robe, Lopez invokes what Chérie Moraga (1983) calls *la fuerza femenina.*

> She [Coyolxauhqui] is la fuerza femenina, our attempt to pick up the fragments of our dismembered womanhood and reconstitute ourselves. She is the Chicana writer's words, the Chicana painter's canvas, the Chicana dancer's step. She is motherhood reclaimed and sisterhood honored. She is the female god we seek in our work, la Mechicana before the "fall." (Moraga 1983, 74)

Coyolxauhqui's dismemberment is taken symbolically by Chicana feminists, like Moraga, to critique how Chicana subjectivity is fragmented due to the multiple forms of oppression they encounter. Chicanas have to contend with multiple discourses of femininity and sexuality that deny their subjectivity and agency. Coyolxauhqui was killed and mutilated by her brother Huitzilopochtli so he could impose patriarchal rule. By reclaiming Coyolxauhqui, Chicanas are reconstructing their fragmented selves. Lopez, then, is constructing a radical Chicana subjectivity where feminism, sexuality, and spirituality are reclaimed in their terms.

Lopez sexualizes Guadalupe, which ultimately humanizes her (Herrera-Sobek, Latorre & Lopez 2007). In this sense, as queer Chicana cultural studies scholar Luz Calvo (2004) proposes, Lopez's art breaks open a public, cultural space for the articulation of queer Chicana desire. This repositioning and articulation of queer Chicana desire is represented more vividly in the series *Lupe & Sirena in Love* (1999). Here, I analyze three digital art vignettes: *Encuentro, Lupe & Sirena in Love,* and *Tattoo,* that depict a romantic relationship between La Virgen de Guadalupe and La Sirena (The Mermaid). La Sirena is drawn from the popular Mexican game of Loteria, a bingo type game, which instead of numbers has cards with pictures of different types of characters, including La Sirena.[15] In *Encuentro,* the Virgen de Guadalupe appears in clouds wearing her traditional attire, stretching her hand to La Sirena. Guadalupe is sustained by the Viceroy butterfly instead of the angel. Her face tilted down, she is looking at Sirena. Sirena appears exactly as she is on the La Loteria card. As a mermaid, she is half-fish and half-woman and is showing her breasts. She is coming out of the water, looking up, and her long curly black hair flows to her back. Her left arm is stretching out of the water as if trying to hold onto someone; the right arm is bent next to her breast. Her red tail is under water. In *Encuentro* (which means finding or meeting), Guadalupe and Sirena are meeting perhaps for the first time. Sirena's stretched out arm is held by Guadalupe. They are not in the ocean, but in the sky surrounded by clouds. In the next vignette, *Lupe & Sirena in Love,* Guadalupe and Sirena embrace. Their poses change strategically a bit. One of Guadalupe's hands is touching Sirena's breast, and the other is holding on to her behind. Sirena's stretched out hand is caressing Guadalupe's hair and starred mantle. They are framed by little angels and roses. In the background, we see the Los Angeles skyline and the wall that marks the México-U.S. border. At the bottom, we see the Viceroy butterfly.

The third installment, or vignette, *Tattoo* represents the tattoos that are more often seen on men's backs on the back of a Chicana, Jill Aguilar. A male tattoo artist is tattooing Guadalupe and Sirena's embrace on Aguilar's back. One of Aguilar's hands is resting on her shoulder, the other on her hips. She is wearing jeans, and her black hair flows to her back, covering just the top of Guadalupe's Mandorla. We can see the profile of Aguilar's face and of her breast. In the background we see Los Angeles' sky line, including East LA and the Mexico-U.S. border. *Tattoo* has recently been used for the cover of two Chicana studies publications: the Spring 2007 issue of *Chicana/ Latina Studies: The Journal of Mujeres Activas en Letras y Cambio Social* special issue on Chicana art; and in *Gender on the Borderlands: The* Frontier *Reader,* edited by Antonia Castañeda with Susan H.Armitage, Patricia Hart, and Karen Weathermon (2007).

Lupe & Sirena in Love not only embodies, thus humanizing, La Virgen, but also embraces the brown body. The embodiment of the brown body, as Cindy Cruz (2001) reminds us, is a "reclamation, for the Chicana social agent, [and] is not only a strategy to make visible Chicana voices and histories, but is also the struggle to develop a critical practice that can propel the brown body from a neocolonial past and into the embodiments of radical subjectivities" (658). Alma Lopez's visual narratives embody the Virgen de Guadalupe with the language of desire and love. She repositions the traditional icons of Guadalupe and Sirena from their traditional meanings, and constructs a Chicana radical queer subjectivity. She enacts the epistemologies of a brown body called for by Cruz.

In *La Ofrenda* (1988), (see Figure 4) a serigraph, and *La Ofrenda II* (1990), a screenprint, Hernández reclaims the female body by placing a tattoo of Guadalupe on a modern-day naked Chicana back. Alma Lopez's *Tattoo* is similar to *La Ofrenda.* Many Chicana cultural critics have given a lesbian reading to *La Ofrenda.* For example, as Chicana lesbian cultural critic Alicia Gaspar de Alba asserts, it "has an overtly lesbian tone" (1998, 141). And, according to Yvonne Yarbro-Bejarano, the image constructs the lesbian body as an altar, "while the lesbian context presses the religious icon transgressively into the representation of lesbian desire" (qtd. in Trujillo 1998, 219). Writer Carla Trujillo proposes that "The transpositional placement of La Virgen on the back of a woman could be regarded as transgressive" (Trujillo 1998, 218). The hand of another woman offering a rose and placing it at the center of Guadalupe's image accentuates the transgressive representation of female desire. Two angels frame Guadalupe's head, sustaining her crown. The woman, in whose back is the Guadalupe icon, has short hair with rays that imitate Guadalupe's mandorla. Although we only see a profile of her face, since her back is at the centre of the artwork, we see that she is wearing red lipstick, which sexualizes Guadalupe. Karen Mary Davalos (2001) proposes, as well, that Hernández "invites the viewer to witness the love between Chicanas as a woman's hand offers a rose to the image of the Virgen and the lover, whose face is turned in profile" (101). However, when Ester Hernández produced *La Ofrenda,* she was not thinking of the artwork piece as sexual. *La Ofrenda* was inspired by henna art and the tattoos of La Virgen de Guadalupe on people's backs. Nevertheless, interpreting *La Ofrenda* as a symbol of women's sexuality, especially lesbian desire, "took a life of its own" (Hernández, personal conversation March 2010).

I believe that because *La Ofrenda* was used for the cover of the anthology *Chicana Lesbians,* it is not uncommon to give it a lesbian reading. Perhaps because this was my first encounter with *La Ofrenda,* I did read it as a representation of lesbian desire. Further, Trujillo adds,

> *La Ofrenda* transfigures the icon and places her into the daily lives and existence of the Chicana lesbian, much like other Chicana artists have re-constructed her in the image of strong women, women we admire, or women who are simply part of our daily existence. Here we see not rejection of the Virgin Mary but, in recognition of her power and cultural significance, a reclamation and reconstruction of La Virgin in our own way and not as historically ascribed. (Trujillo 1998, 219)

The rose at the center of the depiction of Guadalupe could represent a clitoris, the nucleus of women's sexual pleasure. For Gaspar de Alba "the rose is also symbolic of the gift-giver's sexuality" (1998, 141). Hernández represents Guadalupe as a gift of women by women, about the strength of the friendship among women in their own terms and not men's. Yet, due to the readings of *La Ofrenda* as a radical sexuality that contravenes social conventions, *La Ofrenda* is a source of controversy.

Whose Virgen Is She? Who Is Entitled to Claim Her?

Our Lady and *La Ofrenda* have generated anger among some members of the Latino/Hispanic and mainstream communities. Specifically, *Our Lady* produced an immense controversy when it was part of the exhibit "Cyber-Arte: Tradition Meets Technology" at the Museum of International Folk Art in Santa Fe, New Mexico, curated by Tey Marianna Nunn, that opened on February 25, 2001. The protest came mostly from members of the Hispanic and Catholic community in New Mexico: Deacon Anthony Trujillo, Santa Fe Archbishop Michael J. Sheehan,[16] and particularly self-proclaimed Chicano activist Jose Villegas. *La Ofrenda* and *Our Lady* provoked controversy because they both reposition La Virgen de Guadalupe as an embodied Chicana with real sexual desires (Calvo 2004, Herrera-Sobek, Latorre & Lopez 2007, Montoya 2003, Nunn 2007, Lopez 2002).

Lopez responded to her critics in a sort of "matter-of-fact" manner in which she "seems to be surprised" at the controversy generated by *Our Lady* (www.alamalopez.net). She believes that people, particularly men, reacted to the image because they did not understand what she was doing. The accusation that *Our Lady* was blasphemous came from people who read the portrayal of the virgin as if she was "naked." This point of critique seems to be quite disingenuous because Western religious art depicts nudes, so, Lopez asks, "What's wrong with this image?" and further writes:

> Raquel is actually not nude here; she is covered in flowers and a veil. But what many people said to me was the problem rested on her attitude. It is not what she is wearing on her body; it is what she is wearing on her face. It is the attitude she displays; her gaze. Instead of looking down in a passive manner, she is looking straightforward, as if to say: "What?" (Herrera-Sobek, Latorre & Lopez 2007, 81–82)

Repositioning and transcending the patriarchal meanings of Guadalupe did not fit well with the Archdiocese of Santa Fe. The hoopla over *Our Lady* is similar to the controversy about using *La Ofrenda* on the cover of the book *Chicana Lesbians: The Girls Our Mothers Warned Us About.* The center of the controversy is precisely the reconstitution of La Virgen as an everyday *mujer* with feelings and desires as everybody else's. Chicana feminist cultural workers have taken La Virgen de Guadalupe off of her pedestal and embodied her. This, I believe, is a central aspect of the controversy as "nothing provokes the custodians of normality and objectivity more than the excessiveness of a body" (Cruz 2001, 659). And a female and brown body that claims its sexuality and desires for women is a very dangerous body.

There is, of course, another important aspect of the controversies generated by Chicana feminists' transgressive representations of La Virgen de Guadalupe, which is, who is entitled to speak and represent La Virgen. The storms generated by *Our Lady* and *La Ofrenda* amounted to censorship and harassment to the artists. Removing *Our Lady* from the CyberArte exhibit was José Villegas, Sr.'s intentions. Alma Lopez informed her supporters that Villegas "wants the removal of 'Our Lady' from the exhibit, firing of the Director, and an apology" (http://chicanas.com/alma.html) in a letter dated March 26, 2001.

At the heart of Villegas'[17] complaint and anger over *Our Lady* was his belief that Lopez has no right to tinker with the image of La Virgen de Guadalupe. He claims "ownership" of La Virgen de Guadalupe and chastises

Lopez for disrespecting her. Villegas admonishes, "when you cross the sacred boundaries of our gente [sic] traditional values of over five hundred years, you cannot imposed [sic] and/or provoke thought on an issue that will inflame emotions against your own gente. Our Nuestra de Guadalupe does not belong to the new age interpretation of the millienum [sic] century and never will." Further in the letter, Villegas again denies Lopez any right to express her reinterpretation of La Virgen: "you have no say-so regardless on whether you think you have the moral, legal, or ethical right to become irreverence [sic] toward something considered 'sacred' or 'inviolable' with our gente, especially our blessed mother." Villegas takes ownership of La Virgen for his generation and sidesteps the First Amendment declaring that "Copyright and the Freedom of Speech laws that you claim to possess does [sic] not apply to my generation." He ends the letter in anger and with a threat, "Ya! Basta! You started a firestorm in New Mexico and we are going to put it out. . . .

*

Que Viva La Raza!
Que Viva La Causa!
Que Viva Los Brown Berets!
Que Viva Cesar Estrada Chavez!

*

José L. Villegas, Sr.
Chicano Activist"

To a certain extent, the museum did not heed the demands for censorship on the part of the Church and Chicano activists like Villegas, but did cut short the time of the exhibit.[18] The type of censorship demanded by Villegas, the Church, and detractors of *Our Lady* stem from their "ownership" to the Truth and claim to any knowledge or interpretation of La Virgen. Thus, they use their power to silence voices that counter their beliefs. That is, they use their "systems of power that threaten to invalidate certain kinds of knowledges" (Cruz 2001, 662). Villegas claimed an authority based on the hegemony of Chicano nationalist, religious, and male privilege to declare who can represent La Virgen and how. How, or better yet, who, granted Villegas that power is something he does not explain, an explanation he does not have within patriarchal hegemony.

Another case of censorship (to put it mildly) occurred with the publication and subsequent removal (albeit "voluntary") of *La Ofrenda* from the cover of the anthology *Chicana Lesbians,* edited by Carla Trujillo and published by Third Woman Press. Ester Hernández decided not to grant permission to reprint *La Ofrenda* in the subsequent printings of the anthology requested by

Norma Alarcón, editor of Third Woman Press. Hernández stated that "she had been harassed and threatened so intensely by certain people in the community that she felt it was in her best interest to remove the piece from the book's cover for any future printings" (Trujillo 1998, 217). Carla Trujillo was "saddened by Ester's decision but understood her predicament and was respectful of her wishes and needs" (217–18). At the surface level, it might seem that the community members who harassed Hernández so intensely through their actions claimed to have the right and authority to decide how La Virgen can be represented. However, it was not clear who started the harassment that Hernández suffered. Unlike Alma Lopez, Hernández did not know who was behind the harassment that she suffered day and night, and that cost her both materially and emotionally. Thus, literarily and symbolically, "they" tried to silence alternative and transgressive voices. However, neither Lopez nor Hernández have been silenced and have continued their work.

To a certain extent, I can understand (but disagree with) the anger and hurt that Catholics felt by Chicana feminists' reinterpretation of La Virgen de Guadalupe. However, such disagreement should not be a justification for censorship, and much less harassment and intimidation as there is more danger to a community when alternative voices are silenced and threatened. This exercise of power to try to sustain a sole meaning and interpretation of La Virgen de Guadalupe is, in effect, an effort to preserve gender and sexuality oppression within Chicana/o and Mexican communities. Alternative voices are essential to the liberation of *All* the community and *All* of la Raza. Recognizing and honoring multiple subjectivities are necessary steps for critical and feminist pedagogies. The border/transformative pedagogies enacted by Ester Hernández, Yolanda López, Consuelo Jiménez Underwood, and Alma Lopez open a cultural space for the construction of multiple and radical Chicana feminist pedagogies. Their courage to continue their work in spite of the personal material, emotional, and spiritual consequences is a testament to the strength these artists have, and in doing so, they offer a model of Chicana feminist subjectivity and activism in that they do not let conservatives, nationalists, and anonymous communities silence them. Important, also, is that in reclaiming and reimagining La Virgen de Guadalupe, they are insisting that she belongs to women, too. As a Chicana lesbian student in Carla Trujillo's class affirmed, "After all, she's our Virgin too" (Trujillo 1998, 218). And let's not forget that all of these communities express their spiritualities in their own ways.

Guadalupe-Tonantzin: Chicana Feminist Spiritual Activism

Similarly to the Chicana artists I have highlighted in this chapter, I also connect spiritually with the symbolism and reinterpretation of Guadalupe. The cultural expressions of Yolanda López, Consuelo Jiménez Underwood, Ester Hernández, and Alma Lopez are examples of spiritual activism. This is so because spirituality is a way of understanding someone's (or a community's) position in the world and is a guiding source to understand one's position in the world and to give meaning to one's life in relation to one's community. Spirituality includes how a person relates to the totality of life (De Luna 2002). "Spirituality contains our deepest beliefs and thoughts" (Rodríguez 2002, 114). Specifically, Chicana feminist spiritualities try to make sense of unfair economic conditions and gender inequality, and to do something about it. "For women struggling not only to survive but also to prosper spiritually, culturally, and economically, the manner in which they engage in this struggle becomes key to understanding their spirituality" (Medina 2004, 124–5).[19] For many women of Mexican descent, displaying objects of La Virgen, making an altar in their homes, and admiring Chicana feminist art reinscribing her are manifestations of their spirituality and devotion. This understanding of spirituality goes beyond institutionalized religion. In this sense, I agree with Chicana feminist theologian Lara Medina (2004) who proposes that "spirituality emphasizes the multiple ways people relate to the world around them, to their source of life of their Creator, and to themselves" (124).

Spirituality for many Chicanas means more than one's relation with a God or a Creator because it is tied with struggles for social justice and gender equality. For some Chicana scholars, theologians, and cultural workers, spirituality is related to culture, history, economic and material conditions, as well as to pedagogy and epistemology. Spirituality is formed, in part, by "family, teachers, friends, community, class, culture, gender, social location and historical moment" (Rodríguez 2002, 117). Medina (1998) proposes that, among some Chicanas, spiritual practices emerge from the integration of creative inner resources and diverse cultural practices that feed soul and psyche. Many Chicanas link their spiritual beliefs with service to others, especially their communities. For example, Dolores Delgado Bernal (2006) found that some of the Chicana college students in her study linked their spirituality with community service and their education. "(Re)claiming one's spiritual power as an act of self-determination can directly affect our politics" (Medina 1998, 195). By combining an awareness of their structural position within U.S. society with cultural knowledge and spirituality, the young women were able to see that their education not only benefited their personal future, but also, that of their communities, as well.

Chicana spiritual practices connect mind and body, integrating creativity and sexuality. As such, their pedagogies are akin to border/transformative pedagogies. After all, a key aspect of Chicana feminist spirituality is constructed as a critique of Western thought and Christianity's dualism that

separates spirit and body (Medina 1998). Many Chicanas who were alien-
ated from the patriarchal teachings and practices in Christianity (Catholic
and Protestant) returned to indigenous spirituality (Medina 1998; Rodríguez
2002). Recognizing Guadalupe as Tonantzin is one of the ways in which
Chicana's reconstitute their spirituality.

There is a spiritual interconnectedness among all beings, and according to
Laura E. Pérez (1998, 2007), Chicana spiritual practices, which are similar to
American-Indian and African practices, recognize that. This spiritual belief is
antithetical to ideologies that claim there are essential and hierarchal differences that justify the subjugation, exploitation, and abuse of racially different
people (Pérez, L. 1998, 38–9). When Chicana feminists' theorists, cultural
workers, and everyday women rearticulate La Virgen as a feminist figure,
they claim their rights not to be discriminated against and exploited because
of their gender and sexuality. Moreover, when Chicanas invoke these spiritual
practices in their cultural productions, they are linking them to a politics of
memory aimed to maintain one's consciousness about indigenous practices
that recall and reintegrate the spiritual in everyday life. Therefore, Laura Pérez
claims them as decolonizing practices. Yolanda Broyles-González (2002)
argues that indigenous communities adopted Catholic figures, including the
Virgin of Guadalupe, as a form of camouflage in order to maintain their spiritual traditions. Similarly, Rodríguez (1994) documents how women who are
devoted Catholics prefer to pray to La Virgen, as they believe that Guadalupe
understands them better because she is a woman and a mother in ways that God
the Father and Jesus Christ are not able to understand. Indeed, Castillo (1996)
argues that the feminist writers who contributed essays to her anthology, *Goddess of the Americas,* emphasize recapturing La Virgen's omnipotence to offer
"spiritual orphans" a spirituality of love, transformation, and hope.

Guadalupe and Everyday Practices

To say that La Virgen de Guadalupe is an important figure in Mexican and
Chicana/o culture is, to a certain extent, an understatement. Her cultural,
religious, and spiritual significance is unparalleled, but it is also what makes
her a polyvalent symbol for people of Mexican descent across the globe. La
Virgen de Guadalupe has multiple interpretations that can be appropriated by
a multiplicity of discursive practices, from patriarchal to feminist. I assert that
even though the Catholic and patriarchal interpretations are prevalent, from
the outset, Guadalupe has been a woman-centric figure. It is because of her
significance and potential for feminist resignification that Chicana feminists
have viewed her as a source for the formation and transformation of Chicana
feminist subjectivity.

In this chapter, I applied transnational feminist cultural studies perspective to analyze La Virgen de Guadalupe in its multiple meanings and representations, from the object of global consumption to Chicana feminists' deconstructive strategies. Transnational feminism serves as a theoretical framework that assists in the formation of alternative epistemologies associated with collective practices. The multiple meanings and representations of La Virgen de Guadalupe have pedagogical and epistemological functions. Whether we are looking at everyday objects, Chicana spiritual practices, or artistic productions that reclaim Guadalupe, Chicanas are in a constant process of constructing alternative subjectivities. The different meanings and manifestations of Guadalupe make essentialist and unitary readings very tenuous, almost impossible, in spite of what critics of Chicana feminist cultural workers claim.

Chicanas, in their everyday cultural practices which can be manifested in the objects they display, in their spiritual practices, and in their art, are enacting border/transformative pedagogies. Through La Virgen de Guadalupe, Chicanas are reclaiming ancient cultural memories, language, and history. These are the sources of alternative Chicana feminist epistemologies. These pedagogies and epistemologies should be helpful to educators because they can see how Chicanas show their agency, how they produce multiple ways of knowing.

NOTES

1. I am not arguing that social change can be enacted through the transformation of symbols or through cultural productions. However, artistic productions have an important social function in the production of social critique that has an important function in social change. In other words, I do not believe that art is a luxury, but an integral aspect of human life, and artists/cultural workers have an important function in social life.

2. This means The Virgin of Guadalupe defending Xicanos' rights.

3. There is another sixteenth century document, a codex that depicts Guadalupe's apparition to Juan Diego, but Matovina proposes that the Jesuit Xavier Estrada argued it was Juan Diego's death certificate. See Timothy Matovina *Guadalupe and Her Faithful: Latino Catholics in San Antonio, from Colonial Origins to the Present* (Baltimore: The John Hopkins University Press) 2005.

4. Don Fernando de Alva Ixtlixóchitl received the original *Nican Mopohua* after Don Antonio Valeriano's death in 1605. He made it available to Lasso de la Vega.

5. Coatlicue was sweeping on top of a mountain when she found two feathers. She put them in her apron and they began to gestate in her womb, and soon she realizes that, even though she was advanced in age, she is pregnant with Huitzilopochtli.

When Coatlicue's daughter Coyolxauhqui founds out her mother is pregnant, she decides to kill her to avoid the birth of another sibling. Huitzilopochtli is warned by a humming bird and at the moment of birth murders Coyolxauhqui.

6. In Nahuatl tradition flor y canto (literal translation is flowers and song) represented beauty and truth.

7. Grewal argues that under the conditions of globalization, citizenship is redefined beyond nation-state territories as citizen-consumers. Current discussions about undocumented immigration in the U.S. show that the understanding of citizenship is not only territorially-based, but also racially and ethnically. For example, among some of the proposals discussed to curb illegal immigration, some members of congress and groups opposed to immigration would like to amend the U.S. Constitution to deny citizenship status for children of undocumented workers born within the territory of the U.S. Thus, citizenship in the U.S. is based on territorial considerations. Nevertheless, in a consumer-oriented society, groups of people gain status according to their purchasing power regardless of citizenship status. Thus, subjects are citizen- consumers.

8. For a discussion of Chela Sandoval's theories see chapter 2.

9. By commodification, I mean the process by which an object or idea that has not been part of a commercial enterprise becomes one, particularly involving consumption (that is selling and buying).

10. By religious perspectives, I mean the different views on Catholicism that can be expressed by everyday Catholics, which often times differ from the official Vatican dogma.

11. From the standpoint of recognizing that the Mexican community is an integral part of the U.S., one could argue that marketing to them is "the right thing to do." However, I do not want to give the impression that I believe that consumerism is alright. Much of the exploitation of women's labor and environmental problems are the result of consumerism.

12. For a thorough analysis of Yolanda López, see KarenMary Davalos. *Yolanda López* (Minneapolis: University of Minnesota Press), 2009.

13. Laura Pérez (2007) writes that, at the time, Yolanda López was an atheist.

14. In the Judeo-Christian tradition, the snake is associated with the devil. In the biblical creation story, the devil appears to Eve in the form of a snake and tempts her to eat the forbidden fruit. When Adam and Eve eat of the forbidden apple and are expelled from Paradise, it is Eve who is blamed for the downfall of humanity. This creation story is one of the fundamental stories by which women have historically been subordinated.

15. The cards in the Loteria include different characters, many very stereotypical representations, such as "El Negrito" (diminutive for Black and featuring stereotypical representations of Blacks), or "El Valiente" (The brave one, depicting a typical, macho, brave man). Female representations follow traditional views of women, as well. For example "La Dama" (The lady), shows a woman dressed in 1940s elegant and ladylike attire. La Loteria is very popular in Mexico, with generations playing it throughout the years. It is so popular that it is part of Mexican popular culture and

depicted in many art pieces. See Luz Calvo. 2004. "Art comes for the Archbishop: The semiotics of contemporary Chicana feminism and the work of Alma Lopez." *Meridians: feminism, race, transnationalism,* 5(3): 201–24 for a critique of La Loteria.

16. See Alma Lopez's website www.almalopez.net for thorough coverage of the controversy. Alma Lopez decided to include all the letters of protest and of support in her website. She decided to construct the website because, she believes, that the discussion that *Our Lady* provoked is important.

17. The tone of the letter is quite threatening, not only to Lopez, but also to her supporters. The whole letter can be accessed in Alma Lopez's website (www.almalopez.net).

18. See Tey Marianna Nunn's analysis of the controversy in her essay, "The *Our Lady* controversy: Chicana art, Hispanic identity, and the politics of place and gender in Nuevo México." In *Expressing New Mexico: Nuevomexicano creativity, ritual, and memory,* edited by Phillip B. Gonzales (Tuscon: University of Arizona Press, 2007).

19. Lara Medina, in her study of *Las Hermanas,* proposes that they engaged in a transformative struggle in their efforts to work within Liberation Theology and the priest of the organization PADRES. According to Medina, *Las Hermanas* embraced their struggle with faith of a divine presence that desire social justice for women.

Chapter 5

Malintzin/Marina/Malinche

Embodying History/Reclaiming Our Voice

> Not me sold out my people but they me. *Malinali Tenepal* or *Malintzin,* has become known as *La Chingada*—the fucked one. She has become the bad word that passes a dozen times a day from the lips of Chicanos. Whore, prostitute, the woman who sold out her people to the Spaniards are epithets Chicanos spit out with contempt.
>
> The worst kind of betrayal lies in making us believe that the Indian woman in us is the betrayer. We, *indias* y *mestizas,* police the Indian in us, brutalize and condemn her. Male culture has done a good job on us. *Son los costumbres que traicionan. La India en mi es la sombra: La Chingada, Tlazolteotl, Coatlicue. Son ellas que oyemos lamentando a sus hijas perdidads.* (Anzaldúa 1987, 22)

Malintzin/Marina/Malinche, the woman with multiple names, the translator, "the Mexican Eve," embodies the misogynistic fears about women: traitor, *vendida* (sell out), corruptible, sexually active, intelligent. Because she had an active role in the Spanish conquest of Mexico, which included a sexual liaison with Hernán Cortés (Spanish conqueror of México), bearing him a son, and supposedly not repenting for her actions, she has been historically and culturally condemned as the traitor of the Mexican (and Chicano) nation. A condemnation, nevertheless, contested by many Chicana and mexicana feminists.

It was during my childhood when I became acquainted with the story of La Malinche. Through popular narratives presented in the public arena and through family members, I learned that the epitaph *malinchista* referred to Mexicans (and Chicanas/os) who preferred the foreigner over one's own people. When I was growing up, I often heard people referred as *malinches* when they acted in ways that didn't seem "Mexican" enough. Like many

Mexicans, I learned that the negative implications of La Malinche story were not only about a particular woman, Malintzin, but of all women. And while I had not developed a feminist consciousness yet, I did make a connection between gender and treachery. Even though both men and women were (and are) called *malinchistas,* there is a peculiar association in the Malinche story between gender, sexuality, and treachery. The association of treachery with femaleness via La Malinche myth is such a powerful pedagogical tool that serves to inscribe very specific gender meanings onto women's bodies (preferably chaste) and female ways of being (expected to be subservient).

As with the legend of La Llorona and the stories and artistic representations of La Virgen de Guadalupe presented in the previous chapters, there is not one narrative that can offer *the true* story of Malintzin; nor can one offer one specific answer as to why she became the symbol of treachery against the nation. Rather, I take the narratives about Malintzin as constructions that reflect the point of view of its author. Whether the narratives are historical texts (primary and secondary), literature (novels, poems, essays), journalistic accounts, or feminist revisionist texts, they all are ideologically constructed and offer us a rich multiplicity of texts that can be understood as border/ transformative pedagogies.

In this chapter, I explore how the creation of the trope of treachery is imbued with gender meanings. However, as feminist theorists have asserted, the inscription of gender in the body—that is the construction of gender meanings as masculine and feminine—is a fluid process that changes over time. Appropriate notions of femininity and masculinity are not universal, but rather are culturally constructed and historically contingent. I contend that inscriptions of La Malinche as traitor, or what I call the trope of treachery, are extolled and produced through multiple and contradictory discourses about the female gender and vary according to the standpoint of the producer of particular discourses. Three centuries after her death, we witness the transformation of Malintzin into La Malinche, the traitor through the production of a variety of narrative discourses of gender, sexuality, and nationalism.

There are abundant historical, literary, and popular texts on Malintzin/ Malinche. Yet, none are written from her perspective as she did not leave any record of her own life.[1] Malintzin is deemed historically voiceless. But we do have historical narratives about Malintzin's public biography, which is documented in the chronicles of the conquest, indigenous accounts of the conquest, and secondary historical sources. Among the primary historical sources, we find the Spanish chronicles of the conquest, such as Bernal Díaz del Castillo's *Historia Verdadera de la Conquista de la Nueva España,* Francisco López de Gómara's *Historia de la Conquista de México,* Hernán Cortés' *Cartas de Relación,* and Fray Bartolomé de las Casas' *Historia de las Indias.*[2]

The indigenous accounts of the Conquest include *El Lienzo de Tlaxcala, Codex Florentino* (Sagahún's translation) and the recently (1959) edited text *Visión de los Vencidos* by Miguel León Portilla, which provides testimony of the conquest from the point of view of the indigenous people of Tenochtitlan, Tlatelolco, Tezcoco, Chalco and Tlaxcala. Don Fernando de Alva Ixtlilxochiltl's *Obras Históricas* represent a mestizo point of view of the conquest. The secondary historical sources that are often quoted include William H. Prescott's *The Conquest of Mexico,* Mariano G. Somonte's (1969) *Doña Marina, "La Malinche,"* Todorov's *La Conquista de América: El Problema del Otro,* and Federico Gomez de Orozco's (1942) *Doña Marina: La Dama de la Conquista.* Gomez de Orozco claims to be a direct descendant of Malinztin and Hernán Cortés. Recent historical monographs include Ricardo Herrén's *Doña Marina, La Malinche* and Camilla Townsend's *Malintzin's Choices: An Indian woman in the conquest of Mexico.* The *Archivo General de las Indias* in Spain has various documents regarding Malintzin and her children, including the *Probanza*[3] from Don Luis Quesada, husband of Maria Jaramillo (daughter of Malintzin and Juan Jaramillo) to keep their lands near Coatzacualco. I will return to this document below.

These historical narratives tell us the story of the Spanish conquest of México and are helpful to understand the historical context of her life and circumstances. Therefore, these narratives offer the "opportunity" for social critics and historians—or anybody who studies Malintzin—to inscribe their own meanings about Malintzin's life and actions. These meanings and suppositions then become projections of the proponent's ideology onto her life. Malintzin/Marina/Malinche becomes a metaphor on whose body ideologies and viewpoints about colonization are manifested. The formation of the Mexican and Chicana/o nation and gender ideologies are imposed and (re)created.

Given the historical record, it is a flawed strategy to try to determine what her world view was and whether or not she tried to make sense of her life and history. Nevertheless, historian Camilla Townsend (2006) proposes that we can interpret her life and intentions through her actions. We can speculate on the meaning of her actions and try to reconstruct them through our knowledge of Nahua culture and the historical documents about the Spanish conquest of México. Such interpretations must be received as the speculations they are because most of the historical record on Malintzin is vague and suspect. Like all historical sources, those that document Malintzin's life were written from the perspective of its authors. As Townsend writes, "The Spanish chroniclers who mentioned Malinche all wrote with their own agendas, and they were usually distant in time and place when they sat down with their pens in hand. They lied, forgot, and argued with each other" (2006, 6).

Historical documents such as the chronicles of the conquest, the indigenous *codices,* letters, and the like are subject to multiple interpretations as all historical sources are. Additionally, there is barely any "objective" information about her life, including the dates of her birth and death. Those who study Malintzin, including myself, can only but speculate about her life and actions; and we can only imagine what she felt and thought. For me, this is not a problem that needs to be solved. Nor is it necessary to try to uncover the *truth* about Malintzin's story and her actions. I propose to embrace this ambiguity; afterall, it is this uncertainty that permits us to speculate about her life. A more interesting study is to focus the analysis on examinations of the speculations rather than on the historical facts. I am following oral historian Alessandro Portelli's (2003) proposition that "the discrepancies and the errors [of historical sources and memory] are themselves events, clues for the work of desire and pain over time, for the painful search for meaning" (16). The story and the myths surrounding Malinztin produce different epistemological outlooks that can teach us a great deal about different views about women, gender roles, and nationalistic imaginary. Moreover, the generation of new speculations is the source of alternative meanings of Malintzin/Malinche.

The varied viewpoints about Malintzin's life can invoke numerous ideologies; some of which clash with each other. When these interpretations invoke oppositional discourses in the service of social justice—such as Chicana feminists' do—they can result in border/transformative pedagogies. Chicana feminists' re-interpretations of Malinztin, of course, are also invested in the formation of particular epistemologies; in this case, these are alternative epistemologies. In order to return to this point, I will first analyze how historical narratives of the conquest laid the foundations for the gender construction of Malintzin as a "heroine" of the conquest, which later gave way for the construction of the trope of treachery. Next, I examine the formation of the trope of treachery from a gender ideology perspective. Following borderland theories, I analyze how Chicanas re-claim Malintzin as an agent of her life and in doing so exemplify borderland subjectivities.

MAPPING MALINTZIN'S BIOGRAPHY

There are few aspects of Malintzin's life that are readily verifiable. The facts about her life that are known include: her mother tongue was Nahuatl, she was a slave in a Maya region, and she was given to Cortés along with 19 other female slaves. We also know that she served as Cortés translator/ interpreter and secretary. She had two children, a boy with Cortés and a girl with her husband, Juan Jaramillo. Bernal Díaz del Castillo (1632/1960)[4] informs us that Malintzin Tenépal was born in Paynala, near Coatzacualco[5] (or Guazacualco, which is the spelling used by Díaz del Castillo). Chicana feminist anthropologist Adelaida del Castillo (1977) places her birth in 1505, and so does Townsend. Somonte places it around 1502 or 1503. I calculate these years because Somonte writes that she was 16 or 17 years old in 1519 when she was "given" to the Spaniards. Federico Gomez de Orozco believes that she was older than 14 years old in 1519. The 1505 date comes from Luis de Gregoire *Diccionario de Historia, Mitología y Geografía.* What is clear is that she was born early in the sixteenth century, sometime between 1502 and 1505. Coatzacualco is the most accepted place of her birth, although Gómara and others usually following his writings claim that she was born in the Jalisco region (which is toward the Pacific coast region). It is doubtful that she was born in Jalisco because it is quite a distance from Tabasco. Moreover, it is in the region of Coatzacualco where Cortés gave her a land grant after the Conquest.

Chroniclers and biographers tend to agree that Malintzin's parents were from the ruling elite, Caciques. Somonte refers to her as a princess. The most popular account of her life is given to us by Bernal Díaz del Castillo. As a Captain of Cortés' army, Díaz del Castillo spent a lot of time with Malinztin and probably knew her well. However, it is important to take into account that he did not write his chronicle until years after the conquest, and his memory of events could be fuzzy. Malintzin's father died, we are told, when she was young, and her mother remarried another Cacique with whom she had a son. Malintzin's mother and stepfather supposedly had an affinity for this son and decided he should succeed and inherit their fortune (Díaz del Castillo, 1632/1960). They gave the child Malintzin to people of Xicalango during the night and pretended young Malintzin had died. The people from Xicalango gave her to the people of Tabasco. Malintzin's native language was Nahuatl, and she learned Mayan as a slave girl. After Cortés took over Tabasco, the Tabascans gave him twenty women, including Malintzin who was given the Spanish name of Marina after she was baptized (Díaz del Castillo, 1632/1960).

Although this is the story of her life accepted by popular culture and some historians like William Prescott (1900), contemporary historians and literary critics contest Díaz del Castillo's narrative. Cypess (1991), Greer Johnson (1984), Baudot (1993), Herren (1992), and Townsend (2006) find that this version of Malintzin's life is curiously similar to the *Amadís de Gaula,* a famous Medieval Chivalry novel and, therefore, more a fabrication of Díaz del Castillo than "historical fact." Yet, there are reasons to believe that women both bequeathed and inherited property. Early colonial Nahua wills from a variety of communities show women's ownership of houses, land, and a variety of smaller items (Kellogg 2005). Interestingly, Don Fernando de Alva de Ixtlilxhochitl claims that when Malintzin was a child, she was stolen by some merchants during times of war and sold to the people of Xicalango, and later came to the possession of the Señor of Potonchan (Tabascan) (345). Townsend (2006) argues that it is plausible that Malintzin's mother was a concubine of a cacique. Polygamy was customary in Mesoamerica, and in times of economic distress or famine, it was not uncommon to sell young women and girls into slavery. Slave girls were servants and were also asked for sexual favors. It is possible that Malintzin's father's primary wife could be the one who sold her into slavery after his death (Townsen 2006). However, from the moral standpoint of the Spanish, the story of being sold into slavery fits better with a narrative where the Spanish conquerors became the "saviors" of Malintzin from her own culture.

When Cortés first received Malintzin with the other nineteen female slaves, he gave her to one of his senior Captains, Alonso Hernández de Portocarrero (Herren 1992; Díaz del Castillo 1632/1960). Cortés soon realized that her linguistic abilities were beneficial to his enterprise, and not only did she became his translator, interpreter, and secretary, but also his lover.[6] Malinztin had a great ability with languages no doubt. Nevertheless, how she came to be of service to Cortés is also fodder for the development of the Malinche myth. As the Spanish entered the mainland from the Gulf of Mexico, they encountered Totonaca speaking people. Aguilar, a Spaniard who had been marooned in Yucatán, had learned Mayan, served as interpreter for the Spanish and could not translate Totonaca, and neither could Malintzin. But, as Frances Karttunen (1997) documents, Malintzin asked if there were any Nahuatl speaking interpreters, and this is how the chain of translation began. López de Gómara, Cortés biographer, recorded that Cortés was vexed that Aguilar could not translate, but recuperated when he realized that Malintzin understood Nahuatl (Simpson 1964). Eventually, when Cortés and his troops arrived at San Juan de Ulúa, where they met with Moctezuma's emissaries and Aguilar could not understand their language, Malintzin initiated a conversation with the emissaries in Nahuatl and translated into Mayan what they were saying; opening a translating chain from Nahuatl to Mayan to Spanish. When she learned Spanish, (according to Alva Ixtlilxhochitl, she learned it in weeks!) she became even more important for the Spaniards. From the moment she started to translate, she became indispensable for, and inseparable from, Cortés (Karttunen 1997).

As mysterious as her life is, her names are equally mysterious. According to Herren, (1992) it is very likely that her given name was Malinalli, the name of the twelfth day of the month in which she was born. Baudot (1993) tells us that it is a day associated with a disastrous sign: those who were born under this sign were prosperous some of the time but soon would fall from this prosperity. Tenépal is a derivative of "Tene" which means, "who has facility for words" (my translation). The *tzin* is a term of honor and respect, similar to *don/Doña;* thus her name is Malintzin and Doña Marina. There are those who believe that Malinche is a derivative of her Christian name Marina into Malina since many Nahuatl speaking peoples could not pronounce the "r." Adding the possessive "e" to Malintzine, eventually the name becomes Malinche. Malinche is the name that the indigenous people gave to Cortés, which means "Lord of Doña Marina" because they were always together. In this case, a man was named after a woman, reversing the practice of naming women after men (Herren 1992). Baudot (1993) believes that the disastrous sign of Malintzin's birth is the origin of her disgrace, because it justifies her mother giving her away to the merchants from Xicalango to avoid disaster and also comply with the ambitions of her second husband, provided, of course, that the story is accurate.

In order to understand and initiate the process of deconstruction of the trope of treachery, Malintzin's story needs to be contextualized under the conditions she was living. Her status as a slave is crucial for the deconstruction process that takes into account her status and her agency. Even though she was objectified by her condition and was very likely considered a man's "property," she still had to have her sense of self and agency and the capacity of making choices, even though these were made from untenable alternatives. Malintzin's early history is marked by being treated as an object that was passed from one man to the next without her say. When Cortés received twenty slaves, he distributed them among his captains and soldiers. Malintzin is given to Alfonso Hernández Portocarrero and "belongs" to him for four months until she becomes Cortés interpreter, secretary, adviser, and "lover." Cortés' expedition to México was an exploratory one; he did not have the authority to conquer the lands by the Crown of Spain or the Governor of Cuba, Diego de Velázquez (which at the time was the center of the Spanish colonies in the Americas). In order to conquer, he needed the permission of the King or at least the Governor. The Governor of Cuba was not fond of Cortés and would prefer to claim the glory for himself. Thus, Cortés chose to communicate directly with the King. Cortés sent Hernández Portocarrero to Spain with the first *Carta de Relación* and gold for the King of Spain. Some argue that Cortés wanted to keep Malintzin for himself because he was deeply in love with her (Somonte 1969), therefore he asked Hernández Portocarrero to take the letter and the gold to get him out of the way so he could also conquer Malintzin. A more likely scenario is that Cortés did not have to get rid of Hernández Portocarrero in order to seduce (or rape) Malinztin. As the leader of the expedition and *conquistador,* he could have any woman he wanted, including Malintzin. Rather, it is plausible that Cortés trusted Hernández Portocarrero with such an important task.

There is a range of possibilities that can enter into the interpretation of Cortés and Malintzin's relationship. These vary from believing, as Somonte does, that it was a great love story to one of violence: rape. The possibility that Cortés might have raped Malintzin is not far-fetched. As Susan Kellogg notes, "[w]hile it might be going too far to say that rape was a consciously used strategic tool in conquest and colonial rule, that sexual coercion was part of the process of Iberian exploration and conquest cannot be denied. Yet the frequency of sexual violence and the willingness of military leaders such as Cortés and Pizarro to distribute indigenous women among their close lieutenants suggest that conquerors indeed use the 'phallus as an extension of the sword'" (Kellogg 2005, 60). Regardless of the nature of the relationship (consensual or not), it was sexual, as they had a son named Martín Cortés,[7] after Cortés' father. Baudot and Somonte propose that he was one of his favorite children. After the downfall of Tenochtitlan, Malintzin was married to Juan Jaramillo, one of Cortés' captains, with whom she had a daughter, María Jaramillo. Martin Cortés is considered and symbolizes the first mestizo. Yet, he grew up in Spain as a page for Prince Phillip (who became King Phillip), and had a son, also out of wedlock, whom he named Fernando Cortés. Hernán Cortés had the Pope declare Martín a legitimate son. Fernando Cortés settled in Coyoacán, and from him on his descendants, including Gomez de Orozco, have lived in México. Maria Jaramillo had a son, Pedro Quesada, who married a woman by the name of Melchoria and with whom he had four children. Malintzin lives not only in the collective memory of the Mexican and Chicana/o nations, but through her progeny, something Townsend believes would satisfy Malintzin: "Her children and her children's children revered her memory, as any Nahua wife would certainly have wished" (Townsend 2006, 187).

Malintzin's life after the conquest and her death are even more open to conjecture than her public life. Baudot (1993) cites documents that date her death on the 9th of August of 1541. Somonte believes she died before 1529. Baudot is doubtful of all the sources, as he claims there is documentary evidence that she could have been alive in 1551. Unfortunately, the documents that Baudot cite are not from Malintzin, but from another Doña Marina, a daughter of Moctezuma. It seems that Malintzin died in 1529, possibly of smallpox.

Historical Voice

Malintzin's historical voice is absent; the chroniclers of the conquest such as Díaz del Castillo, Cortés, Gómara, and some of the indigenous codices documented what we know of her. There are scholars and historians, such as Mexican historian Ricardo Herren, who wish she had left a written record of her life. But the need to have written documents is perhaps a twentieth century sensibility that was not that important or relevant to sixteenth century Mesoamerican life and culture. Herren blames Malintzin, herself, for the not leaving documentary evidence of her life: "Parece que, come el zorro del Artico, Marina quiso borrar or desfigurar con el rabo las huellas de sus pasos antes de su encuentro con los españoles. Y en eso se asemeja a su amo y amante, Hernán Cortés" (Herren 1992, 37).[8] Herren's assessment of her historical voicelessness is a twentieth century interpretation of individual agency. Given how the historical events of the conquest were recorded, it seems more plausible that indigenous people did not write individualistic accounts or autobiographical texts, but rather produced communal cultural productions. The codices were group efforts, not the work of individual artists.

Interpretations of her life are mostly produced through popular culture and literature. During Spanish colonial times, she was pretty much forgotten except for a few sources. The contemporary and popular construction of La Malinche as a traitor began after independence (Cypess 1991). The first construction of Malintzin as a traitor is the anonymous novel *Jicotencal,* or *Xicótencatl,* published in Philadelphia in 1826 (Leal 1983, Cypess 1991). According to Leal, *Jicotencal* represents Doña Marina as "the forces of evil and is characterized as wily, perfidious, deceitful, and treacherous" (228). In the twentieth century, the trope of treachery is consolidated with Octavio Paz's *El Laberinto de la Soledad* (1950) and in José Clemente Orozco's murals (Leal 1983).

Díaz del Castillo (1632/1960) refers to Malintzin in a very positive, kind, and deferential manner. He always referred to her by her Christian name Doña Marina, the Doña being a term of respect. Díaz del Castillo described her as a "gran cacica, beautiful, self-assured, and willing to insert herself in the unfolding events of her time" (120–121). In the *Códice Ramírez* and *Códice Aubin,* which are native narratives of the conquest documented in *Visión de los Vencidos* (1959/1992), Malinche is referred to as Malintzin, also with respect since the "tzin" reflects respect and honor. *El Lienzo de Tlaxcala* documents the importance of her translating functions and her direct participation in the conquest. Gómara, on the other hand, has great contempt toward her and barely mentions her, seldom by name, and most often in a matter of fact fashion only says that the "lengua" or "farute" translated.

Malintzin performed an important function in the conquest of México, not only for her translating abilities, but also as a source of information and diplomacy. According to Díaz del Castillo (1632/1956), her translating functions were essential for the Spanish conquest. Although she was not a conquistadora, her function in the conquest went beyond that of a translator. Examples of her strategic importance in the conquest abound. There are two significant events that are often cited as examples of her supposed treachery, in which Malintzin was able to provide key information to Cortés that avoided a catastrophe for the Spanish. The first one is when the Spanish were in Cholula; as they moved toward Tenochtitlan, the Cholutecas were planning a surprise attack. An old Indian woman approached Malintzin and told her what they were planning and that she should leave with her. The old lady befriended and confided in Malintzin because she was beautiful and rich and promised to marry her to her son. Malintzin pretended to agree to leave with her, and told the old woman that she needed to gather her belongings that were of significant value. Instead, she informed Cortés of the plan. With this information, Cortés was able to avoid a costly catastrophe for the Spanish (Díaz del Castillo 1631/1960, 242–243, Herren 1992). The second event occurred during the expedition to Honduras, when she was already married to Jaramillo. The Spanish suspected that Cuauhtemoc, the last ruler of Tenochtitlan, was plotting to escape. There are speculations that she told Cortés about Cuauhtemoc's intentions, but not much evidence.

Her function as a translator and diplomat became very significant once the Spanish entered Tenochtitlan. When Cortés decided that he needed to place Moctezuma under house arrest, some Spaniards were talking very loud and rude. Moctezuma could not understand what they were saying, and was nervous about the tone of voice. He asked Malintzin what they were saying. Instead of simply translating, she inserted her own position. According to Díaz del Castillo (1631/1960) she told him: "Lord Montezuma: what I advise you is to go with them to your quarters, in silence, because I know they will honor you as the great lord you are. Any other way and you will be dead. In your quarters the truth will be known"[9] (294). After hearing this, Moctezuma agreed to the house arrest. Todorov (1984) believes that she sided with the Spanish because her own people gave her in slavery, and therefore we can imagine that she held certain rancor against them. Regardless of what her motivations were, Todorov's point that she clearly took sides and adapted to the Spaniards' values is one of the reasons why she is so maligned in post-independence Mexico. Indeed, as Kellogg argues, Malinztin's actions were consistent with an anti-Mexican sentiment, but were also the result of living under extremely difficult circumstances that offered a virtually impossible set of options presented by others (56). What is significant, then, is that Malintzin interpreted not only language, but also the indigenous cultural practices and ways of being, an interpretation and information that gave Cortés an advantage that was more powerful than the numerical superiority of the Mexicas.

The Trope of Treachery

During colonial times, Malintzin was pretty much forgotten; indeed, it is not until the nineteenth century that she becomes the "Mexican Eve," as Sandra Messinger Cypess proposes in her book (1991), *La Malinche in Mexican Literature: From History to Myth.* The construction of Malintzin as a traitor, symbolized in her designation as *La Malinche,* is a Mexican post-independence move reflected in popular culture, essays, and literature, especially in the novel *Xicoténcatl* published in 1826 (Cypess 1991, Franco 1989). A close reading of the aforementioned historical record shows that her contemporaries did not consider her a traitor, although some of the indigenous codices did show her in a negative way. For example, Brotherston (1994) argues that codices produced by those who were loyal to Tenochtitlan disapproved of her behavior, while those who sided with Cortés presented her as an indigenous woman who knew how to navigate the new political and religious values brought by the Spanish. Nevertheless, the formation of the trope of treachery and of the concept of *Malinchista* as one who prefers the foreigner is a nineteenth century phenomenon. Mexican writer Carlos Monsiváis (1994) proposes that the myth of La Malinche makes sense in nineteenth century Mexico (but does not justify it) as the country was establishing its cultural identity after independence and later on suffered foreign interventions by the U.S. and France.

It is not surprising, then, that throughout the nineteenth century, Mexicans developed a skeptical view of foreigners. But this skepticism does not answer the question why Malintzin became the symbol of betrayal and preference for the foreigner. Why or how does she become the scapegoat of Mexico's conquest? Mexican feminist Juana Armanda Alegría (1975) believes that history judges Malintzin harshly because she was a woman. While I do believe that how Malintzin's gender is viewed is a decisive factor in her construction as a traitor, I want to put into question whether her place in history can be reduced to gender. I believe that her gender per se does not answer the question, even though a gender analysis can illuminate the development of the trope of treachery. Rather, such analysis must be complicated by examining how gender ideologies are invoked by those who opt to judge or defend her. It is gender ideology, such as the belief that women should be submissive and chaste (even at the expense of their lives) that is enacted in the historical judgment of Malinztin. An analysis of the trope of treachery entails an examination of the intersections of nationalism, nation, gender, and sexuality. To understand how this operates, it is necessary to appreciate how Mexican and eventually Chicano nationalism developed.

The turmoil that characterized most of post-independence México in the nineteenth century was considered to be the result of foreign influence and efforts to bring back monarchic forms of government. The historical events of the nineteenth century show not only the effects of foreign influence, but the devastating effects of foreign invasion as well. For example, México lost more than half of its territory to the U.S after the war in 1848, and later suffered from the French invasion, which indeed imposed a monarchy (1864–1866). However, the desire on the part of conservative forces to establish a monarchy and empire in early independent México dates back to 1821, when Agustín de Iturbide (one of the heroes of the Mexican independence war) was named Emperor Agustín I (Cypess 1991). Iturbide did not last long, as he tried to maintain a hierarchical order that did not sit well with the republican and democratic ideals of the independence movement. In 1824, a republican constitution was adopted. However, throughout the ninteenth century, there was a struggle between liberal and conservative forces which facilitated foreign influence and invasion.[10]

It is under the backdrop of the struggle between liberal democratic republican ideologies and conservative hierarchical perspectives that nationalist discourses emerged in México. Mexican nationalist discourses that started to develop in the nineteenth century and continued throughout the twentieth century were critical of colonialism and looked at the pre-Hispanic past in favorable ways. As Cypess writes, "Destigmatization of the pre-Hispanic Indians was the necessary first step toward integrating into Mexican nationhood the Amerindian and mestizo figures who were appearing on the political scene" (42). Thus, a way to develop a notion of Mexican identity was to break with the Spanish and reassert the indigenous cultures of the past. As México began its life as a new nation, it was necessary to construct a unique cultural identity; this identity looked at the indigenous past, particularly the Aztec empire, and rejected Spanish culture. This not withstanding that, Spanish became the official language of the new nation, and the majority of the population is Catholic. Nevertheless, as Carlos Monsiváis (1994) asserts, a nation needs to construct symbols that depict their sense of identity. According to anthropologist Natividad Gutiérrez (1999), Mexican nationalism relies on two ethnic myths: (1) foundation and (2) descent. The foundational myth is the adoption of the foundation of Tenochtitlan as the emblem of the nation.[11] The myth of descent is reflected in mestizaje.

Mexican nationalism developed by re-imagining and reconstructing an idealized glorious indigenous past. Proponents of Chicano nationalism of the

1960s followed a similar process. Both are based on a desire to bring back an utopian idyllic indigenous past. As Wallerstein (1991) theorizes, "pastness" is an important element for the construction of nationalism and nation:

> Pastness is a central element in the socialization of individuals, in the mainte-
> nance of group solidarity, in the establishment of or challenge to social legiti-
> mization. Pastness therefore is preeminently a moral phenomenon, therefore a
> political phenomenon, always a contemporary phenomenon. That is, of course
> why it is so inconsistent. Since the real world is constantly changing what is
> relevant to contemporary politics is necessarily constantly changing. (78)

Given that the past is considered to be constant "no one can ever admit that any particular past has ever changed or could possibly change"(Wallerstein 1991, 78). That is, proponents of such notions of nationalism need to articu-late their nationalist sentiments by representing the past as a constant. But, as I elaborated previously, historical events and texts can have multiple interpre-tations. That is, while the past per se cannot change, our understanding and interpretations of it can change.

Discursively, Mexican nationalism idealizes indigenous cultures, but this does not necessarily translate into contemporary solidarity or as a radical restructuring of conditions for the disenfranchised. A distinction between the "dead" and the "living" Indian is made, where the "dead" Indian becomes the authentic Indian. Mexican nationalism that idealizes the indigenous past has not benefited México's indigenous population; yet, it is a discursive strategy that helped mark Malinztin as a traitor. The Mexican state invokes an indig-enous past at the same time that it uses the symbols to unify the nation and to "assimilate" the living Indian (Gutiérrez 1999). It helps develop a belief in cultural unity and nationalism while it does little to maintain the current indigenous cultures and spirituality. But, hegemonically, it helps the state position itself as a liberal entity that is capable of reconciling with a lost past that projects onto the future and off which it can profit (e.g., via tourism of archeological sites).

Because nationalist discourses tend to be patriarchal, they also have a propensity to glorify masculinity. In the case of the Spanish conquest of México, the masculinity of the nation can be put into question if the warriors who were responsible for defending it were militarily defeated. Mexican and Chicano nationalism honor the male warriors, like Cuauhtémoc, who is perceived as standing up to the Spaniards.[12] Thus, it was necessary to find a scapegoat for the loss of the past. But why single out one individual? It is logical that one person cannot single-handedly be responsible for the fall of an empire. As we know, there were plenty of men who allied themselves with Cortés. For example, the cacique of Cempoala, who was under the rule of the Mexicans and allied himself to Cortés, can, under the same logic, be considered a traitor. Yet, his place in history is negligent. The Tlaxcaltecas could also be stigmatized given that they allied with Cortés and gave him plenty of troops. Moctezuma has been criticized for his role in the conquest and seen as an incompetent ruler, though ironically, not ostracized in the historical and national imagination as responsible for the downfall of his empire and nation. Instead of vilifying him, there seems to be an historical amnesia regarding his role in the conquest. The codices documenting the conquest testify that Moctezuma's people were upset with him and perhaps wished he would take a more proactive attack and resistance against the Spanish. There is even speculation that he might have been killed by his people (see *Visión de los Vencidos*). Yet, neither the cacique of Cempoala nor Moctezuma nor the Tlaxcaltecas are blamed for the conquest or considered traitors for the most part.[13] They are not blamed because it would put Mexican and Chicano masculinity into question. Ironically, masculinity and the nation are seen as rather fragile, as they can be undermined by a woman, thus constructing quite a contradictory discourse.

The interrelationship between gender ideology and the formation of the Malinche myth is played out, for example, in the novel *Xicoténcal*. This novel is one of the first texts to articulate the trope of treachery and was published anonymously in Spanish in Philadelphia in 1826. Literary critics Luis Leal and Rodolfo J. Cortina (1995), in the Spanish edition of *Jicoténcal,* attribute authorship to the Cuban priest Félix Varela.[14] Nevertheless, the "anonymous" novelist presents Malintzin as a treacherous, conniving seductress, while the Tlaxcaltecas are absolved from their role in the conquest. The Tlaxcaltecans were, according to the novelist, misled by a scheming senator by the name of Magicatzin into joining Cortés and marching with him to Tenochtitlán.

All of the characters in the novel are stereotypical representations of good and evil. Malintzin—referred in the novel by her Spanish name Doña Marina—is contrasted with Teutila, a Zocoltlan Indian woman who is Xicontécal's (the General of the Tlaxcalan army) wife. Zocoltán was a national enemy of Tlaxcala and was allied with the Mexicas. Teutila is then from an enemy nation of Xicontécatl and thus their love, at the beginning of the novel, is prohibited. But the arrival of the Spanish changes those dynamics; as former enemies must ally together in order to defeat the new, and more powerful, enemy. The contrast between Teutila and Malinztin is evident in that both are living similar situations and both have to make decisions in order to survive; Teutila is virtuous while Malintzin is not. In doing so, the author is evoking the virgin/whore dichotomy to establish the differences between these two different women with similar histories; and to set the stage for the development of the La Malinche paradigm as a traitor who prefers the foreigner (see Cypess 1991). The anonymous writer does recognize that Malintzin was a slave and alone in the world, which is exemplified through a dialogue with Teutilia in which Marina expresses her feelings about her lot in life: "Woe is me! What would you have me do without support, without defenders, without friends, without family, alone and abandoned by everyone?" (50). Yet, the author forecloses the possibility that her actions were the result of survival strategies, by ascribing only negative characteristics to Marina and positive ones to Teutilia. Teutilia has also lost her family and is imprisoned by Cortés, yet she never wavers in her virtue and prefers to die rather than be in the arms of Cortés or betray her nation. Teutilia maintains her loyalty to her people, which in the novel eventually means the Tlaxcalans and most Amerindian or American peoples (the author refers to all indigenous peoples as Americans).

The purpose of the novel is more than to fictionalize the history of the conquest as Guillermo I. Castillo-Feliú (*Xicoténcalt* translator into English) asserts. The novel has a pedagogical function to teach the public about how the struggle for freedom can be undermined when the nations of peoples with similar interests are divided. Cypess makes a similar argument that the point of the novel is to show the negative effects of civil war on the development of a republic. If one thinks of the author of *Xicotécatl* as a Mexican national, and taking into consideration that in post-independence México there was a struggle between republican and monarchic ideologies, it is very plausible that the anonymous author wanted to present such a theme; and that is precisely why "he" chose to remain anonymous. But, if Leal and Cortina are correct, and Varela is the author, the warnings offered are beyond the Mexican context. Thus, this interpretation needs to be put in light of Latin American independence movements and the need to maintain unity in order to attain autonomy of independence (Leal & Cortina 1995). Regardless of whether the novel speaks to a specific Mexican or a broader Latin American context in the era of struggles for independence, the argument does not help explain why he opted to present Malinche as a traitor, as the point could have been said without creating such a character. I argue, then, that the author's representation of La Malinche, through the symbolism of Eve, invoked his own gender ideology and in doing so "warn" of the "consequences" for society when women act outside acceptable gender roles. As a Catholic priest, he imposed his idea of gender subordination within the Catholic Church and used Malintzin as an example of why such subordination must exist.

The author/Varela explains the Spanish's success in conquering the Mexicas beyond military strategies. I agree with Cypess' reading that in addition to military might, sexuality was an important tactic in the conquest. Columbus compared the take-over of land with the conquest of women (see Castañeda 2005, Pendleton Jiménez 2006, Zamora 1993). The novel *Xicoténcatl* was written in the format of the romantic genre, and as such, it has several love triangles between various characters: between Teutilia, Xicoténcatl, and Ordoñez (a "good" Spanish soldier); Xicoténcatl, Marina, and Cortés; and Cortés, Teutilia, and Xicontécatl. Teutilia maintains her honor and refuses any sexual activity outside marriage, while Marina is represented as a seductress who not only has sexual relations with Cortés but successfully seduces Ordoñez. When he believed he had lost Teutilia, Xicontécatl falls in love with Marina, believing that she is as pure and innocent as Teutilia. Xicoténcatl realizes his mistake when he finds out that not only is Marina pregnant, but that the father of the baby is Cortés. Xicoténcatl calls Marina names and questions her patriotism,

> "Is it possible, great lord!" he exclaimed after a long and deep silence, "is it possible for there to be such treachery, and so much duplicity, and so much falseness, and so much artifice, and so much infamy? That unworthy American, spurious daughter of these simple regions, a thousand times more detestable than those who have corrupted her, has unworthily abused the sincerity of my heart. Who could have discovered the poison in her tender words? Those kind and modest looks, that heartbeat, those continuous displays of alarm against her weakness: does all of this befit a betrayer as she leaves her adulterous bed?" (65)

The association of the conquering of women and the land is symbolized in Marina's pregnancy. The son Martín Cortés has come to symbolize the formation of a new race: the mestizo.

Teutilia does not have children, and thus she is not conquered (or raped) by the Spanish (keeping in mind that she could have had children with her legitimate and Indian husband Xicontécatl). In the novel, women have (or must have) the ability to refuse sex even in cases of attempted rape. Teutilia symbolizes the resistance against the Spanish by refusing Cortés and thus maintaining not only her honor, but that of her land and nation (whichever it might be) (see Cypess 1991). After Xicontécatl is murdered, Teutilia decides that she must kill Cortés, but fails. She ingests poison before she tries to stab Cortés in order to die and avoid punishment. She is able to conceal her face with a veil and does have access to Cortés, but there is a disturbance that he must attend to. In the meantime, the poison takes effect, and Teutilia is dying an agonizing death. When Cortés reappears, Teutila is able to say her last words: "Damn you, vile murderer of my Xicoténcatl!—Xicontécatl—Xiconténcalt—"(155). Cortés represents more than the murderer of Xiconténcatl, but of the indigenous nations.

The Mexican journalist Ignacio Ramírez in 1890 also deploys a binary form of thinking in his "contribution" to the development of La Malinche myth. He compares Malintzin to doña Josefa de Ortiz (heroine of Mexican independence war when she informed Father Miguel Hidalgo y Costilla that the Spanish were aware of the rebellion and precipitating the *grito de Dolores* that started the War of Independence in 1810) as one that reproduced the myths of Eve and Mary:

> Es uno de los misterios de la fatalidad que todas las naciones deben su pérdida y su baldón a una mujer, a otra mujer su salvación y su gloria; en todas partes se reproduce el mito de Eva y de María: nosotros recordamos con indignación a la barragana de Cortés, y jamás olvidaremos en nuestra gratitud a doña María Josefa de Ortiz, la Malintzin inmaculada de otra época que se atrevió a pronunciar el *fiat* de la Independencia para que la encarnación del patriotismo la realizara. (Ramírez 1890/1984, 490)[15]

Ramírez, who was a strong proponent of the liberal policies of the Reforma (which include a democratic republican form of government and strict separation of Church and state), deploys an ironic tone to explain how the fate of nations can rest on the actions of women. In the case of Doña Josefa Ortiz de Domíguez, her patriotism made her heroine of the Independence movement, and she is presented as someone who helps build a future while Malintzin is reduced to being Cortés' concubine and who through her sexuality destroys the "nation."

At the beginning of the twentieth century, during the Mexican Revolution of 1910, La Malinche myth continued to be represented in popular culture, literature, and textbooks (Monsiváis 1994, Gutiérrez 1999). As Monsiváis has asserted, México is a country that has been invaded, and those who do not defend her are called *Malinchistas*. The educational system serves as instrument to reproduce nationalist sentiments, and through the distribution of state sponsored books (*libros de texto gratuitos*), it disseminated the Malinche myth.

Octavio Paz was instrumental in the consolidation of the trope of treachery in *El Laberinto de la Soledad* (*The Labyrinth of Solitude*). Paz takes a psychoanalytic perspective in his analysis of the Mexican psyche. Moreover, Paz views women as a negation, as an inferior Other who is invisible and incapable of knowing. He thus constructs Malintzin as *La Chingada*, as the symbol of the violated mother. Yet, in Paz's view, she is a "violated" mother who "gave herself voluntarily to the conquistador" (86). He chastises Malinztin as a traitor the following way,

> Doña Marina becomes a figure representing the Indian women who were fascinated, violated or seduced by the Spaniards. And as a small boy will not forgive

his mother if she abandons him to search for his father, the Mexican people have
not forgiven La Malinche for her betrayal. (86)

Textually, Paz not only consolidates the definition of *malinchista* as a traitor
who prefers the foreigner for the Mexican; but in doing so he develops such
a notion with gender undertones that have an ugly misogynistic ring. As he
argues that in the 1950s newspapers in Mexico started to circulate the term
malinchista as a critique of "those who have been corrupted by foreign influences" (86).

Chicano nationalist Armando Rendón in his 1971 *Chicano Manifesto* continued the definition of *malinchista* as those who are traitors to the Chicano
movement by allying with the "gringo."

> We Chicanos have our share of malinches, which is what we call traitors to la
> raza who are of la raza, after the example of an Aztec woman of that name who
> became Cortez' concubine under the name of Doña Marina, and served him as
> an interpreter and informer against her own people. The malinches are worse
> characters and more dangerous than the Tio Tacos, the Chicano euphemism for
> an Uncle Tom. The Tio Taco may stand up in the way of progress only out of
> fear or misplaced self-importance. In the service of the gringo, malinches attack
> their own brothers, betray our dignity and manhood, cause jealousies and misun-
> derstandings among us, and actually seek to retard the advance of the Chicanos,
> if it benefits themselves—while the gringo watches. (Rendón 1971, 96–97)

The examples that Rendón offers of malinches are not necessarily female,
yet his definition of malinchista and the gender undertones of his text can be
interpreted as an indictment against women (see Contreras 2008). The sexual
voyeurism implied in the words "while the gringo watches" not only indicate
the problematic for Chicano nationalism (and manhood) when Chicanas
prefer white man over Chicanos, but that the Chicana (and the gringo) enjoy
such relationships. (Rendón is equally critical of Chicanos who married
white women.) Moreover, Rendón's prose is written with a clear masculinist
perspective that endorses the maintenance of patriarchal power, even when
he provides a self-critique of the male-centered practices within the Chicano
movement. He argues that one of the consequences of U.S. assimilation policies are manifested in the "decrease in the authority of the male" (171) in the
family, and that Chicanas who try to maintain several roles inside and outside
of the home, "have to answer for themselves, individually, [. . .] whether they
can live more than one of these roles at a time" (187).

Therefore, to reduce Malinztin's gender as the primary source that marks
her as a traitor is somewhat reductive. The combination of traditional ideologies of gender and sexuality, added to her intelligence and patriarchal

ideologies of nation, nationalism, and power, offer a nuanced analysis. Malintzin is vilified because she is viewed as a skilled woman who was sexually active. Mexican nationalism and patriarchy do not forgive her, not because she was a woman, but because she was a woman who acted outside the narrow confines of gender ideology through her sexuality and the posses-sion of knowledge held by only a few. Malinztin's sexuality became particu-larly problematic because she bore a son with Cortés out of wedlock, Martín Cortés, who symbolizes the birth of the mestizo nation. Additionally, she is viewed as exercising her linguistic abilities in the service of the Spanish. As Cypess (2005) writes, "La Malinche disrupted the general Amerindian curb on 'women's tongues in public spaces' as well as the Christian restrictions against women as speakers in public" (17). Malintzin is constructed as a trai-tor mostly by male writers/narrators who were in a position of power to offer their fictional version of history and the conquest. Thus, her status as a traitor and scapegoat is linked to her status as a woman who is seemed to have devi-ated in her own volition from traditional norms of womanhood as defined by nineteenth and twentieth century ideologies but not necessarily of her time.

Susan Kellogg (2005) in her book *Weaving the Past: A History of Latin America's Indigenous Women from the Prehispanic Period to the Present* shows how indigenous women have been active agents in shaping the regions history. As such, she argues that women have been creators of change and served as transformative agents in responding to forces of change, whether resisting or embracing them. Malintzin, as I have already argued, is clearly an example of an indigenous woman who acted as a transformative agent by embracing the change brought by the Spanish. While Malinztin's role in the conquest offered her a public role and material gain, other women experienced diminished roles. Kellogg argues that Mexica women were not subordinate, passive, or dominated by patriarchal fathers and husbands, as is often inferred from stone and paper portrayals.

Nahua views on gender were not ideal, as gender inequality and oppres-sion existed. Nevertheless, Kellogg and others (e.g., Joyce 2000) document that Nahua society followed a philosophy of gender parallelism that defined men's and women's gender roles as complementary opposites. For example, spinning and weaving were central to all women's work, noble or commoner, while men were responsible for farming and fighting, hunting, fishing, pro-duction of many crafts, and long distance trading of those items. Women performed vital household labor including cooking, cleaning, spinning and weaving, rearing and socializing children. Outside the home, commoner women provided labor in market exchange, worked as midwives, healers, and marriage brokers, and served as teachers and priestesses in temples and song houses. These activities were not drudge, unvalued labor, and some women had control over the fruits of their labor. Kellogg argues that some women were able to perform these activities due to the militarization of Mexica society and occupations outside of the home open for women.

In Aztec society, women could attend schools like the Calmecac and Telpochcalli, but it was not compulsory and was left as a family decision (Kellogg 2005; Joyce 2000). Yet, some prestigious occupations were not accessible for women such as those related to war activities. Many have looked at the transformation of Aztec symbolism toward male figures associated with strength and victory and femaleness with defeat and subjugation as examples of the establishment of patriarchal ideology. Yet, as Kellogg argues, paradoxically, the increasing militarization of Mexica society opened up a social space for women to play important—often parallel—social roles. Moreover, Nahua women held positions of authority that were hierarchically organized. They gained respect and access to material goods through their activities in homes, markets, neighborhoods, song houses, and temples. Also, women's property earned through dowry and inheritance was kept separate from men's at marriage, and the Mexica made distinctions between those household goods belonging to men and women (Kellogg 2005).

Although Mexica women, especially those who were of the noble class, were taught to be chaste, circumspect, and dutiful in fulfilling their wifely and maternal obligations, Mexica's views of sexuality were much more open than the Spanish's. Still, women who transgressed social and legal responsibilities could be punished for their behavior or crimes. Willful female children, prostitutes, female adulterers, and women who had abortions were subject to strong social sanctions and punishments, including death (Kellogg 2005). Yet, sexuality was associated with pleasure for both men and women, and not viewed as inherently sinful. "Sex carried with it the obligation for men and women to please each other and behave responsibly both toward one another and the children they jointly created" (Kellogg 2005, 28).

Varela, Ramírez, Paz, and Rendón construct Malintzin as a traitor based on their particular interpretations of history and gender roles. They created in their imagination an ideal nation that was destroyed by Malintzin's actions, and these actions in turn transformed her into a treacherous and "sinful" woman. Her perceived sexual transgressions are exacerbated by the usage of her knowledge in the service of the "enemy" or herself, not her community. This type of critique of Malintzin is based on contemporary notions of nation and community. Which community did Malintzin betray? Following her history, Malinztin did not have a community, as she was a slave who was passed from one group to the next. According to Joyce (2000), in Aztec society, to be without a place was the worst condition that could be imagined. It is possible that Malintzin, given her condition of a slave that begins in her childhood, developed a strong sense of survival by learning how to adapt to new circumstances. But it is very likely, as well, that she was seeking to establish a sense of home, to have a place, to belong; and she found this sense of belonging in the new society brought by the Spanish. She has become ostracized for almost 200 years because her behavior did not conform to norms of sexuality and passivity that were not part of her cultural milieu. As Norma Alarcón writes,

> Because Malintzin the translator is perceived as speaking for herself and not the community, however it defines itself, she is a woman who has betrayed her primary function: maternity. The figure of the mother is bound to a double reproduction, *strictu sensu* that of her people and her culture. In a traditional society organized along metaphysical or cosmological figurations of good and evil, cultural deviation from the norm is not easily tolerated nor valued in the name of inventiveness or "orgininality." In such a setting, to speak or translate in one's behalf rather than the perceived group interests and values is tanta-mount to betrayal. (Alarcón 1989/1991, 63)

Another way to see how idealized notions of gender operate in the trope of treachery is that her survival strategies jettisoned self-sacrifice. All she had available for herself was to survive; thus, acting on behalf of herself was an act of survival, not of treachery. But in the narratives of treachery, there is an impli-cation, as in *Xicotencatl,* that the noble act would be to die defending her honor (sexuality) and in doing so, the nation. To say that she allied with the foreigner is her ultimate betrayal is an a-historical interpretation that views all indigenous people as one nation. Her attributed sin is one created in the nineteenth and twentieth centuries and continues with contemporary interpretations. The trope of treachery had a particular pedagogical function to discipline women who might consider violating cultural rules and mores. Indeed, early critiques of la Malinche myth centered on Chicana feminists' struggles against being labeled Malinches.

GENDER, SEXUALITY, AND THE BODY

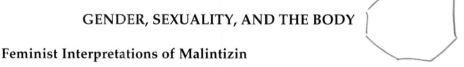

Feminist Interpretations of Malintizin

The examination of the historical record of the Spanish conquest of México, the cultural texts that facilitated the development of the trope of treachery, and feminist reinterpretations reduce Malintzin's life to her sexuality and her translation abilities. These two traits are converted into a boilerplate of her life, used when needed to give a quick explanation of her life. This reductive strategy produces binary discourses practices, where her sexuality, of course, is particularly depicted within the virgin/whore dichotomy. She is either ostracized as Cortés "traitorous whore," (Pérez, E 1999, 102) or reinscribed as an intelligent woman who used her linguistic abilities in order to survive. In what follows, I will examine Chicana feminist discursive strategies about Malintzin that go beyond this dichotomy. Even though, at times, feminists, including myself, also tend to describe her life through her sexuality and her translating abilities. Yet, there is the possibility of offering alternative feminist readings that go beyond the reversing of the interpretations of the myth.

Rebolledo and Rivero (1993), in their anthology of Chicana literature *Infinite Divisions,* propose that Chicana writers' relationship to Malintzin is constantly changing and revaluated. Thus, they identify four aspects on the revision of La Malinche myth: (1) La Malinche as conquered and raped, and, thus victim of her historical circumstances; (2) the recognition of mestizaje is recognition of indigenous inheritance; (3) Malinche exercised power and knowledge through her translating abilities; and (4) La Malinche as survivor. I propose that there is a fifth strategy that centers on reclaiming her body and sexuality. Moreover, this fifth strategy offers a differential consciousness (Sandoval 2000) that produces the enactment of border/transformative pedagogies.

Although Malintzin has achieved a mythical representation in historical, literary, and popular culture texts, she was a real in-the-flesh woman. As an individual or subject, her body becomes fragmented as her embodiment centers on her translation abilities represented through her tongue and her sexuality. Her tongue (*lengua* in Spanish) is reified as the organ that is primarily seen as responsible for speech (ignoring other organs needed for speech such as the lungs, throat, and vocal cords); but *Lengua* was also how Cortés and other Spaniards refer to her due to her translating abilities. Malintzin's sexuality is reduced to her extra marital relationship with Cortés. Malintzin's brown body and her sexuality cannot be avoided in any re-reading and re-definition. This is the case because, ironically, while her tongue is prominent in the descriptions of her life, her voice is absent. Without her voice, without any testimony from herself explaining her actions, we can only infer her motivations. As I mentioned at the beginning of this chapter, those who offer explanations of her life and her motivations end up making projections of one's own viewpoints (which, of course, includes feminists). Or, as Emma Pérez (1999) writes, "feminists have remade La Malinche into an agent of her own desires, and not just Cortés's whore" (102).

Remaking Malinche

When Chicanas first developed and articulated a feminist consciousness about the myth in the 1960s and 70s, they were answering to the epithets against Chicana feminists that named them Malinches, traitors to *La Raza* (Alarcón 1989/1990). Thus, Chicana feminists initiated the process that rearticulated the myth. As cultural critic Debra A. Castillo (2005) writes, Chicana rearticulations of the myth "have turned this negative image of the indigenous woman on its head, rewriting her story as that of an empowered woman" (68). Poet and historian Naomi Quiñones (2002) in her essay "Re(riting) the Chicana postcolonial: From traitor to twenty-first century interpreter" compares the first wave of Chicana writers to La Malinche in their role as interpreters of culture. Yet, when some of these early Chicana critics re-wrote the myth, the patriarchal tenets were still present. For example, Cordelia Candelaria (1980) proclaimed La Malinche as paradigmatic of Chicana feminism because "La Malinche embodies those personal characteristics—such as intelligence, initiative, adaptability, and leadership—which are most often associated with Mexican-American women unfettered by traditional restraints against activists public achievement" (6). She identified a new model for reconstituting Chicana subjectivity by reversing the terms of the arguments about La Malinche; the elements that marked La Malinche, and Chicanas, as traitors—intelligence and sexuality—became the symbols of feminist politics. Chicana feminist anthropologist Adelaida del Castillo (1977) looked at how Malinche had been distorted due to misinterpretations of her role in the conquest and the misogynistic characteristics ascribed to Malinche. Del Castillo, then, helped in the development of new discourses on Chicana womanhood that were not readily available for Chicanas.

Intelligence is a characteristic valued by Chicana feminists, but to reclaim Malintzin as a decolonial figure necessitates more than reversal of patriarchal discourses. Feminist interpretations that center on her intelligence and survival strategies (as important as these are), tend to limit the discussion as well. Particularly, there is an urgency to move beyond sexual victimization (a point of which I will return to further down). In order to offer transformative discourse, it is important to take into account the conditions of her life, specifically as a slave and concubine. Malintzin made choices under untenable conditions; indeed, Norma Alarcón makes a distinction between options and choices and prefers to look at Malintzin's actions and behaviors as selecting among untenable options, rather than as rational choices. "There are no choices for slaves, only options between lesser evils" (Alarcón 1989/1990, 83). That is, Alarcón ascribes a form of agency that takes into consideration Malintzin's social position. Alarcón is able to offer an agentic reading of Malintzin's behavior because she challenges the foundations of treachery and betrayal. Alarcón's reading contrasts with Rodriguez Kessler's (2005) psychological analysis based on the Stockholm Syndrome, Traumatic

Psychological Infantilism, and Traumatic Bonding Theory that helps her "justify" Malinztin's betrayal and bonding with Cortés:

> Knowing "right" from "wrong" in a society where slavery is part of the accepted norm is different from being expected to behave in a way that displays cultural loyalty when one has been sold into slavery from her parents, is powerless and threatened, and is under the command of a master from a different society. Marina's behavior clearly displays her inability to be personally efficacious in her private environment even though she can control the negotiations among military leaders. She is not only a slave; she is also a young woman suffering from psychological dysfunction created by her environment and her alternatively abusive and rewarding treatment by Cortés. (Rodriguez Kessler 2005, 95–96)

Following Alarcón, I see Malintzin's actions beyond the dualities that nationalism, treachery, psychological dysfunction, and gender ideology dictate, and argue that she navigated her world and circumstances in ways that neither totally assimilated the Spanish discourses nor repudiated her Mesoamerican traditions. Therefore, in agreement with Alarcón, I propose that by taking into account the structural constrains of her choices, we can make sense of her decisions that ensured her survival, and which, while consistent with Mexica gender practices, enacted new gender practices that neither the Spanish nor mestizos were willing to accept. As Marx argued, people may make their own history, but not under circumstances of their own choosing. That is, individuals can will their agency even under the direst conditions.

Reclaiming the Body and Sexuality

For Chicanas, a revision La Malinche myth that is "truly" decolonial requires the activation of a new epistemological stance. This epistemology moves beyond responding to patriarchal discourses in binary opposite terms. In order to re-claim La Malinche as a feminist figure, cultural critics and theorists need to change the terms of the discussion about her life. This point was brought up by Chicana feminist theorist Norma Alarcón's early critical writing on Malintzin in 1981, when she published the essay "Chicana's Feminist Literature: A Re-Vision Through Malintzin/ or Malintzin: Putting Flesh Back on the Object" in *This Bridge Called My Back*. Alarcón proposed that Chicanas "attempt[ed] to restore balance in ways that are sometimes painfully ambivalent, and at other times attempt[ed] to topple the traditional patriarchal mythology through revision and re-vision" (182). For Alarcón, this re-vision was manifested in the ways Chicana authors (particularly poets) re-claimed their self and subjectivity as sexual beings. By resisting the male-centric reading of Malinztin in particular and women in general as sexual pawns, Chicana poets such as Lorna Dee Cervantes and Carmen Tafolla reclaim their sexuality and humanism.

Chicana feminist essayist and play writer Cherrie Moraga in her 1993 essay "A long line of Vendidas" offers an early feminist examination of La Malinche myth from the perspective of her sexual identity and relationship with other women (100). For Moraga, the myth centers on the belief on the inherent unreliability of women, on women's natural propensity for treachery, and their incapacity of making choices. But for Moraga, the myth continues to have currency because it deals specifically with women's sexuality and subordination in the family and culture. That is, the legacy of La Malinche myth is that women who do not act in the traditional norms ascribed to women, such as being subservient to men, or who act upon their own sexual desires are considered traitors. In this way, Moraga twists the myth by proposing that the betrayal is not committed by women, but by a community that refuses to see our weakness as a people. Particularly, she argues that Chicana lesbians bear the brunt of this betrayal, for they are the most visible manifestation of a woman taking control of her sexuality. Reclaiming a voice, challenging women's subordination, and making choices are perceived as acts of betrayal. If this is the case, then, as the title of the essay implies, Chicanas come from a long line of vendidas. Instead, in disassociating Chicanas from the notion of selling out; she deconstructs the whole notion, and reclaims it as a source of power. Moraga's interpretation changes the terms of discussion.

Rita Cano Alcalá (2001) suggests, as well, an innovative viewpoint that offers a radical reinterpretation of La Malinche by focusing on the feminine aspects of the myth. Alcalá re-symbolizes La Malinche myth by linking her to a "long line of *hermanas*" (33): Malinaxochitl and Coyolxauhqui, siblings of Huitzilopochtli. Their brother Huitzilopochtli, representing the triumph of patriarchy over matrilocality in Aztec mythology, overpowers these two Aztec female deities. Malinaxochitl was removed from the nation; Coyolxcauhqui suffered a violent death when she opposed to the birth of her brother, Huitzilopochtli, who subsequently dismembered her. Alcalá argues that La Malinche's struggle and agency are better understood through these two female symbolic figures, rather than continuing to focus on her role as the raped mother of the mestizo nation.[16]

Emma Pérez (1999) suggests that in order to understand Malinche beyond the two oppositional meanings ascribed to her as either heroine of the conquest or the traitor *La Chingada*,[17] it is necessary to deploy a third space

feminist strategy that will "reinscribe her as a feminist icon . . . [and] identify her as an agent of her own desires" (Pérez, E. 1999, 103). According
to Pérez, the feminist move of remaking Malinche into an agent reinscribes
her as a complex subject "and not only [as] Cortés's whore" (102). That is,
Malinche becomes a decolonial subject: a powerful mother. But the powerful mother that she represents is not the traditional submissive and "virginal"
mother endorsed by patriarchal ideology. Rather, she is a mother who has
subverted patriarchal power and colonialism as Malintzin physically and
symbolically exercised her sexuality. As Antonia Castañeda (2005) argues in
her essay "Malinche, Calafia y Toypurina: Of Myths, Monsters and Embodied History," native women, including Malintzin, "used their bodies both
symbolically and materially, as instruments of opposition, resistance, and
subversion of colonial domination" (87). That is, it is necessary to construct
an understanding of women's sexuality that does not define sexual activity
and agency within the confines of marriage and reproduction. But also one
that does not idealize sex, and leaves room to comprehend that women, like
men, can use their sexuality for survival.

These interpretations point to the crucial aspects of border/transformative
pedagogies that seek to understand the complex and paradoxical meanings
of culture. In the case of Malintzin/Malinche, these constructions are based
on a variety of gender ideologies that have had the function of subordinating women. The female-centric interpretations that deconstruct the binary
terms under which Malinche has been historically constructed point to the
significance of border/transformative pedagogies. The strategies, proposed
by Chicana feminists such as Norma Alarcón, Emma Pérez, and Rita Alcalá,
are examples of border/transformative pedagogies because they transform
through their feminist deconstructive interpretations the terms of discussion
that constructed her as a treacherous woman.

These pedagogical strategies are not easily enacted, and there is the constant fear of falling back into comfortable binaries. Reconstructing Malintzin
is not easy, as it is too simplistic to either define her as a traitor or to idealize
her. My view is that Malintzin, like many of us, made decisions based on her
own interests and survival. In this sense, she is neither a traitor nor a heroine,
but a woman who lived under extremely difficult circumstances and used her
skills (linguistic, diplomatic, and perhaps sexual) to create a new life for herself and her children. What is the price of survival? Is survival opportunist?
Are these readings really progressive, or are we invoking an individualistic
Western liberal model? Gayatri Spivak proposed that the subaltern cannot
speak, and many have argued that the subaltern indeed can speak. In Malintzin's case, the issue is not weather she could speak; the question becomes
what happens when the subaltern acts?

NOTES

1. I am not arguing that Malintzin should have left a written record of her life, because this demand is an anachronism. In Aztec society, history was not recorded by individual voices; rather recording of events was done as a communal process. Thus, it is "logical" that Malintzin did not leave her own record and interpretation of her life. This circumstance leads to much speculation and projections onto her life.

2. This is by no mean an exhaustive list of sources of the Spanish Conquest of Mexico. See Miguel León Portilla, *Visión de los Vencidos* (México: Universidad Nacional Autónoma de México, 1959, pp. 207–219) for a complete list. It is beyond the scope of this study to analyze all of the existent historical texts on the Spanish Conquest.

3. Probanza is not easily translated into English, but is a document presented as evidence in a lawsuit by Maria Jaramillo and her husband to keep the land grant Cortés gave as a dowry when Malintzin married Juan Jaramillo.

4. According to the introduction to the fifth edition by Editorial Porrúa by Joaquin Ramírez Cabañas, the first edition of *Historia Verdadera* was published in Madrid in 1632. Del Castillo's original manuscript in draft form was finished in 1568 (forty-seven years after the Conquest). The manuscript was sent to Spain the same year, which was later found in the early 17th century by Fray Alfonso Remón in the library of Lorenzo Ramírez Prado, the Counselor of the Indies. This is the manuscript that was used for the first edition with editorial changes by Remón. Subsequent editions came from the manuscript and *códices* archived in Guatemala based on Del Castillo's draft.

5. Coatzacualcos (today's spelling) is in the Gulf of México coastal region in what is today the state of Veracruz.

6. The type of sexual relationship between Cortés and Malintzin is unknown. What I mean by this is that given that Malintzin arrived at Cortés's side as a slave, the issue of consent is difficult to assert. Many feminists argue (e.g., Alarcón) that slaves do not have choices. I agree with Alarcón that slaves do not have choices, but that does not mean they do not have agency. She could, as well, use her sexuality as a tool of survival. If we are redefining gender roles and feminist sensibilities, I believe that we need to move away from notions of female sexuality in which women who act in sexual ways or use their sexuality for survival are denigrated. I am not advocating for women to use their sexuality to get ahead in the world, but to a recognition that in terrible and oppressive circumstances like the one Malintzin was living, if her access to survival and material gain was through her sexual relationships with Cortés, I do not want to judge her for doing so.

7. At the time of Martín Cortés's birth, Hernán Cortés was married to Catalina Juárez, who was not able to give him children. There is much speculation and belief that Hernán Cortés murdered Catalina after a party in their home in México City. During a party, she and her husband had a heated argument, and the next day she was found dead in her bedroom with marks on her neck. The cause of death was declared to be natural causes, but years later, the conqueror was accused of murdering his

wife. Once a widower, Cortés married a Spanish woman who gave him also a son who was named Martín Cortés and who is the one who inherited his father's wealth and nobility title.

8. The Spanish translation into English reads, "It seems that like a fox in an attic, Marina tried to erase or distort with her tail the footprints of her encounter with the Spanish. In this she is very similar to her lord and lover Hernán Cortés." (My translation).

9. The Spanish text reads, "Señor Montezuma: lo que yo os aconsejo es que vais luego con ellos a su aposento, sin ruido ninguno, que yo sé que os harán mucha honra, como gran señor que sois, y de otra manera aqui quedaréis muerto, y en su aposento se sabrá la verdad." (My translation to English).

10. The liberal factions exemplified by President Benito Juárez advocated a democratic republican and secular government. This faction is associated with the Reforma Laws while conservatives were somewhat in favor of the Monarchy and close relations with the Catholic Church.

11. The emblem on the Mexican flag of the eagle standing on a cactus with a serpent in its beak comes from the story of the foundation of Tenochtitlan. The Aztec legend was that they would settle where they would find an eagle on a cactus eating a serpent.

12. Las Adelitas during the Mexican revolution might seem to contradict the emphasis on the male warriors. I believe they complement the warrior as even though they fought during the revolution, the historical image of the Adelitas is of women who did their patriotic duty, and even though they acted outside acceptable gender norms, they did it in the service of the cause by following the men to battle.

13. Recently, Monsiváis does include Cortés's allies in his discussion of the development of La Malinche myth.

14. Leal and Cortina offer a thorough analysis about the possible Mexican and Latin-American writers who plausibly could have authored the novel. While they recognize that there is no empirical evidence due to the lack of attribution in the texts, Leal and Cortina suggest that Varela left tell-tale signs in his writing that "reveal" his authorship. Some of these signs are his writing style, spelling of Mexican words (e.g., spelling Mexico with a "j," which Mexicans did not do, and lack of knowledge of central Mexico's landscape).

15. The Spanish text reads: "It is one of the mysteries' of fate that all nations owe their fall and disgrace to one woman, and to another their salvation and glory; everywhere Eve's and Mary's myth is reproduced, we recall with indignation Cortés's concubine, and we will never greatfully forget Doña María Josefa Ortiz, the immaculate Malintzin of another time who had the courage to announce the Independence's Decree in order for patriotism's embodiment became a reality." (My translation).

16. Alcalá argues that masculinist viewpoints that have condemned Malinche for mothering the first mestizo have erased the even more significant role, for the creation of mestizaje is through Malinche's legitimate daughter, María Jaramillo.

17. *La Chingada* means the "raped one." Literally, it means "the fucked one."

Chapter 6

Re-Mapping Transformative Pedagogies

New Tribalism and Social Justice

The practices of domination within educational institutions exemplified in hegemonic epistemologies, theories, and methodologies tend to privilege monocausal accounts of educational practices. The faith on positivism, objectivity, neutrality, and meritocracy, coupled with a myopic view of the U.S. as a monocultural and homogeneous society (if not in fact but in desire), is manifested not only in limited and oversimplified educational discourses and practices, but in the marginalization of knowledge produced by people of color. Ideologies, such as assimilation, are not new; they date back to the nineteenth century; historically one of the schools' functions was to assimilate immigrants to Anglo-American culture (Kliebart 1992).[1] Yet, in spite of how obsolete and ineffective these ideas are, they continue to hold currency in contemporary conservative rhetoric as demonstrated in attacks on bilingual education, ethnic studies, women's studies, immigrant rights, and affirmative action. For example, the Arizona legislature passed in 2010 H.B. HB 2281 that bans the teaching of ethnic studies in public and charter schools in Arizona. Specifically, Section A of HB 2281, prohibits instruction or classes that:

1. Promote the overthrow of the U.S. Government
2. Promote resentment toward a race or class of people
3. Are designed primarily for pupils of a particular ethnic group
4. Advocate ethnic solidarity instead of treatment of pupils as individuals.

Arizona State Superintendent of Public Instruction, Tom Horne, is behind this legislation. Specially, the law targets the Tucson Unified School District (TUSD) Raza Studies Program. In an interview with local PBS affiliate KAET program *Horizonte*, Horne explained that for years he worked with the legislature to pass the ban on ethnic studies because among other things, La Raza Studies program segregated students by race (e.g., African American students taking African American classes, Chicanos taking La Raza Studies, etc.), and that the curriculum in these classes created resentment among students and in doing so treated them as members of a group and not as individuals.

The purpose of ethnic studies is to provide an interdisciplinary and comprehensive examination of ethnic, racial, and indigenous diversity in the U.S. La Raza Studies curriculum at TUSD covers a variety of themes that offer interdisciplinary and in-depth examination of Mexican-American culture, literature, history, politics, and social movements. For example, the elementary school curriculum includes lessons in Mexican intellectual and indigenous traditions and cultural practices (e.g., Día de los Muertos, Piñatas); family life; literature, labor and social justice; gender; and assimilation. The middle school curriculum covers literature, history, diversity, and oral history; education; cultural practices; Mexican-American (Chicana/o) civil rights movements and leaders; math; and music. And at the high school level, the curriculum covers U.S. and Mexican history; Chicana/o cultural practices; Literature and social justice; contemporary Chicana/o politics, status, and civil right leaders; and literature and culture. Additionally, at all levels, there is an examination of the Mexico-U.S. border. More importantly, an intrinsic aspect of this curriculum is to develop critical thinking skills, which, I argue, are necessary for democratic citizenship.

Conservative views such as those exposed by Horne are not only incapable of understanding cultural practices and social relations as complex, but they continue to set their priorities based on the perceived "cultural deficit" of, and quite frankly hostility toward, communities of color. Access to quality education, whether in the public schools, community colleges, universities, community agencies, museums, or popular culture is essential for a truly democratic and just society. When a community is denied a basic right such as education (broadly defined), its material conditions suffer. Therefore, the decolonial feminist narratives on La Llorona, La Virgen de Guadalupe, and Malintzin/Malinche offer alternatives to such dominant discursive practices. Activism in the service of social justice can be exercised in multiple fronts; the decolonial differential consciousness expressed in Chicana/o popular culture in the representations and re-imagining of La Llorona, La Virgen de Guadalupe, and Malintzin/Malinche offer a language that connects everyday cultural productions with larger socio-structural struggles against poverty, racism, sexism, homophobia, globalization, and capitalism.

To show the significance of Chicana/o popular culture, I offered a historical and borderland analysis of the narratives on La Llorona, La Virgen de

Guadalupe, and Malintzin/Malinche. The array of meanings in the narratives I analyzed in this book—ranging from colonial, patriarchal, and nationalist to feminist and decolonial—demonstrate the richness of such popular cultural productions, and the complexities of the social world Chicanas occupy. Such narratives offer new transformative epistemological and pedagogical strategies that take into account alternative modes of being in and interacting in the world for Chicanas. Through feminist narratives, Chicana cultural workers/educational actors enact border/transformative pedagogies that articulate ways in which Chicanas understand the world and how to act in it order to change unequal social conditions that affect their lives and the lives of their communities.

As I demonstrated in my analysis of the three figures, their representation in popular culture is not one-dimensional. Rather, the manner in which the figures are re-configured in oral narratives, visual art, essays, and poems emerge from a multi-dimensional approach capable of recognizing multiple and contradictory viewpoints. In this sense, La Llorona is neither an evil terrifying ghost nor an innocent victim; La Virgen de Guadalupe is not only the asexual passive mother endorsed by the Catholic Church and protector of the disenfranchised, but she is also a sexual being; and Malintzin/Malinche is not Cortés' *puta* or our raped mother, but a woman who, like ourselves, made difficult and unpopular decisions under extreme circumstances. The analysis of the multiple meanings of the three figures is testament of how Chicana/o identity is not static. Rather, it is between the gaps and fissures of these narratives that third space feminism, the decolonial imaginary, and differential consciousness emerge (Pérez, E. 1999, Sandoval, C. 2000). I offer the results of this exegetical analysis as a strategy toward the development of transformative epistemological and pedagogical strategies as alternatives to prevailing Western epistemologies. I know that this is a daunting task given that the hegemony of mainstream positivistic approaches to education and social policy is very entrenched in policy and in contemporary popular imaginary; therefore, I am not naïve in my approach. But, I strongly believe that alternative viewpoints must be voiced and every effort made to transform our society and the world we live in.

Any understanding of cultural productions as complex will recognize that when multiple meanings are articulated, they will create conflicts. This is the case with feminist re-imagining of La Llorona, La Virgen de Guadalupe, and Malintzin/Malinche. Those who have access to power, such as the Catholic Church, find alternative viewpoints threatening, and instead of exercising democratic practices, move to silence dissenting voices. This is exemplified in the controversy over the exhibition of Alma López digital print *Our Lady* in the Museum of Santa Fe, when Chicano nationalist Villegas claimed that

López had no right to re-imagine Our Lady of Guadalupe. These debates, while painful, are reminders that cultural productions that manifest conflicts over meaning suggest a very powerful pedagogical practice.

Border/transformative pedagogies are in line with other transformative pedagogical discourses such as critical, feminist, queer, and multicultural. By looking at the significance of the history of the México-U.S. border and ensuing colonial relations between people of Mexican descent within the U.S. social, economic, and political system, border/transformative pedagogies recognize how these institutional practices affect the material conditions of Chicanas and Chicanos. Such socio-historical, political, cultural, and economic structures are significant in the formation of borderland subjectivities. The knowledge that Chicanas produced through their decolonial narratives is critical of those conditions. That is, the cultural workers/educational actors that I have highlighted in this book did not produce popular culture devoid of a language of critique and activism. Rather, through these productions, they connect their cultural identity and subjectivity with larger socioeconomic and political structures. And, more importantly, this connection between self and community is carried out in the service of social, gender, and spiritual justice. By recognizing people's subjectivity as a whole, border/transformative pedagogies connect mind/body/spirit as a source of transformation. Finally, border/transformative pedagogies take into account the significance of race, ethnicity, class, gender, and sexuality as both historical forms of oppression, but as the sources of identities and liberation. In this sense, border/transformative pedagogies do not focus on only one axis of analysis, but follows an intersectional approach that connect economic issues with cultural ones, and the micro and the macro structural.

An Apartheid of Knowledge: Re-mapping Pedagogical Discourses

It is difficult to situate border/transformative pedagogies within singular or specific transformative pedagogical projects. They can be situated within critical/feminist/queer/multicultural pedagogies; and yet I cannot map it within any of the particular discourses. This is the situation because transformative pedagogies suffer from an "apartheid of knowledge" (Sandoval, C. 2000). While Sandoval discusses the concept of apartheid of knowledge in reference to cultural studies, I find her elaboration similar to the situation of critical and feminist pedagogies. She notes that critical and cultural studies in the U.S., including the domains of difference, "have been developed as divided, racialized, genderized, and sexualized theoretical domains" (70). Further, she writes, "[i]n spite of the profoundly similar theoretical and methodological foundations that underlies such seemingly separate domains, there is a prohibitive and restricted flow of exchange that connects them, and their terminologies are continuing to develop in a dangerous state of theoretical apartheid that insists on their differences" (70). Likewise, Dolores Delgado Bernal and Octavio Villalpando (2002) propose that "an apartheid of knowledge . . . is sustained by an epistemological racism that limits the range of possible epistemologies considered legitimate within the mainstream research community" (169). An apartheid of knowledge occurs within transformative pedagogies in the following way: critical pedagogies seems to be the domain of white leftist males; feminist pedagogy of white women; queer pedagogy of gays and lesbians; and the misappropriated, but useful for lack of a better word of multicultural pedagogies, or those based on racial and ethnic identity, the realm ethnic based pedagogies (including Chicana feminist). As if individuals could only live one identity at the time.

These transformative pedagogies share a commitment to social justice and to a struggle against multiple forms of oppression, be they by race, class, gender, and sexuality. Many proponents share a critique of capitalism and economic exploitation. The goal of developing transformative educational praxis is central in these discourses. Yet, while they share in this vision toward a society free of inequality, we continue to witness divisions among different proponents based more on their theoretical visions, understanding of subjectivity, and perspectives that often times remain unchecked, than on the transformative project itself. I find this situation unfortunate because as Sandoval proposes in respect to cultural studies, "This divisive and debilitating phenomenon plagues intellectual production" (69). Moreover, in agreement with Sandoval, both in cultural studies and transformative pedagogies, this divisiveness can be understood as the "racialization of theoretical domains" (68), and unwittingly the product of binary thinking.

As I discussed in the introduction to this book, many scholars involved in critical and/or feminist pedagogies have expressed their concern with the lack of participation of scholars of color in critical pedagogy (Allen 2006, Elenes 2002, hooks 1994, Grande 2004, Kinchloe 2007). Nevertheless, it is important to note that there are scholars of color who have contributed to transformative pedagogies (e.g., Delgado Bernal 2006, Elenes 2002, 2006, Grande 2004, Godinez, 2006, Haymes 2003, hooks 1994, 2003, Hernández 1997, Kumashiro 2001,Trinidad Galván 2001, 2006, Trueba 1999, Varney 2001, Villenas 2006, 2010). Unfortunately, not much of this scholarship makes an appearance on the pages of critical and feminist pedagogies. The consequences are the apartheid of knowledge within transformative pedagogies.

This, I believe, is the effect of the under theorization of race, gender, class, and heterosexual privileges that ensue from systems of domination. One of the legacies of Western thought is the unmarking of the aforementioned

advantages and to produce binaries such as white/black, male/female, rich/
poor, and straight/gay which privilege the term on the top of the duality. Privilege is surreptitious, and the knowledge produced by those who benefit from
the unmarked categories is more likely to be universalized. The knowledge
produced by white males is more likely to be considered universal, while the
knowledge produced by those on the bottom of the hierarchy is viewed as
local and not capable of being generalized to the population as a whole. Of
course, the system is much more complicated because as African American
feminist scholar Patricia Hill Collins (2000) has proposed, race, class, and
gender operate within the matrix of domination. That is, different groups of
people and individuals have different gradations of privilege and oppression,
and we all move back and forth from privilege and oppression. In the case
of transformative pedagogies, for example, even though white males do have
more access to symbolic power in society and the academy, they certainly do
not have the same type of power than conservative white males. The Marxist
view of many of their proponents, for example, Peter McLaren's, positions
him toward the margins of academic discourses. Yet, his theories, even
though come from an embodied human being (white, male, middle class, heterosexual and Canadian), are seen as applicable to all groups; while the work
of Chicanas (and of women of color) are seen as applicable only to Chicanas
and women of color.[2] I am not arguing that McLaren's theories do not have
applicability to a whole variety of contexts, because they do. But they are also
limited to explain the circumstances of people of color, and he is also limited
in how he can approach the critical work produced by scholars of color. A
similar case can be made between feminist pedagogies, which tend to be
produced mainly by white women. In this case, the work of white women is
more likely to seen as universal than the work of women of color.

New Tribalism and Transformative Pedagogies

Social relations are much more complex than the scenario I presented, which
is what why transformative pedagogies can benefit from the relational theory
of difference. The relational theory of difference articulated by Yvonne
Yarbro-Bejarano (1999), which I presented in the introduction to this book,
explains that race, class, gender, and sexuality are relational terms, that is "the
theory is also relational within each binary set, for example, a man lives his
masculinity through his cultural, sexual and class identifications, but also in
relation to a certain construction of femininity which for the man is essential
for his manhood" (430). In other words, the relational theory of difference
is capable of recognizing that all groups construct their identities through,
among other definitional categorizations, their race, class, gender, and

sexuality. The relational theory of difference permits us to start theorizing the historically unmarked categories such as "white," "male," "heterosexual," and "middle class" (Allen 2006). For transformative pedagogies, theorizing these unmarked categories will help us re-conceptualize their contours and perhaps move beyond the apartheid of knowledge.

Chela Sandoval (2000) suggests that "the theoretical project of U.S. third world feminism insists on a standpoint, the theory and method of oppositional consciousness, Anzaldúa's *'la conciencia de la mestiza,'* which is, [she argues], capable of aligning such divided theoretical domains into intellectual and political coalition" (70–1). The conceptualizations of new tribalism, nepantla, and nos/otras that Anzaldúa developed in more recent publications (and which were published after Sandoval's *Methodology of the Oppressed*) offer a more nuanced framework for transformative pedagogical projects.

In her efforts to move beyond binary opposites, Anzaldúa's theorization open intellectual and activist spaces where the best interests of the whole, not just of a particular group (which usually is the one an individual belongs) were central (Lara 2005). The best interests of the whole, I argue, can be achieved via a social justice agenda that focus on the rights of all members of society globally to have access to the means to satisfy their material needs (food, clothing, shelter); intellectual (recognition of multiple epistemologies and cultural practices); and personal well being (to live life without violence and persecution, and to love and being loved). This utopian view is not a relativistic approach that places all discourses on the same plane. There are discourses that are oppressive and harmful. The best interests of the whole cannot be accomplished by policies and practices that are based on power and domination and serve the interests of the rich and powerful. For example, the neoliberal ideology of global capitalism that gives more power to transnational corporations than to individuals and permits the exploitation of workers and the decimation of the environment is not one that looks at the best interests of the whole. Neoliberalism benefits those few on the top of the social hierarchy.

Transformative projects recognize how inequality operates on a global scale and the ways in which a variety of communities struggle against those inequalities from an array of perspectives and praxis. That is, the theoretical space offered by new tribalism, nos/otras, third space feminism, nepantla, and spiritual activism cannot be reduced to single analysis of political economy, racism, sexism, and homophobia, and the policies that ensue from multiple forms of oppression such as neoliberalism, anti-immigration, attacks on affirmative action, and bilingual education. Moreover, Anzaldúa, although speakingfrom her position and identity as a Chicana, did not wish to address Chicanas' primarily.

In an interview with Irene Lara (2005), Anzaldúa explained that as early as *Borderlands* she was looking to theorize beyond the label Chicana, which she strived to accomplish through her conceptualization of mestiza consciousness. When she wrote *Borderlands* and coined the term mestiza consciousness, Anzaldúa was trying to find a term that could express the necessity to embrace ambiguity and the connection among different cultures and perspectives that would not limit the analysis to one group or particular context. While Chicana scholars (e.g., Alarcón 2002, Delgado Bernal 1998, 2006, Elenes 2006, Godinez 2006, Pérez, E. 1999, Sandoval, C. 1998, 2000, Téllez 2005, Trinidad Galván 2001, 2006), and feminist of color such as (e.g., Alexander 2005, Keating 2002, 2005, 2008)[3] embraced mestiza consciousness as theoretical and methodological tools and standpoints, the concept did not seem to gain traction outside of Chicana/o studies and feminist scholars. I believe this is the case, in part, because *Borderlands* is a text that speaks of Chicana and Chicano experiences and therefore might be read as localized, and non-Chicanos/as might not see how it could apply in other contexts. That is, in an environment of intellectual apartheid, the knowledge produced by and about groups that historically have been marked by way of race, class, gender, and sexuality is not considered to have relevance for other groups.

Granted, *Borderlands* is indeed a book that deals specifically with Chicana and Chicano experiences, and the epistemology in the book is constructed out of unique cultural and intellectual mythologies of Nahua intellectual traditions. But the beauty of metaphors lays in their abstractions and the ability to express values that can be shared among a various temporal and cultural contexts. Western intellectual traditions since the Renaissance looked at Greek and Roman myths to develop their epistemologies and values. Why are Greek mythologies applicable to the whole world, and not Nahua's? We understand these myths in their abstract nature and not in their localized racial, gendered, classed, sexualized perspectives. The history of colonialism, augmented with a globalization of communication technologies, has resulted in global mestizaje where most groups adopt different cultural, intellectual, and political practices from different milieus. The ability to embrace this ambiguity is the hallmark of mestiza consciousness, therefore, one that could be embraced by non-Chicanos. Thus, Anzaldúa moved toward reconceptualization of mestiza consciousness to new tribalism.

Anzaldúa was concerned with the difficulty we have in understanding differences in a nuanced way. New tribalism, "define who we are by what we include" (Anzaldúa 2002, 3), rather than by what we exclude. True to her anti-binary position, Anzaldúa looked at differences as operating in two simultaneous ways: 1) she tried to look at difference by not only what separates us from others; and 2) not gloss over those differences. Here Anzaldúa is linking the universal and the local, and in doing so, giving us a new language that is neither nested in cultural nationalism nor it is not color-blind. New tribalism, then, opens up epistemological spaces that can benefit transformative pedagogies. We can avoid wasting time and energy arguing over the intellectual conceptualizations that separate different critical and feminist pedagogical discourses (e.g., Marxist privilege of class or feminist privileging gender) and how all theories should follow suit, to a recognition that those who are not centering one form of analysis over another might indeed be using that axis of analysis with the other formations.

For example, when McLaren (2006) proposes that revolutionary pedagogy "insist on understanding social life from the standpoint of the strategic centrality of class and class struggle" (86), and that, "race, class, and gender, while they intersect and interact, are not coprimary. This triplet approximates what the philosophers might call a 'category mistake'" (87), he is, unwittingly, looking at intellectual difference by theoretical separation and binary thinking that insist on glossing over, or outright dismissing, other perspectives such as intersectionality. I do not disagree with McLaren that class is a significant mode of analysis. The border/transformative pedagogies articulated in the feminist narratives on La Llorona, La Virgen de Guadalupe, and Malintzin/Malinche all conduct a class analysis; yet this class analysis does not subsume the significance of gender, race, ethnicity, and sexuality. Moreover, an examination of transnational education and feminist scholarship produced by some Chicana scholars (Bejarano 2002, Trinidad Galván 2001, 2006, Téllez 2005, 2006) shows that Mexican women activists employ a distinctive cultural repertoire in their struggle against the forces of globalization, gender violence, and neoliberalism that point to the significance of class in a global scale. At the same time, this class analysis intersects with a gendered examination. Similarly, Chicana feminist sociologist María Soldatenko (2005), in her study of the Justice for Janitors movement in Los Angeles, concludes that "Latinas/os' language, cultural memory, and street theater have activated a political voice among Latinas/os in Los Angeles that enriches and transforms labor organization through the United States" (243). Race, class, gender, and sexuality are important axis of analysis that help us understand that all of these forms of consciousness and struggle are key in the activism deployed by women of color. The conceptualization of new tribalism helps us take off the theoretical blinders that maintain academic and intellectual apartheid.

Of course, taking off blinders is not easy, and I am sure I have a few that someone will point out. However, we can try to become nepantleras/os who seek to bridge what might seem to be theoretical impasses. As I mentioned in the first two chapters of this book, *nepantla* is the Nahuatl word for the land in the middle, and Anzaldúa uses it "to theorize liminality and to talk about those who facilitate passages between worlds, whom [she] named nepantleras" (2002, 1). Nepantla is unstable, unpredictable, precarious, and an uncomfortable space in transition (1). For Anzaldúa, nepantleras have to construct bridges that "span liminal (threshold) spaces between worlds" (1), yet it is in these in-between spaces where transformation occurs. What I am arguing here is that we need to construct bridges among the different transformative pedagogies discourses, and become nepantleras/os transformative pedagogues.

The work of border/transformative pedagogies benefits from new tribalism in that it helps us shift our categories (Lara 2005). Identities are intertwined, so for Anzaldúa, it was important to use the categories or labels that mark out identities without locking ourselves into those categories (Lara 2005). At the beginning of the twenty-first century, boundaries are less rigid and we need to account for that, "as time went by and las 'otras' ('us') partook more of the dominant culture—in terms of education and better living wages—the us/them boundary seems less rigid" (Anzaldúa qtd. in Lara 2005, 43). Further, Anzaldúa adds, "we have some of whites' privileges and whites have acquired some of our otherness; so then I started thinking of us as "nos/otras" with a slash in the middle" (43). The struggle for social change is to remove the slash, to recognize that we are all in this together. In line with her anti-binary logic, this does not mean that Anzaldúa favored color-blind views that plague liberal and conservative views in the U.S. As usual, Anzaldúa refuses to take an either/or position and favors a holistic one that is capable of keeping together two or more contradictory statements at the same time. Through this interconnectedness, according to AnaLouise Keating,

> Anzaldúa dismantles these walls by building bridges. She adopts flexible, context-specific perspectives enabling her simultaneously to see and see through exclusionary identity classifications. She does not ignore the importance of color, class, gender and other identity markers; however, she puts these perspectives into a more holistic perspective. (Keating 2008, 62)

This is a position that all, regardless of where one fits on the hierarchies that grant advantages or disadvantages, can take. All of the categories that privilege some and underprivilege others are social constructions whose meanings change over time. Their significance lays in the meanings that societies, groups, and individuals give to them. That is, while classification of human beings based on race, class, gender, and sexuality result from histories of colonization with the purpose of colonizing, enslaving, and subordinating the groups that were marked on the bottom of the hierarchy; many of those who have been marked by these classifications have in turn claimed their identities by honoring their race, class, gender, and sexuality.

New tribalism, differential consciousness, third space feminism, mestiza consciousness, and decolonial imaginary permits us to theorize a cultural identity beyond binary thinking and acknowledge that classifications can be both oppressive and liberatory. As such, we need to understand that race, class, gender, and sexuality are contingent and flexible and its meanings have to be understood as unstable. Nepantleras/os appreciate that our standpoints can emerge out of our experiences of privilege and oppression; it is not only people of color, women, the working class, and gay/lesbian/bisexual/transgender who use their experiences as epistemic sources. This is a point that Supreme Court Justice Ruth Bader Ginsburg noted in her dissent on the *Ricci*[4] case that favored white firefighters when she wrote that the conservative majority in the Court were sympathetic to the white firefighters, because they "understandably attract this court's sympathy" (www.courant.com). Very astutely, Justice Ginsburg used her dissenting voice to show that, in spite of conservative ideology, conservative judges are not as objective as they claim to be, and indeed do invoke their experiences and identities to decide their cases.

Border/Transformative Pedagogies in the Era of "Hope"

Recognizing cultural identities—as well as other markers of difference—as contingent, flexible, and unstable does not mean that they will lose their significance over time. The diversity of human expression is significant and necessary to counter the practices of domination and imperialism. The border/transformative pedagogies that Chicanas enact through their re-imagining of La Llorona, La Virgen de Guadalupe, and Malinztin/Malinche attest to the significance of the understanding of cultural identity as multifaceted and unstable. They are expressions of subjugated knowledges that offer practices that will lead toward a world free of social inequality and one where social justice prevails. In her articulation of pedagogies of crossing, feminist scholar M. Jacqui Alexander (2005) proposes that "subordinated knowledges that are produced in the context of the practices of marginalization in order that we might destabilize existing practices of knowing and thus cross the fictive boundaries of exclusion and marginalization" (7). These practices are akin to border/transformative pedagogies.

Centering the work of Chicanas within the discourses of transformative pedagogies is done to recognize that subjugated knowledges find a way to voice their contributions to social and intellectual life. Clearly, the pedagogies enacted by Chicanas are situated within a specific cultural and social space. It is imperative to give voice to these cultural expressions for both Chicanas/os and non-Chicanas/os alike. To speak against colonization and imperialism, against the forces of globalization, Chicana and Mexicana voices are necessary. Not to create another hierarchy, or to speak as victims, but because in order to create a just society, all voices must be heard.

I offer border/transformative pedagogies as epistemological, methodological, and ontological strategies that, by placing Chicanas as the center of the discourse, offer their visions of society. Their distinctive viewpoints offer both universal and localized knowledges, and as such can help us develop another strategy for social transformation. In the way that Chicana border/transformative pedagogies developed feminist praxis by centering spirituality, I hope that these strategies can also help transform educational praxis.

NOTES

1. Indeed, Native American scholar Sandy Grande documents that since 1611, French Jesuits developed mission schools to educate Indian children "in the French manner." (Sandy Grande. *Red Pedagogy: Native American Social and Political Thought,* Lanham, MD: Rowman & Littlefield, 2004, 11.)

2. In my experience reviewing articles for a variety of educational journals or papers for national conferences (including NACCS) I have noticed that scholars writing on Chicana feminist pedagogies make sure to quote and rely on white male authors (which is fine), yet neglect to refer to the work of Chicana feminist education scholars. This occurs even with self-identified Chicana/Latina scholars (which I know because they identify in the body of the paper). My concern with this is that even scholars of color tend to see mainstream and white scholars as universal, and in doing so neglect significant research that should inform their work.

3. Anzaldúa's work is cited by a variety of scholars, including white feminists such as Judith Butler and Donna Haraway. Additionally, Anzaldúa's essays, especially "La Conciencia de le mestiza" are anthologized. However, these citations and anthologizing are not necessarily translating to an adaptation of her work in any significant way outside Chicana and women of color contexts.

4. In the *Ricci v. DeStefano* (2009) case, the Supreme Court ruled in a five to four decision that white firefighters in New Heaven, Connecticut had been the victims of racial discrimination when the city invalidated a promotional exam that would have not promoted black applicants.

Bibliography

Acuña, Rodolfo. *Occupied America: A History of Chicanos.* 4th ed. New York: Longman, 2000.

Alarcón, Norma. "Chicana's Feminist Literature: A Re-vision Through Malintzin/ or Malintzin: Putting Flesh Back on the Object." In *This Bridge Called My Back: Writings by Radical Women of Color.* 2nd ed, edited by Cheríe Moraga and Gloria Anzaldúa, pp. 182–196. New York: Kitchen Table Women of Color Press, 1983.

———. "Traddutora, Traditora: A Paradigmatic Figure of Chicana Feminism." *Cultural Critique* 13 (Fall 1989): 57–87.

———. "Chicana Feminism: In the Tracks of 'the' Native Woman." *Cultural Studies* 4, no. 3 (1990): 248–256.

———. "Conjugating Subjects in the Age of Multiculturalism." In *Mapping Multiculturalism,* edited by Avery F. Gordon and Christopher Newfield, pp. 127–148. Minneapolis: University of Minnesota Press, 1996.

———. "Making 'Familia' From Scratch: Split Subjectivities in the Work of Helena María Viramontes and Cherríe Moraga." In *Chicana Creativity & Criticism: New Frontiers in American Literature,* edited by María Herrera-Sobek and Helena María Viramontes, pp. 220–232. Albuquerque: University of New Mexico Press, 1996.

———. "Anzladúa's *Frontera:* Inscribing Gynetics." In *Decolonial Voices: Chicana and Chicano Cultural Studies in the 21st Century,* edited by Arturo J. Aldama and Naomi H. Quiñonez, pp. 113–129. Bloomington: Indiana University Press, 2002.

Alcoff, Linda and Elizabeth Potter. "Introduction: When Feminisms Intersect Epistemology." In *Feminist Epistemologies,* edited by Linda Alcoff and Elizabeth Potter, pp. 1–14. New York: Routledge, 1993.

Aldama, Arturo. *Disrupting Savagism: Intersecting Chicana/o Mexican Immigrant, and Native American Struggles for Self-Representation.* Durham, NC: Duke University Press, 2001.

Aldama, Arturo and Naomi H.Quiñones, eds. *Decolonial Voices: Chicana and Chicano Cultural Studies in the 21st Century.* Bloomington & Indianapolis: Indiana University Press, 2002.

Alegría, Juana. *Psicología de las Mexicanas.* 2nd ed. Coyoacán, Mexico: Editorial Samo, 1975.

Alexander, M. Jacqui. *Pedagogies of Crossing: Meditations on Feminism, Sexual Politics, Memory, and the Sacred.* Durham, NC: Duke University Press, 2005.

Allen, Ricky Lee. "The Race Problem in the Critical Pedagogy Community." In *Reinventing Critical Pedagogy: Widening the Circle of Anti-Oppression Education,* edited by César Augusto Rossatto, Ricky Lee Allen, and Marc Pruyn, pp. 3–20. Lanham, MD: Rowman & Littlefield, 2006.

Almaguer, Tomás. *Racial Fault Lines: The Historical Origins of White Supremacy in California.* Berkeley & Los Angeles: University of California Press, 1994.

Alvarez, Robert, Jr. "The Border as Social System: The California Case." *New Scholar* 9 (1984): 119–129.

———. "Mexican-U.S. Border: The Making of an Anthropology of Borderlands." *Annual Review of Anthropology* 24 (1995): 447–464.

Anaya, Rudolfo. "La Llorona, El Kookooee, and Sexuality." *The Bilingual Review* (1992): 50–55.

Anaya Rudolfo and Francisco Lomelí, eds. *Aztlán: Essays on the Chicano Homeland.* New Mexico: Academia/El Norte Publications, 1989.

"Andrea Yates Returned to Prison After Hospital Stay." *The Associated Press,* 17 July 2004.

Anzaldúa, Gloria. *Borderlands/La Frontera: The New Mestiza.* San Francisco: Spinsters/Aunt Lute, 1987.

———. "Chicana Artists: Exploring *Nepantla, el Lugar de la Frontera.*" In *The Latino Studies Reader,* edited by Antonia Darder and Rodolfo D. Torres, pp. 163–169. Malden, MA: Blackwell Publishers, 1998a

———. "To(o) Queer the Writer-Loca, escritora y chicana." In *Living Chicana Theory,* edited by Carla Trujillo, pp. 263–276. Berkeley: Third Woman Press, 1998b.

———. *Borderlands/La Frontera: The New Mestiza.* 2nd ed. San Francisco: Spinsters/Aunt Lute, 1999.

———. ed. *Making Face, Making Soul Haciendo Caras.* San Francisco: Aunt Lute, 1990.

———. "now let us shift . . . the path of conocimiento . . . inner work, public acts." In *this bridge we call home: radical visions for transformation,* edited by Gloria Anzaldúa and AnaLouise Keating, pp. 540–578. New York: Routledge, 2002.

———. *Friends from the Other Side/Amigos del Otro Lado.* San Francisco: Children's Book Press/Libros para niños, nd.

Anzaldúa, Gloria and Keating, AnaLouise, eds. *this bridge we call home: radical visions for transformation.* New York: Routledge, 2002.

Archival Collection of Oral Histories of "The Legend of La Llorona." Southwest Folklore Center, University of Arizona.

Arora, Shirley L. "La Llorona: The Naturalization of a Legend." *Southwest Folklore* 5, no. 1 (1981): 23–40.

Arredondo, G.F., Aida Hurtado, N. Klahn, O. Nájera-Ramírez, and Patricia Zavella. Introduction to *Chicana Feminisms: A Critical Reader*. Durham, NC: Duke University, 2003.

Arteaga, Alfred. "Introduction: The Here, the Now." In *An Other Tongue: Nation and Ethnicity in the Linguistic Borderlands*, edited by Alfred Arteaga, pp. 1–7. Durham, NC: Duke University Press, 1994b.

———. "An Other Tongue." In *An Other Tongue: Nation and Ethnicity in the Linguistic Borderlands*, edited by Alfred Arteaga, pp. 9–33. Durham, NC: Duke University Press, 1994c.

———, ed. *An Other Tongue: Nation and Ethnicity in the Linguistic Borderlands*. Durham, NC: Duke University Press, 1994a.

Banks, James A., ed. *Handbook on Research on Multicultural Education*. New York: MacMillan, 1995.

Bannon, John Francis, ed. *Bolton and the Spanish Borderlands*. Norman: University of Oklahoma Press, 1964.

Barakat, Robert. "Aztec Motifs in 'La Llorona'" *Southern Folklore Quarterly* 29 (1987): 288–296.

Barthes, Roland. *Mythologies*. New York: The Noonday Press, 1973.

———. *The Rustle of Language*. New York: Hill and Wang, 1986.

Baud, Michael. "Toward a Comparative History of Borderlands." *Journal of World History* 8, 2 (Fall 1997): 211–242.

Baudot, Georges. "Malintzin, Imagen y Discurso de Mujer en el Primer Méjico Virreinal." *Cuadernos Americanos* 40 (1993): 181–207.

Baughman Collection. University of New Mexico Center for Southwest Research.

Bejarano, Cynthia. "Las Super Madres de Latino America: Transforming Motherhood by Challenging Violence in Mexico, Argentina, and El Salvador." *Frontiers: A Journal of Women Studies* 23, no. 1 (2002): 126–150.

———. *¿Qué onda? Urban youth cultures and border identity*. Tucson: University of Arizona Press, 2005.

———. "Latino Youths at the Crossroads of Sameness and Difference: Engaging Border Theory to Create Critical Epistemologies on Border Identity." In *Reinventing Critical Pedagogy: Widening the Circle of Anti-Oppression Education*, edited by César Augusto Rossatto, Ricky Lee Allen, and Marc Pruyn, pp. 49–62. Lanham, MD: Rowman & Littlefield, 2006.

Bhabha, Homi K. *The Location of Culture*. London: Routledge, 1994.

Bierhorst, John, tr. *History and Mythology of the Aztects: The Codex Chimalpopoca*. Tucson: University of Arizona Press, 1992.

Blake, Debra. *Chicana Sexuality and Gender: Cultural Refiguring in Literature, Oral History, and Art*. Durham, NC: Duke University Press, 2008.

Blanco, Iris. "Participación de las Mujeres en la Sociedad Prehispanica." In Pt. 1 in *Essays On La Mujer*, edited by Rosaura Sánchez, pp. 48–81. Los Angeles and Berkeley: University of California Press, 1977.

Blayne, Culter. "Welcome to the Borderlands." *American Demographics* 13, 2 (February 1991): 44–57.

Bolton, Herbert Eugene. *The Spanish Borderlands: A Chronicle of Old Florida and the Southwest.* With an introduction by Albert L. Hurtado. Albuquerque: University of New Mexico Press, 1921.

———. *Wider Horizons of American History.* Edited by William E. Lingelbach. New York: D. Appleton-Century Company Incorporated, 1939.

———. *Bolton and the Spanish Borderlands.* Edited and with an introduction by John Francis Bannon. Norman: University of Oklahoma Press, 1964.

Bouvier, Virginia M. *Women and the Conquest of California, 1542–1840: Codes of Silence.* Tucson: University of Arizona Press, 2001.

Brandenburg, Frank. *The Making of the Modern Mexico.* Englewood Cliffs: Prentice-Hall, 1964.

Bright, Brenda Jo. "Introduction." In *Looking High and Low: Art and Cultural Identity,* pp. 1–18. Tucson: University of Arizona Press, 1995.

Bright, Brenda Jo and Bakewell, Liza, eds. *Looking High and Low: Art and Cultural Identity.* Tucson: University of Arizona Press, 1995.

Brotherston, Gordon. "La Malintzin de los Códices." In *La Malinche, Sus Padres y Sus Hijos,* edited by Margo Glantz, pp. 13–29. Mexico D.F.: Ciudad Universitaria, 1994.

Broyles-González, Yolanda. "Indianizing Catholicism: Chicana/India/Mexicana Indigenous Spiritual Practices in Our Image." In *Chicana Traditions: Continuity and Change,* edited by Norma E. Cantú and Olga Nájera-Ramírez, pp. 117–132. Urbana and Chicago: University of Illinois Press, 2002.

Buell, Susan D. "Our Lady of Guadalupe: A Feminine Mythology for the New World." *Historical Magazine for the Protestant Episcopal Church* 51 (1982): 399–404.

Bustamante, Jorge. "Demystifying the United States-Mexico Border." *William and Mary Quarterly* 49 (1992): 321–334.

Butler, Judith. *Gender Trouble: Feminism and the Subversion of Identity.* New York: Routledge, 1990a.

———. *The Psychic Life of Power: Theories in Subjection.* Palo Alto, CA: Stanford University Press, 1990b.

———. *Excitable Speech: A Politics of the Performative.* New York: Routledge, 1997.

Calderón, Héctor. "Texas Border Literature: Cultural Transformation in the Works of Américo Paredes, Rolando Hinojosa and Gloria Anzaldúa." *Dispositio* 26, 41 (1991): 13–28.

Calderón, Héctor and José David Saldívar, eds. *Criticism in the Borderlands: Studies in Chicano Literature, Culture and Ideology.* Durham: Duke University Press, 1991.

Calvo, Luz. "Art Comes for the Archbishop: The Semiotics of Contemporary Chicana Feminism and the Work of Alma Lopez." *Meridians: Feminism, Race, Transnationalism* 5, no. 1 (2004): 201–224.

Camarillo, Albert. *Chicanos in a Changing Society: From Mexican Pueblos to American Barrios in Santa Barbara and Southern California, 1848–1930.* Cambridge, MA: Harvard University Press, 1979.

Cano Alcalá, Rita. "From Chingada to Chingona: La Malinche Redefined Or, A Long Line of Hermanas." *Aztlan: A Journal of Chicano Studies* 26, no. 2 (2001): 33–61.

Candelaria, Cordelia. "The Market Place." *Agenda 7* (1977): 46–47.

———. "La Malinche, Feminist Prototype." *Frontiers* 5, no. 2 (1980): 1–6.

———. "Letting La Llorona Go, or, Re/reading History's 'Tender Mercies.'" In *Literatura Chicanas 1965–1995: An Anthology in Spanish, English, and Caló,* edited by Manuel de Jesús Hernández-Gutiérrez and David William Foster, pp. 93–97. New York: Garland Publishers, 1993/1997.

———. "Différance and the Discourse of 'Community' in Writings By and about the Ethnic Other(s)." In *An Other Tongue: Nation and Ethnicity in the Linguistic Borderlands,* edited by Alfred Arteaga, pp. 185–202. Durham, NC: Duke University Press, 1994.

Cantú, Norma. *Canícula: Snapshots of a Girlhood en la Frontera.* Albuquerque: University of New Mexico Press, 1995.

Carbonell, Ana María. "From Llorona to Gritona: Coatlicue in Feminist Tales by Viramontes and Cisneros." *Melus* 24, no. 2 (Summer 1999): 53–74.

Carrasco, Davíd. *Religions of Mesoamerica: Cosmovision and Ceremonial Centers.* Prospect Heights, IL: Waveland Press, 1990.

Castañeda, Antonia I. "Gender, Race, and Culture: Spanish-Mexican Women in the Historiography of Frontier California." *Frontiers* 11, no. 1 (1990a): 8–20.

———. "The Political Economy of Nineteenth Century Stereoptypes of Californianas." In *Between Borders: Essays on Mexicana/Chicana History,* edited by Adelaida R. Del Castillo, pp. 213–236. Encino, CA: Floricanto Press, 1990b.

———. "Language and Other Lethal Weapons: Cultural Politics and the Rites of Children as Translators of Culture." In *Mapping Multiculturalism,* edited by Avery F. Gordon and Christopher Newfield, pp. 201–214. Minneapolis: University of Minnesota Press, 1996.

———. "Malinche, Calafia y Toypurina: Of Myths, Monsters and Embodied History." In *Feminism, Nation and Myth: La Malinche,* edited by Rolando Romero and Amanda Nolacea Harris, pp. 82–97. Houston: Arte Público Press, 2005.

Castañeda, Antonia I., Susan Armitage, Patricia Hart, and Waren Weathermom. *Gender on the Borderlands: The Frontiers Reader.* Lincoln: University of Nebraska Press, 2007.

Castillo, Ana. *Massacre of the Dreamers: Essays on Xicanisma.* Albuquerque: University of New Mexico Press, 1994.

———, ed. *Goddess of the Americas: Writings on the Virgin of Guadalupe.* New York: Berkeley Publishing Group, 1996.

Castillo, Debra A. "Coagulated Words: Gaspar de Alba's Malinche." In *Feminism, Nation and Myth,* edited by Rolando Romero and Amanda Nolacea Harris, pp. 67–80. Houston: Arte Público Press, 2005.

Chabram-Dernsersesian, Angie. "Chicano Critical Discourse: An Emerging Cultural Practice." *Aztlan: Journal of Chicano Studies* 18, no. 2 (1989): 45–90.

———. "I Throw Punches for My Race, but I Don't Want to be a Man: Writing Us-Chican-nos (Girl, Us)/Chicanas—into the Movement Script." In *Cultural Studies,* edited by Lawrence Grossberg, Cary Nelson and Paula Treichler, pp. 81–95. New York: Routledge, 1992.

———. "And, Yes . . . The Earth Did Part: On the Splinting of Chicana/o Subjectivity." In *Building With Our Hands: New Directions in Chicana Studies,* edited by Adela de la Tore and Beatríz M. Pesquera, pp. 34–56. Berkeley and Los Angeles: University of California Press, 1993.

———. "'Chicana! Rican? No, Chicana-Riqueña!' Refashioning the Transnational Connection." In *Multiculturalism: A Critical Reader,* edited by David Theo Goldberg, pp. 269–295. Cambridge: Blackwell, 1994.

———. "Introduction: Chicana/o Latina/o Cultural Studies: Transnational and Transdisciplinary Movements." *Cultural Studies* 13, no 2 (1999): 173–194.

Chambers, Iain. *Border Dialogues: Journeys in Postmodernism.* New York: Routledge, 1990.

Chavero, Alfredo. *Obras Históricas de Don Fernando de Alva Ixtlilxochitl: Tomo II Historia Chichimeca.* México: Oficina Tip. de la Secretaria de Fomento, 1892.

Cisneros, Sandra. *Woman Hollering Creek and Other Stories.* New York: Vintage Contemporaries, 1991.

———. "Guadalupe the Sex Goddess." In *Goddess of the Americas: Writings on the Virgen of Guadalupe,* edited by Ana Castillo, pp. 46–51. New York: Riverhead Books, 1996.

Cline, Zulmara., Juan Necochea, and Francisco Ríos. "The Tyranny of Democracy: Deconstructing the Passage of Racist Propositions." *Journal of Latinos and Education* 3 (2004): 67–85.

Cline, Zulmara and Juan Necochea. "Teacher Dispositions for Effective Education in the Borderlands." *The Educational Forum* 70 (Spring 2006): 268–282.

Collins, Patricia Hill. *Black Feminist Thought, 2nd edition.* New York: Routledge.

———. *Fighting Words: Black Women & the Search for Justice.* Minneapolis and London: University of Minnesota Press, 1998.

Concannon, Kevin. "The Contemporary Space of the Border: Gloria Anzaldúa's *Borderlands* and William Gibson's *Neuromancer.*" *Textual Practice* 12, no. 3 (1998): 429–442.

Contreras, Sheila M. *Blood Lines: Myth, Indigenism, and Chicana/o Literature.* Austin: University of Texas Press, 2008.

Córdova, Teresa. ed. *Chicana Voices: Intersections of Class, Race, and Gender.* NP: National Association for Chicano Studies, 1990.

Cortez, Constance. "History/Whose-Story? Postcoloniality and Contemporary Chicana Art." *Chicana/Latina Studies: The Journal of Mujeres Activas en Letras y Cambio Social* 6, no. 2 (2007): 22–54.

Cortés, Hernando. *Hernán Cortés: Letters from México.* Edited by Anthony Pagden. New Haven: Yale University Press, 1986.

Cruz, Cindy. "Toward an Epistemology of a Brown Body." *International Journal of Qualitative Studies in Education* 14 (2001): 657–669.

Cuádraz, Gloria H. Chicanas and Higher Education: Three Decades of Literature and Thought." *Journal of Hispanic Higher Education* 4 no. 3 (July 2005): 215–234.

Cypess, Sandra Messinger. *La Malinche in Mexican Literature: From History to Myth.* Austin: University of Texas Press, 1991.

———."'Mother' Malinche and Allegories of Gender, Ethnicity and National Identity in México." In *Feminism, Nation and Myth: La Malinche,* edited by Rolando Romero and Amanda Nolacea Harris, pp. 14–27. Houston: Arte Público Press, 2005.

Darder, Antonia. *Culture and Power in the Classroom: A Critical Foundation for Bilingual Education.* Edited by Henry Giroux and Paulo Freire. New York: Bergin & Garvey, 1991.

———. *Culture and Difference: Critical Perspectives on the Bicultural Experience in the United States.* Westport, CT: Bergin & Garvey, 1995.

———. "Creating the Conditions for Cultural Democracy in the Classroom." In *Latinos and Education: A Critical Reader,* edited by Antonia Darder, Rodolfo D. Torres, and Henry Gutiérrez, pp. 331–350. New York: Routledge, 1997.

Darder, Antonia, Rodolfo D. Torres & Henry Gutiérrez, eds. *Latinos and Education: A Critical Reader.* New York: Routledge, 1997.

Darder, Antonia and Rodolfo D. Torres. "Shattering the 'Race' Lens: Toward a Critical Theory of Racism." In *Critical Pedagogy Reader,* edited by Antonia Darder, Marta Baltodano, and Rodolfo D. Torres, pp. 245–261. New York: Routldege, 2003.

Dávalos, Karen Mary. *Yolanda M. López. A Ver: Revisioning Art History,* Vol.2, UCLA Chicano Studies Research Center press, distributed by the University of Minnesota Press, 2008.

———. *Exhibiting Mestizaje: Mexican (American) Museums in the Diaspora.* Albuquerque: University of New Mexico Press, 2001.

Davidson, Miriam. *Lives on the Line: Dispatches from the U.S. Mexico Border.* Tucson: The University of Arizona Press, 2000.

Dávila, Arlene. *Latinos Inc.: The Marketing and Making of a People.* Berkeley & Los Angeles: University of California Press, 2001.

De Alva Ixtlixochitl, Don Fernando. *Obras Históricas,* publicadas y anotadas por Alfredo Chavero, Tomo I. México: Oficina Tip. De la Secretaria de Fomento, 1891.

De la Garza, Sarah Amira. *María Speaks: Journeys into the Mysteries of the Mother in My Life as a Chicana.* New York, NY: Peter Lang Publishing, Inc., 2004.

De Luna, Anita. *Faith Formation and Popular Religion: Lessons from the Tejano Experience.* Lanham, Boulder, New York, Oxford: Rowman & Littlefield, 2002.

De la Torre, Adela, and Beatriz M. Pesquera, eds. *Building with Our Hands: New Directions in Chicana Studies.* Berkeley and Los Angeles: University of California Press, 1993.

De Leon, Arnoldo. "Whither Borderlands History? A Review Essay." *New Mexico Historical Review* 64 (1989): 349–360.

Del Castillo, Adelaida R. "Malintzin Tenepal: A Preliminary Look into a New Perspective." In Pt. 2 in *Essays on La Mujer,* edited by Rosa Martínez Cruz, pp. 124–149. Los Angeles and Berkeley: University of California Press, 1977.

———, ed. *Between Borders: Essays on Mexicana/Chicana History.* Encino, CA: Floricanto Press, 1990.

Delgado, Richard. "Storytelling for Oppositionists and Other." In *The Latino Condition: A Critical Reader,* edited by R. Delgado and J Stefancic, pp. 259–270. New York and London: New York University Press, 1998.

Delgado Bernal, Dolores. "Using a Chicana Feminist Epistemology in Educational Research." *Harvard Educational Review* 68 (Winter 1998): 555–579.

———. "Chicana/o Education From the Civil Rights Era to the Present." In *The Elusive Quest for Equality: 150 Years of Chicano/Chicana Education,* edited by José E. Moreno, pp. 77–108. Cambridge: Harvard Educational Review, 1999.

———. "Learning and Living Pedagogies of the Home: The Mestiza Consciousness of Chicana Students." In *Chicana/Latina Education in Everyday Life,* edited by Dolores Delgado Bernal, C. Alejandra Elenes, Francisca E. Godinez, Sofia Villenas, pp. 113–132. Albany, NY: State University of New York Press, 2006.

Delgado Bernal, Dolores, and C. Alejandra Elenes. "Chicana Feminist Theorizing: Methodologies, Pedagogies, and Practices." In *Chicano School Failure and Success,* 3rd edition, edited by R. Valencia. New York: Routledge, in press.

Delgado Bernal, Dolores, and Octavio Villalpando. "An Apartheid of Knowledge in Academia: The Struggle over the "Legitimate" Knowledge of Faculty of Color." *Equity & Excellence in Education* 32, no. 2 (2002): 169–180.

Demas, Ellen D. and Saavedra, Cinthya M. "(Re)conceptualizing Language Advocacy: Weaving a Postmodern *mestizaje* Image of Language. In *Decolonizing Research in Cross-Cultural Contexts Personal Narratvies,* edited by K. Mutua and B. B. Swadener, pp. 215–233. Albany: State University of New York Press, 2004.

Derrida, Jacques. *Writing and Difference,* Chicago: University of Chicago Press, 1978.

———. *Positions.* Translated by Alan Bass. Chicago: University of Chicago Press, 1981.

———. *The Post Card: From Socrates to Freud and Beyond.* Translated by Alan Bass. Chicago and London: The University of Chicago Press, 1987.

———. *Limited Inc.* Translated by Samuel Weber. Evanston: Northwestern University Press, 1988.

Desai, Manisha. "Transnational Solidarity: Women's Agency, Structural Adjustment, and Globalization." In *Women's Activism and Globalization: Linking Local Struggles and Transnational Politics,* edited by Nancy A. Naples and Manisha Desai, pp. 15–33. New York: Routledge, 2002.

Díaz Del Castillo, Bernal. *The Discovery and Conquest of Mexico.* Edited by Genaro Garcia. New York: Farrar, Straus, and Cudahy, 1956.

———. *Historia Verdadera de la Conquista de la Nueva España.* 5th ed. Con Introducción de Joaquín Ramírez Cabañas. México, D.F.: Editorial Porrúa, 1632/1960.

Dicochea, Perlita R. "Environmental Justice on the Mexico-U.S. Border: Toward a Borderlands Methodology." In *Chicana/Latina Education in Everyday Life: Feminista Perspectives on Pedagogy and Epistemology,* edited by Dolores Delgado Bernal, C. Alejandra Elenes, Francisca E. Godinez, and Sofia Villenas, pp. 231–243. Albany: State University of New York Press, 2006.

Dillard, Cynthia. "The Substance of Things Hoped For, the Evidence of Things Not Seen: Examining an Endarkened Feminist Epistemology in Educational Research and Leadership." *Qualitative Studies in Education* 13, no. 6 (2000): 661–681.

Donato, Rubén. *The Other Struggle for Equal Schools: Mexican Americans During the Civil Rights Era.* Albany: SUNY Press, 1997.

Du Bois, W. E. B. *The Illustrated Souls of Black Folk,* edited and annotated by Eugene F. Provenzo Jr. Boulder and London: Paradigm Publishers, 2005.

Dussel, Enrique. "A Nahuatl Interpretation of the Conquest: From the 'Parousia' of the Gods to the 'Invasion.'" In *Latin American Identity and Constructions of Difference,* edited by Amaryll Chanady, pp. 104–129. Minneapolis, University of Minnesota Press, 1994.

Easton, Pam. "Andrea Yates' Husband Files for Divorce." *The Associated Press* 2 August 2004.

Elenes, C. Alejandra. "Reclaiming the *Borderlands:* Chicana/o Identity, Difference, and Critical Pedagogy" *Educational Theory* 47 (Summer 1997): 359–375.

———. "Malinche, Guadalupe, and Llorona: Patriarchy and the Formation of Mexican National Consciousness." In *Latin America: An Interdisciplinary Approach,* edited by Gladys Varona-Lacey and Julio López-Arias, pp. 87–103. New York: Peter Lang, 1999.

———. "Border/Transformative Pedagogies at the End of the Millennium: Chicana/o Cultural Studies and Education." In *Decolonial Voices: Chicana and Chicano Studies in the 21st Century,* edited by Arturo Aldama and Naomi Quiñonez, pp. 245–261, 2002.

———. "*Transformando Fronteras:* Chicana Feminist Transformative Pedagogies." In *Chicana/Latina Education in Everyday Life: Feminista Perspectives on Pedagogy and Epistemology,* edited by Dolores Delgado Bernal, C. Alejandra Elenes, Francisca E. Godinez, Sofia Villenas, pp. 245–259. Albany: State University of New York Press, 2006.

Elenes, C. Alejandra, Dolores Delgado Bernal, Francisca E. Godinez, and Sofia Villenas. "Introduction: Chicana/Mexicana Feminist Pedagogies: *Consejos, Respeto y Educación* in Everyday Life." *Qualitative Studies in Education* 14 (2001): 595–602.

Elenes, C. Alejandra and Dolores Delgado Bernal. "Latina/o Education and the Reciprocal Relationship between Theory and Practice: Four Theories Informed by the Experiential Knowledge of Marginalized Communities." In *Handbook of Latinos and Education,* edited by Enrique Murillo, Jr. pp. 63–89. New York: Routledge, 2010.

Fernández, Adela. *Dioses Prehispánicos de Mexico: Mitos y Deidades del Panteón Nahuátl.* México: Panorama Editorial, 1993.

Fernández-Kelly, María Patricia. *For We Are Sold, I and My People: Women and Industry in Mexico's Frontier.* Albany: State University of New York Press, 1983.

Fine, Michelle, et. al, eds. *Off White: Readings on Race, Power, and Society.* New York: Routledge, 1997.

Flax, Jane. "Postmodernism and Gender Relations in Feminist Theory." *Signs: Journal of Women in Culture and Society* 12 (1987): 621–643.

Flores, Juan and George Yúdice. "Living Borders/Buscando America: Languages of Latino Self-Formation." In *Latinos and Education: A Critical Reader,* edited by Antonia Darder, Rodolfo Torres, Henry Gutiérrez, pp. 174–200. New York: Routledge, 1997.

Flores, Lisa. "Reclaiming the "Other": Toward a Chicana Feminist Critical Perspective." *International Journal of Intercultural Relations* 24 (2000): 687–705.

Florescano, Enrique. *Memory, Myth, and Time in Mexico: From the Aztecs to Independence.* Translated by Albert Bork. Austin: University of Texas Press, 1994.

Fox, Claire F. *The Fence and the River: Culture and Politics at the U.S.-Mexico Border.* Minneapolis: University of Minnesota Press, 1999.

Fowkles, Diane. "Moving From Feminist Identity Politics to Coalition Politics Through A Feminist Materialist Standpoint of Intersubjectivity in Gloria Anzaldúa's *Borderlands/La Frontera: The New Mestiza.*" *Hypatia* 12, 2 (Spring 1997):105–124.

Franco, Jean. *Plotting Women: Gender and Representation in Mexico.* New York: Columbia University Press, 1989.

———. "Border Patrol." *Travesía* (1992): 134–142.

Fregoso, Rosa Linda. "Born in East L.A. and the Politics of Representation." *Cultural Studies* 3 (1990): 264–281.

———. *The Bronze Screen: Chicana and Chicano Film Culture.* Minneapolis: University of Minnesota Press, 1993.

———. "Imagining Multiculturalism: Race and Sexuality on the Tejas Borderlans." *The Review of Education/Pedagogy/Cultural Studies,* 21 no. 2 (1999): 133–148.

———. *meXicana encounters: The Making of Social Identities on the Borderlands.* Berkeley & Los Angeles: University of California Press, 2003.

Fregoso, Rosa Linda and Angie Chabram. "Chicana/o Cultural Representations: Reframing Alternative Critical Discourses." *Cultural Studies* 4, 3 (1990): 203–216.

Freire, Paulo. *Pedagogy of the Oppressed.* Translated by Myra Bergaman Ramos. New York: Continuum, 1970.

———. *La Educación Como Práctica de la Libertad.* México: Siglo Veintiuno Editores, 1982.

Gamio, Manuel. *Consideraciones Sobre el Problema Indígena.* México, D.F.: Ediciones del Instituto Indigenista Interamericano, 1948.

García, Alma. "The Development of Chicana Feminist Discourse, 1970–1980." *Gender & Society* 3, no. 2 (June 1989): 217–238.

———, ed. *Chicana Feminist Thought: The Basic Historical Writings.* New York: Routledge, 1997.

García, Eugene E. *Hispanic Education in the United States: Raíces y Alas.* Lanham, MD: Rowman & Littlefield, 2001.

García Canclini, Néstor. *La Producción Simbólica: Teoría y Método en Sociología del Arte.* 5a Edición. México: Siglo Veintiuno Editores, 1993.

Garibay, Angel Ma. K. *Visión de los Vencidos: Relaciones Indígenas de la Conquista.* México, D.F: Universidad Nacional Autónoma de México, 1992.

Garza, Sabino. "La Llorona: An Omen of Doom." In *El Quetzal Emplumece,* edited by Carmela Montalvo, OSB, and Leonardo Anguiano, pp. 444–454. San Antonio: Mexican American Cultural Center, 1976.

Gaspar de Alba, Alicia. "The Alter-Native Grain: Theorizing Chicano/a Popular Culture" In *Culture and Difference: Critical Perspectives on the Bicultural Experience in the United States,* edited by Antonia Darder, pp. 103–122. Westport, CT: Bergin & Garvery, 1995.

———. *Chicano Art: Inside/Outside the Master's House: Cultural Politics and the CARA Exhibition.* Austin: University of Texas Press, 1998.

Giroux, Henry. *Border Crossings: Cultural Workers and the Politics of Education.* New York: Routledge, 1992.

Giroux, Henry and Peter McLaren, eds. *Between Borders: Pedagogy and the Politics of Cultural Studies.* New York: Routledge, 1994.

———. *Critical Pedagogy, the State, and Cultural Struggle.* Albany: State University of New York Press, 1989.

Giroux, Henry and Roger Simon. "Popular Culture and Critical Pedagogy: Everyday Life as a Basis for Curriculum Knowledge." In *Critical Pedagogy, the State and Cultural Struggle,* edited by Henry Giroux and Peter McLaren, 236–252. Albany: State University of New York Press, 1989.

Glass, John B. *Sahagun: Reorganization of the Manuscrito de Tlatelolco, 1566–1569.* Part 1. Massachusetts: Coneme Associates, 1978.

———. *Catálogo de la Colección de Códices.* México: Instituto Nacional de Antropología e Historia, 1964.

Godinez, Francisca E. "*Haciendo que Hacer:* Braiding Cultural Knowledge into Educational Practices and Policies." In *Chicana/Latina Education in Everyday Life: Feminista Perspectives in Pedagogy and Epistemology,* edited by Dolores Delgado Bernal, C. Alejandra Elenes, Francisca E. Godinez and Sofia Villenas, pp. 25–38. Albany: State University of New York Press, 2006.

Goldman, Shifra M. "The Iconography of Chicano self-determination: Race, Ethnicity,and Class." *Art Journal* 49 (Summer 1990): 167–173.

Gomez de Orozco, Federico. *Doña Marina: La Dama de la Conquista.* Mexico: Ediciones Xochitl, 1942.

Gonzáles, Sylvia. "La Chicana: Malinche or Virgin." *Nuestro* 3 (1979): 41–45.

———. "Toward a Feminist Pedagogy of Self-Actualization." *Frontiers* 5 (1980): 49–51.

González, Deena J. *Refusing the Favor: The Spanish-Mexican Women of Santa Fe, 1820–1880.* New York: Oxford University Press, 1999.

González, Diana. *América Jamas Descubierta,* Mexico: Ediciones Castillo, 1992.

González, Francisca E. "Formation of *Mexicana*ness: *Trensas de identidades múl-tiples* Growing up *Mexicana:* Braids of Multiple Identities." *Qualitative Studies in Education* 11 (1998): 81–102.

González, Norma. *I am my Language: Discourses of Women and Children in the Borderlands.* Tucson: University of Arizona Press, 2001.

González Obregón, Luis. . . . *Las Calles de México . . . Leyendas y Sucedidos.* México: Ediciones Bota, 1944.

Gordon, Avery and Christopher Newfield, eds. *Mapping Multiculturalism.* Minneapolis: University of Minnesota Press, 1996.

Gordon, Linda. "On 'Difference.'" *Genders* 10 (Spring 1991): 91–111.

Gore, Jennifer. *The Struggle for Pedagogies: Critical and Feminist Discourses as Regimes of Truth.* New York: Routledge, 1993.

Grande, Sandy. *Red Pedagogy: Native American Social and Political Thought.* Lanham, MD: Rowman & Littlefield, 2004.

Graves, Robert and Raphael Patai. *Hebrew Myths: The Book of Genesis.* Garden City, New York: Doubleday & Company, Inc., 1963/1964.

Greer Johnson, Julie. "Bernal Díaz and the Women of the Conquest." *Hispanofila* 82 (1984): 67–77.

Grewal, Inderpal. "Autobiographic Subjects and Diasporic Locations: *Meatless Days* and *Borderlands.*" In *Scattered Hegemonies: Postmodernity and Transnational Feminist Practices,* edited by Inderpal Gewal and Caren Kaplan, pp. 231–257. Minneapolis: University of Minnesota Press, 1994.

———. *Transnational America: Feminisms, Diasporas, Neoliberalisms.* Durham, NC: Duke University Press, 2005.

Grewal, Inderpal and Caren Kaplan, eds. *Scattered Hegemonies: Postmodernity and Transnational Feminist Practices.* Minneapolis: University of Minnesota Press, 1994.

Griffith, James S. *Southern Arizona Folk Arts.* Tucson: The University of Arizona Press, 1988.

———. *A Shared Space: Folklife in the Arizona-Sonora Borderlands.* Logan: Utah State University Press, 1995.

Griswold del Castillo, Richard, Teresa McKenna, and Yvonne Yarbro-Bejarano, eds. *Chicano Art: Resistance and Affirmation, 1965–1985.* Los Angeles: Wight Gallery.

Grossberg, Lawrence. "Introduction: Bringing it all Back Home-Pedagogy and Cultural Studies." In *Between Borders,* edited by Henry Giroux and Peter McLaren, pp. 1–25. New York: Routledge, 1994.

———. *Bringing It All Back Home: Essays on Cultural Studies.* Durham: Duke University Press, 1997.

Grossberg, Lawrence, Cary Nelson, Paula Treichler, eds. *Cultural Studies.* New York and London: Routledge, 1992.

Guarnizo, Luis Eduardo and Michael Peter Smith. "The Locations of Transnationalism." In *Transnationalism from Below, Vol. 6 Comparative Urban and Community Research,* edited by Michael Peter Smith and Luis Eduardo Guarnizo, pp. 3–34. New Brunswick: Transaction Publishers, 1998.

Guerra, Verónica. "The Silence of the Obejas: Evolution of Voice in Alma Villanueva's 'Mother, May I' and Sandra Cisneros's 'Woman Hollering Creek.'" In *Living Chicana Theory,* edited by Carla Trujillo, pp. 320–351. Berkeley: Third Woman Press, 1998.

Guevarra, Anna R. *Marketing Dreams, Manufacturing Heroes: The Transnational Labor Brokering of Filipino Workers.* New Brunswick: Rutgers University Press, 2010.

Gutiérez, Laura. "Sexing Guadalupe in Transnational Double Crossings." *El Aviso* 6, no. 2 (2006): 8–9.

Gutiérrez, Natividad. *Nationalist Myths and Ethnic Identities: Indigenous Intellectuals and the Mexican State.* Lincoln: University of Nebraska Press, 1999.

Gutiérrez-Jones, Carl. *Rethinking the Borderlands.* Berkeley: University of California Press, 1995.

Harasym, Sarah, ed. *The Post-Colonial Critic: Interviews, Strategies, Dialogues.* New York: Routledge, 1990.

Haraway, Donna. *Simians, Cyborgs, and Women: The Reinvention of Nature.* New York: Routledge, 1991.

Haymes, Stephen Natha. "Toward a Pedagogy of Place for Black Urban Struggle." In *The Critical Pedagogy Reader,* edited by Antonia Darder, Marta Baltodona, and Rodolofo D. Torres, pp. 211–237. New York: RoutledgeFalmer, 2003.

Heidenreich, Linda. "The Colonial North: Histories of Women and Violence from Before the U.S. Invasion." *Aztlán: A Journal of Chicano Studies* 30, no. 1 (Spring 2005): 23–54.

Heinz Dieterich, Steffan, ed. *La Interminable Conquista: Emancipación e Identidad de America Latina, 1492–1992.* Mexico: Editorial Joaquin Mortiz / Planeta, 1990.

Henderson, Mae G. *Borders, Boundaries, and Frames: Essays in Cultural Criticism and Cultural Studies.* New York: Routledge, 1995.

Hernández, Adriana. *Pedagogy, Democracy and Feminism: Rethinking the public sphere.* Albany: State University of New York Press, 1997.

Hernández, Ellie D. "The Futureperfect: Chicana Feminist Critical Analysis in the Twenty-First Century." *Chicana/Latina Studies: The Journal of Mujeres Activas en Letras y Cambio Social* 5, no. 2 (Spring 2006): 59–91.

Hernández, Ester. "La Virgen de Guadalupe Defendiendo los Derechos de los Xicanos." *Third Women* 4 (1989): 42–43.

Hernández, Inés. "Cascadas de Estrellas: La Espiritualidad de la Chicana/Mexicana/Indígena." In *Este Puente mi Espalda: Voces de Mujeres Tercermundistas en los Estados Unidos,* edited by Cherríe Moraga and Ana Castillo, translated by Ana Castillo and Norma Alarcón, pp. 256–266. San Francisco: ISM Press, 1988.

Herzog, Lawerence. *Where North Meets South: Cities, Space, and Politics on the U.S.-Mexico Border.* Austin: Center for Mexican American Studies, University of Texas Press, 1990.

Herren, Ricardo. *Doña Marina, La Malinche.* Barcelona: Editorial Planeta, 1992.

Herrera-Sobek, María. *Chicana Creativity and Criticism: Charting New Frontiers in American Literature.* 2nd ed. Albuquerque: University of New Mexico Press, 1996.

Herrera-Sobek, María, Guisela Latorre, and Alma Lopez. "Digital Art, Chicana Feminism, and Mexican Iconography: A Visual Narrative by Alma Lopez in Naples, Italy." *Chicana/Latina Studies: The Journal of Mujeres Activas en Letras y Cambio Social* 6, no. 2 (2007): 68–91.

Hicks, D. Emily. *Border Writing: The Multidimensional Text.* Minneapolis: University of Minnesota Press, 1991.

Holley, Joe. "Confronting La Frontera: Who's Watching the Boom Along the Border?" *Columbia-Journal Review* 33, 1 (1994): 46–48.

hooks, bell. *Teaching to Transgress.* New York: Routledge, 1994.

Hurtado, Aída. "Relations to Privilege: Seduction and Rejection in the Subordination of White Women and Women of Color." *Signs: Journal of Women in Culture and Society* (Summer 1989): 833–855.

———. "The Politics of Sexuality in the Gender Subordination of Chicanas." In *Living Chicana Theory,* edited by Carla Trujillo, pp. 383–428. Berkeley: Third Woman Press, 1998.

Hurtado, Albert. "Parkmanizing the Spanish Borderlands: Bolton, Turner, and the Historians' World." *The Western Historical Quarterly* 26, 2 (Summer 1995): 149–167.

Iglesias Prieto, Norma. *Beautiful Flowers of the Maquiladora: Life Histories of Women Workers in Tijuana.* Translated by Michael Stone with Gabrielle Winkler. Austin: University of Texas Press, 1997.

Infante, Judith. "La Llorona." *Blue Mesa Review* 4 (Spring 1992): 5–7.

Irigaray, Luce. *This Sex Which is Not One.* New York: Cornell University Press, 1977.

JanMohamed, Abdul. "Some Implications of Paulo Freire's Border Pedagogy." In *Between Borders,* edited by Henry Giroux and Peter McLaren, pp. 242–252. Routledge: New York, 1994.

Janvier, Thomas A. *Legends of the City of Mexico.* New York: Harper & Brothers, 1910.

Johnson, Lyndon B. Foreword to *The Texas Rangers,* by Walter Webb. Austin: University of Texas Press, 1965

Jones, Pamela. "'There Was a Woman': La Llorona in Oregon." *Western Folklore* 47 (Summer 1988): 195–211.

Joyce, Rosemary A. *Gender and Power in Prehispanic Mesoamerica.* Austin: University of Texas Press, 2000.

Kaplan, Caren and Inderpal Grewal. "Transnational Feminist Cultural Studies: Beyond the Marxism/Postculturalism/Feminism Divides." In *Between Woman and Nation,* edited by Caren Kaplan, Norma Alarcón, and Minoo Moallem, pp. 349–363. Durham, NC: Duke University Press, 1999.

Karttunen, Frances. "Rethinking Malinche." In *Indian Women of Early Mexico,* eds. Susan Schroder, Stephanie Wood, and Robert Haskett, pp. 291–312. Norman and London: University of Oklahoma Press, 1997.

Kearney, Michael. "La Llorona as a Social Symbol." *Western Folklore* 28, 3 (July 1969): 199–206.

Keating, AnaLouise, ed. *"Interviews/Entrevistas: Gloria E. Anzaldúa."* New York and London: Routledge, 2000.

———, ed. *EntreMundos/AmongWorlds: New Perspectives on Gloria Anzaldúa.* New York: Palgrave McMillan, 2005.

———. "'I'm a citizen of the universe': Gloria Anzaldúa's spiritual activism as catalyst for social change. *Feminist Studies* 34 (Spring/Summer 2008): 53–69.

Keister, Kim. "Borderlands." *Historic Preservation* 46, 4 (July 1994): 50–98.

Kellogg, Susan. *Weaving the Past: A History of Latin America's Indigenous Women from the Prehispanic Period to the Present.* New York: Oxford University Press, 2005.

Kincheloe, Joe L. "Critical Pedagogy in the Twenty-First Century: Evolution for Survival." In *Critical Pedagogy: Where Are We Now?,* edited by Peter McLaren and Joe L. Kincheloe, pp. 9–42. New York: Peter Lang, 2007.

Kirtely, Bacil. "'La Llorona' and Related Themes." *Western Folklore* 19 (1960): 155–168.

Kliebard, Herbert M. *Forging the American Curriculum: Essays in Curriculum History and Theory.* New York: Routledge, 1992.

Kolodny Annette. "Among The Indians: The Uses of Captivity." *Women's Studies Quarterly* 3, no. 4 (Fall/Winter 1993): 184–195.

Korte, Tim. "Feds unveil new steps to combat drug cartels." *The Arizona Republic* (Saturday, 6 June 2009), A4.

Kossan, Pat. *The Arizona Republic* retrieved online http://www.azcentral.com/community/phonix/articles. 17 June 2009.

Kumashiro, Kevin K., ed. *Troubling Intersections of Race and Sexuality: Queer Students of Color and Anti-Oppressive Education.* Lanham, MD: Rowman and Littlefield, 2001.

Kunow, Marianna Appel. "Gonzalo Guerrero and La Malinche: Symbols of Mestizaje." *Human Mosaic* 26 (1992): 12–22.

LaCapra, Dominick. *History & Criticism.* Ithaca, NY: Cornell University Press, 1985.

Ladson-Billings, Gloria. "Racialized Discourses and Ethnic Epistemologies." In *Handbook of Qualitative Research,* edited by Norman K. Denzin and Yvonna S. Lincoln, 2nd. ed, pp. 257–277. Thousand Oaks, CA: Sage Publications, Inc., 2000.

Lafaye, Jaques. *Quetzlalcoatl and Guadalupe: The Formation of Mexican National Consciousness, 1531–1813.* Translated by Benjamin Keen. Chicago: University of Chicago Press, 1974.

Lampe, Philip, E. "Our Lady of Guadalupe and Ethnic Prejudice." *Borderlands Journal* 9 (Spring 1986): 91–120.

Lara, Irene. "Bruja positionalities: Toward a Chicana/Latina spiritual activism." *Chicana/Latina Studies: The Journal of Mujeres Activas en Letras y Cambio Social* 4, no. 2 (2005a): 10–45.

———. "Daughter of Coaltlicue: An Interview with Gloria Anzaldúa." In *EntreMundos/AmongWords: New Perspectives on Gloria Anzaldúa,* edited by AnaLouise Keaning, pp. 41–56. New York: Palgrave McMillan, 2005b.

———. "Goddess of the Americas in the decolonial imaginary: Beyond the virtuous Virgen/Pagan puta dichotomy." *Feminist Studies* 43 (1/2) (Spring/Summer 2008a): 99–127.

———. "Tonalupanisma: Re-membering Tonantzin-Guadalupe in Chicana visual art." *Aztlán: A Journal of Chicano Studies* 33(2) (Fall 2008b): 61–90.

Lather, Patti. *Getting Smart: Feminist Research and Pedagogy with/in the Postmodern*. New York: Routledge, 1991.

Latina Feminist Group. 2001. *Telling to Live: Latina Feminist Testimonios*. Durham, NC: Duke University Press.

Leddy, Betty. "La Llorona in Southern Arizona." *Western Folklore* 7 (1948): 272–277.

———. "La Llorona Again." *Western Folklore* 9 (1950): 363–365.

León-Portilla, Miguel. *Los Antiguos Mexicanos: A Traves de sus Crónicas y Cantares*. México: Fondo de Cultura Económica, 1983.

———. *La Filosofía Nahuatl: Estudiada en Sus Fuentes*. México: UNAM, Instituto de Investigaciones Históricas, 1983.

———. *The Aztec Image of Self and Society: An Introduction to Nahua Culture*. Salt Lake City: University of Utah Press, 1992.

———. *Visión de los Vencidos: Relaciones indígenas de la Conquista*. México: Universidad Autónoma de México, 1992.

———. *Tonantzin Guadalupe: Pensamiento náhuatl y mensaje cristiano en el 'Nican mopohua.'* México: Fondo de Cultural Económica, 2000.

Limerick, Patricia Nelson. *The Legacy of Conquest: The Unbroken Past of the American West*. New York: W. W. Norton & Company, 1987.

Limón, José. "La Llorona, the Third Legend of Greater Mexico: Cultural Symbols, Women, and the Political Unconscious." In *Between Borders: Essays on Mexican/Chicana History,* edited by Adelaida del Castillo, pp. 399–432. Encino: Floricanto Press, 1990.

———. *Mexican Ballads, Chicano Poems: History and Influence in Mexican-American Social Poetry*. Berkeley and Los Angeles: University of California Press, 1993.

Lipsitz, George. *The Possessive Investment in Whiteness: How White People Profit From Identity Politics*. Philadelphia: Temple University Press, 1998.

Lomax Hawes, Bess. "La Llorona in Juvenile Hall." *Western Folklore* 27 (1968): 153–170.

Lopez, Alma. *Frontiers: A Journal of Women Studies* 23, no. 1 (2002): 90–95.

López de Gómara, Francisco. *Historia de la Conquista de México*. Caracas: Biblioteca Ayacucho, 1979.

López de Marical, Blancal. *La Figura Femenina en los Narradores Testigos de la Conquista*. México: El Colegio de México, 1997.

López-Pérez, René. "Barrios and Borderlands: Cultures of Latinos and Latinas in the United States." *Library Journal* 119 (November 1994): 91.

Loustaunau, Martha Oemke. "'La Llorona' Tales of the Weeping Woman." *The World and I* (October 1990): 660–663.

Lugones, Maria. "On Borderlands/La Frontera: An Interpretative Essay." *Hypatia* 7, 4 (Fall 1992): 31–37.

Matovina, Timothy. *Guadalupe and Her Faithful: Latino Catholics in San Antonio, from Colonial Origins to the Present.* Baltimore: Johns Hopkins University Press, 2005.

Mahler, Sarah J. "Theoretical and Empirical Contributions: Toward a Research Agenda for Transnationalism." In *Transnationalism from Below,* edited by Michael Peter Smith and Luis Eduardo Guarnizo, pp. 64–100. New Brunswick: Transaction Publishers, 1998.

Martínez, Jacqueline. *Phenomenology of Chicana Experience and Identity: Communication and Transformation in Praxis.* Lanham, MD: Rowman & Littlefield, 2000.

Martínez, Oscar. "Transnational Fronterizos: Cross-Border Linkages in Mexican Border Society." *Journal of Borderlands Studies* 5 (Spring 1990): 79–94.

———. ed. *U.S.-Mexico Borderlands: Historical and Contemporary Perspectives.* Wilmington: Scholarly Resources, 1995.

———. *Troublesome Border.* Tucson: University of Arizona Press, 1995.

———. *Border People: Life and Society in the U.S.—Mexico Borderlands.* Tucson: University of Arizona Press, 1998.

Martinez, Theresa A. "Toward A Chicana Feminist Epistemological Standpoint: Theory at the Intersection of Race, Class, and Gender." *Race, Gender & Class* 3, 3 (1996) 107–128.

———. "The Double-Consciousness of DuBois and the 'Mestiza Consciousness' of Anzaldúa." *Race, Gender & Class* 9, 4 (2002), 159–171.

Mattingly, Doreen and Ellen R. Hansen, eds. *Women and Change at the U.S.-Mexico Border: Mobility, Labor, and Activism.* Tucson: University of Arizona Press, 2006.

McCann, Carole R. and Seung-Kyung Kim. *Feminist Theory Reader: Local and Global Perspectives.* New York and London: Routledge, 2003.

McLaren, Peter. *Critical Pedagogy and Predatory Culture: Oppositional Politics in a Postmodern Era.* New York: Routledge, 1995.

———. *Revolutionary Multiculturalism: Pedagogies of Dissent for the New Millenium.* Boulder: Westview Press, 1997.

———. *Che Guevara, Paulo Freire, and the Pedagogy of Revolution.* Lanham: Rowman & Littlefield, 2000.

———. "Some Reflections on Critical Pedagogy in the Age of Global Empire." In *Reinventing Critical Pedagogy: Widening the Circle of Anti-Oppression Education,* edited by César Augusto Rossatto, Ricky Lee Allen, and Marc Pruyn, pp. 79–98. Lanham, MD: Rowman & Littlefield, 2006.

McLaren, Peter and Peter Leonard *Paulo Freire: A Critical Encounter.* New York: Routledge, 1993.

Marx, Karl. *The 18th Brumaire of Louis Bonaparte.* London: Electric Book Company, Ltd., 2001.

Medina, Lara. "Los Espíritus Siguen Hablando: Chicana Spiritualities." In *Living Chicana Theory,* edited by Carla Trujillo, pp. 189–213. Berkeley: Third Woman Press, 1998.

————. *Las Hermanas: Chicana/Latina Religious-Political Activism in the U.S. Catholic Church.* Philadelphia: Temple University Press, 2004.

Mendez, Jennifer B. "Creating Alternatives from a Gender Perspective: Transnational Organizing for Maquila Workers' Rights in Central America." In *Women's Activism and Globalization: Linking Local Struggles and Transnational Politics,* edited by Nancy A. Naples and Manisha Desai, pp. 121–141. New York: Routledge, 2002.

Mesa-Bains, Amalia. "El Mundo Femenino: Chicana Artist of the Movement—A Commentary on Development and Production." In *Chicano Art: Resistance and Affirmation, 1965–1985,* edited by Richard Griswold del Castillo, Teresa McKenna and Yvonne Yarbro-Bejarano, pp. 131–140. Wright Art Gallery, Catalog, University of California, Los Angeles, 1991.

————. "*Domesticana:* The Sensibility of Chicana *Rasquachismo.*" In *Chicana Feminisms: A Critical Reader,* edited by Gabriela F. Arredondo, Aída Hurtado, Norma Klahn, Olga Nájera-Ramírez, and Patricial Zavella, pp. 298–315. Durham, NC: Duke University Press, 2003.

Meza, Otilia. *Leyendas del Antiguo Mexico; Mitologia Prehispanica.* Mexico: EDAMEX, 1985.

————. *Leyendas Prehispanicas Mexicanas.* Mexico: Panorama Editorial, S.A., 1992.

Mignolo, Walter D. *Local Histories/Global Designs: Coloniality, Subaltern Knowledges, and Border Thinking.* Princeton: Princeton University Press, 2000.

Miller, Beth, ed. *Women in Hispanic Literature.* Berkeley and Los Angeles: University of California Press, 1983.

Miller, Toby. *Cultural Citizenship: Cosmopolitanism, Consumerism, and Television in a Neoliberal Age.* Philadelphia: Temple University Press, 2007.

Mohanty, Chandra Talpade. "On Race and Voice: Challenges for Liberal Education in the 1990s." *Cultural Critique* 8 (1989–1990): 179–208.

————. "Introduction: Cartographies of Struggle: Third World Women and the Politics of Feminism." In *Third World Women and the Politics of Feminism,* edited by Chandra Talpade Mohanty, Ann Russo, and Lourdes Torres, pp. 1–47. Bloomington: Indiana University Press, 1991.

————. "Under Western Eyes: Feminist Scholarship and Colonial Discourses." In *Third World Women and the Politics of Feminism,* edited by Chandra Mohanty, Ann Russo, and Lourdes Torres, pp. 51–80. Bloomington: Indiana University Press, 1991.

————. *Feminism Without Borders: Decolonizing Theory, Practicing Solidarity.* Durham & London: Duke University Press, 2003.

Mohanty, Chandra Talpade, Ann Russo and Lourdes Torres, eds. *Third World Women and the Politics of Feminism.* Indianapolis: Indiana University Press, 1991.

Molina, Ida and Oleg Zinam. "The Historical Role of a Woman in the Chicano's Search for Ethnic Identity: The Case of Dona Marina." *Quarterly Journal of Ideology* 14 (1990): 39–53.

Monsiváis, Carlos. "La Malinche y el Primer Mundo." In *La Malinche, sus Padres y sus Hijos,* edited by Margo Glantz, pp. 139–147. México: Facultad de Filosofía y Letras Universidad National Autónoma de México: 1994.

Montejano, David. *Anglos and Mexicans in the Making of Texas, 1836–1986*. Austin: University of Texas Press, 1987.

Montoya, Margaret E. "Border Crossings." In *The Latino/a Condition,* edited by Richard Delgado and Jean Stefancic, pp. 639–643. New York: New York University Press, 1998.

Mora, Pat. *Nepantla: Essays from the Land in the Middle.* Albuquerque: University of New Mexico Press, 1993.

Moraga, Cherríe. *Loving in the War Years: Lo que nunca paso por sus labios.* Boston: South End Press, 1983.

———. *The Last Generation.* Boston: South End Press, 1993.

———. "El mito azteca." In *Goddess of the Americas: Writings on the Virgin of Guadalupe,* edited by Ana Castillo, pp. 68–71. New York: Riverhead Books, 1996.

Morrison, Tony. *Beloved.* New York: Knopf, 1987.

Mufti, Aamir and Ella Shohat, eds. "Introduction." In *Dangerous Liasons: Gender, Nation, and Postcolonial Perspectives,* edited by Anne McClintock, Aamir Mufti and Ella Shohat, pp. 1–12. Minneapolis: University of Minnesota Press, 1997.

Mukerji, Chandra, and Schudson, Michael, eds. *Rethinking Popular Culture: Contemporary Perspectives in Cultural Studies.* Berkeley: University of California Press, 1991.

Murrillo Jr., Enrique. "Mojado Crossings along Neoliberal Borderlands." *Educational Foundations* 13, no. 1 (Winter 1999): 7–30.

Naples, Nancy A. "Changing the Terms: Community Activism, Globalization, and the Dilemma of Transnational Feminist Praxis." In *Women's Activism and Globalization: Linking Local Struggles and Transnational Politics,* edited by Nancy A. Naples and Manisha Desai, pp. 3–14. New York: Routledge, 2002a.

———. "The Challenges and Possibilities of Transnational Feminist Praxis." In *Women's Activism and Globalization: Linking Local Struggles and Transnational Politics,* edited by Nancy A. Naples and Manisha Desai, 267–281. New York: Routledge, 2002b.

Nebel, Richard. *Santa María Tonántzin Virgin de Guadalupe: Continuidad y Transformación Religiosa en México.* Translated in Spanish by Carlos Warnholtz Bustillos. México, D.F.: Fondo de Cultura Económica, 1995.

Nieto-Gomez de Lazarín. "Woman in Colonial Mexico." *Regeneración* 2, 4 (1975): 18–19.

No More Deaths. http://www.facebook.com (retrieved 10 June 2009).

Noriega, Chon. "Editor's Introduction." *Aztlan* 24, 2 (1999): vii–viii.

Nunn, Tey Marianna. "The *Our Lady* Controversy: Chicana Art, Hispanic Identity, and the Politics of Place and Gender in Nuevo México." In *Expressing New Mexico: Nuevomexicano Creativity, Ritual, and Memory,* edited by Phillip B. Gonzales, pp. 162–183. Tucson: University of Arizona Press, 2007.

Obregón, Luis. *Las Calles de México,* 1924.

Ochoa, Enrique. "Constructing Fronteras: Teaching the History of the U.S. Mexico Borderlands in the Age of Proposition 187 . . ." *Radical History Review* 70 (1998): 119–130.

Ochoa, Marcia. *La Ofrenda,* Ann Arbor: University of Michigan Press, 1991.

Ong, Aihwa. *Spirits of Resistance and Capitalist Discipline: Factory Workers in Malaysia.* Albany: State University of New York Press, 1987.

Omi, Michael and Howard Winant. *Racial Formation in the United States.* New York: Routlege & Kegan Paul, 1986.

Ortega, Mariana. "'New Mestizas,' 'World-Travelers,' and '*Dasein*': Phenomenology and the Multi-Voiced, Multi-Cultural Self." *Hypatia* 16, 3 (Summer 2001): 1–29.

———. "Apertures of In-Betweeness, of Selves in the Middle." In *EntreMundos/ AmongWorlds: New Perspectives on Gloria Anzladúa,* edited by AnaLouise Keating, pp. 77–84. New York: Palgrave McMillan, 2005.

Ortiz Dunbar, Roxanne. "Invasion of the Americas and the Making of the Mestizo-coyote Nation: Heritage of the Invasion." *Social Justice* 20, 1–2 (Spring-Summer 1993): 52–56.

Palacios, Monica. "La Llorona Loca: The Other Side." In *Chicana Lesbians: The Girls Our Mothers Warned Us About,* edited by Carla Trujillo, pp. 49–51. Berkeley: Third Woman Press, 1991.

Paredes, Américo, *"With His Pistol in His Hand": A Border Ballad and Its Hero.* Austin: University of Texas Press, 1958.

Patai, Raphael. *The Hebrew Goddess.* Detroit, MI: Wayne State University Press, 1990.

Paz, Octavio. *El Laberinto de la Soledad.* México: Fondo de Cultura Económica, 1950.

———. *Sor Juan Inés de la Cruz o Las Trampas de la Fé.* México: Fondo de Económica, 1982.

Peña, Devon Gerardo. *The Terror of the Machine: Technology, Work, Gender, and Ecology on the U.S.-Mexico Border.* Austin: Center for Mexican American Studies, University of Texas at Austin, 1997.

Peña, Milagros. *Latina Activists across Borders: Women Grassroots Organizing in Mexico and Texas.* Durham, NC: Duke University Press, 2007.

Pendleton Jiménez, Karleen. Lengua Latina: Latina Canadians (Re)constructing Identity Through a Community of Practice. In *Learning, Teaching and Community: Participatory Approaches to Educational Innovation,* eds. C. Pease-Alvarez and S. Schecter, pp. 235–255. Mahwah, NJ: Lawrence Erlbaum Associates, 2005.

———. "'Start with the Land': Groundwork for Chicana Pedagogy." In *Chicana/ Latina Education in Everyday Life: Feminista Perspectives on Pedagogy and Epistemology,* edited by Dolores Delgado Bernal, C. Alejandra Elenes, Francisca Godinez and Sofia Villenas, pp. 219–230. Albany: State University of New York Press, 2006.

Penn-Hilden, Patricia. "How the Border Lies: Some Historical Reflections." In *Decolonial Voices: Chicana and Chicano Cultural Studies in the 21st Century,* edited by Arturo J. Aldama and Naomi H. Quiñonez. Bloomington & Minneapolis: Indiana University Press, 2002.

Pérez, Domino Renee. "Caminando con La Llorona: Traditional and Contemporary Narratives. In *Chicana Traditions: Continuity and Change,* edited by Norma E.

Cantú and Olga Nájera-Ramírez, pp. 100–116. Urbana and Chicago: University of Illinois Press, 2002.

Pérez, Emma. *The Decolonial Imaginary: Writing Chicanas into History*. Bloomington: Indiana University Press, 1999.

Pérez, Laura E. "Spirit Glyphs: Reimagining Art and Artists in the Work of Chicana *Tlamatinime*." *Modern Fiction Studies* 44, no. 1 (1998): 36–76.

———. *Chicana Art: The Politics of Spiritual and Aesthetic Altarities*. Durham, NC: Duke University Press, 2007.

Pérez-Torres, Rafael. "Nomads and Migrants: Negotiating a Multicultural Postmodernism." *Cultural Critique* 26 (Winter 1993–94): 161–189.

———. *Movements in Chicano Poetry: Against Myths, Against Margins*. New York: Cambridge University Press, 1995.

Peterson, Jeanette Favrot. "The Virgin of Guadalupe: Symbol of Conquest or Liberation?" *Art Journal* 51 (Spring 1992): 39–47.

Pizarro, Marcos. "'Chicana/o Power!' Epistemology and Methodology for Social Justice and Empowerment in Chicana/o Communities." *Qualitative Studies in Education* 11, no. 1 (1998): 57–80.

———. *Chicanas and Chicanos in School: Racial Profiling, Identity Battles, and Empowerment*. Austin: University of Texas Press, 2005.

Poole, Stafford. *Our Lady of Guadalupe: The Origins and Sources of a Mexican National Symbol, 1531–1797*. Tucson: University of Arizona Press, 1995.

———. ed. *In Defense of the Indians: The Defense of the Most Reverend Lord, Don Fray Bartolomé de Las Casas, of the Order of Preachers, Late Bishop of Chiapa, Against the Persecutors and Slanderers of the Peoples of the New World Discovered Across the Seas*. Translated by Stafford Poole, C. M. Dekalb, IL: Northern Illinois Press, 1974.

Portelli, Alessandro. *The Order has been Carried Out: History, Memory, and Meaning of a Nazi Massacre in Rome*. New York: Palgrave McMillan, 2003.

Poyo, Gerald and Gilbert Hinojosa. "Spanish Texas and Borderlands Historiography in Transition: Implications for United States History." *Journal of American History* 75, 2 (September 1988): 393–417.

Prescott, William H. *History of the Conquest of Mexico with a Preliminary View of the Ancient Mexican Civilizations and the Life of the Conqueror Hernando Córtes*. Vol. 2. New York: John W. Lovell Company, 1900.

Preston, James J., ed. *Mother Worship: Theme and Variations*. Chapel Hill: University of North Carolina Press, 1982.

Quintana, Alvina E. *Home Girls: Chicana Literary Voices*. Philadelphia: Temple University Press, 1996.

Quiñonez, Naomi H. "Re(Riting) the Chicana Postcolonial: From Traitor to 21st Century Interpreter." In *Decolonial Voices: Chicana and Chicano Cultural Studies in the 21st Century*, edited by Arturo J. Aldama and Naomi H. Quiñonez, pp. 129–151. Bloomington: Indiana University Press, 2002.

Quirarte, Jacinto. "Sources of Chicano Art: Our Lady of Guadalupe." *Exploration in Ethnic Studies* 15 (1992): 13–26.

Ramirez, Ignacio. *Obras Completas, Vol 2.* México: Centro de Investigación Científica, 1984.

Ramos, Samuel. *Profile of Man and Culture in Mexico.* Austin: University of Texas Press, 1962.

Rebolledo, Tey Diana and Eliana S. Rivero. *Infinite Divisions: An Anthology of Chicana Literature.* Tucson & London: University of Arizona Press, 1993.

Rendón, Armando. *Chicano Manifesto.* New York: Macmillan, 1971.

Rendón, Laura I. "Recasting Agreements that Govern Teaching and Learning: An Intellectual and Spiritual Framework for Transformation." *Religion and Education* 32, no. 1 (2005): 79–108.

Reyes, Alfonso. *Visión de Anahuac, 1519.* Madrid: Indice, 1923.

———. *Mexico in a Nutshell: and Other Essays.* Berkeley: University of California Press, 1964.

Rivero, Eliana S. "The 'Other's Others': Chicana Identity and Its Textual Expressions." In *Encountering the Other(s): Studies in Literature, History, and Culture* edited by Gisela Brinker-Gabler, pp. 239–260. Albany: State University of New York Press, 1995.

Robelo, Cecilio. *Diccionario de Mitologia Nahuatl.* Second ed. México: Edicones Fuentes Cultural, 1951.

Robles, Martha. *Mujeres, Mitos y Diosas.* México: Consejo Nacional para la Cultura Económica, 1996.

Rodríguez, Jeanette. *Our Lady of Guadalupe: Faith and Empowerment Among Mexican-American Women.* Austin: University of Texas Press, 1994.

———. "Guadalupe: The Feminine Face of God." In *Goddess of the Americas: Writings on the Virgin of Guadalupe,* edited by Ana Castillo, pp. 25–31. New York: Riverhead Books, 1996.

———. "Latina Activists: Toward an Inclusive Spirituality of Being in the World." In *A Reader in Latina Feminist Theology: Religion and Justice,* edited by María Pilar Aquino, Daisy L. Machado, and Jeanette Rodríguez, pp. 114–130. Austin: University of Texas Press, 2002.

Rodríguez-Kessler, Elizabeth. "She's the Dreamwork Inside Someone Else's Skull: La Malinche and the Battles Waged for Her Autonomy." *Chicana/Latina Studies: The Journal of Mujeres Activas en Letras y Cambio Social* 5, no. 1 (Fall 2005): 76–109.

Roman, Leslie. "White is a Color! White Defensiveness, Postmodernism, and Anti-Racist Pedagogy." In R*ace, Identity and Representation in Education,* edited by Cameron McCarthy and Warren Crichlow, pp. 71–88. New York: Routledge, 1993.

Romero, Mary and Michelle Habell-Pallán. "Introduction." In *Latino/a Popular Culture,* edited by Michelle Habell-Pallán and Mary Romero, pp. 1–21. New York: New York University Press, 2002.

Romo, Jaime J. and Claudia Chavez. "Border Pedagogy: A Study of Preservice Teacher Transformation." *The Educational Forum* 70 (Winter 2006): 142–153.

Roof, Wade Clark. "Religious Borderlands: Challenge for Future Study." *Journal for the Scientific Study of Religion* 37 (March 1998): 1–14.

Rosaldo, Renato *Culture and Truth: The Remaking of Social Analysis.* Boston: Beacon Press, 1989.

———. "Surveying Law and Borders." In *The Latino Condition,* edited by Richard Delgado and Jean Stefancic, pp. 631–643. New York: New York University Press, 1998.

Rosales, Arturo F. "Chicano Art: A Historical Reflection of the Community." *The Americas Review* 18 (Summer 1990): 58–70.

Roschelle, Anne, Theresa Martinez and William Vélez. "Race, Gender, Class and U.S Latinas and Latinos." *Race, Gender & Class* 3, 3 (1996): 107–128.

Ross, Stanley R., ed. *Views Across the Border: The United States and Mexico.* Albuquerque: University of New Mexico Press, 1978.

Ruiz, Vicki. *From Out of the Shadows.* New York: Oxford University Press, 1998.

Ruiz, Vicki and Susan Tiano, eds. *Women on the U.S.-México Border.* Boulder: Westview Press, 1991.

Russel y Rodríguez, Mónica. "(En)Countering Domestic Violence, Complicity, and Definitions of Chicana Womanhood." *Voces: A Journal of Chicana/Latina Studies* 1, 2 (Summer 1997): 104–141.

———. "Mexicans and Mongrels: Policies of Hybridity, Gender and Nation in the U.S.-Mexican War." *Latino Studies Journal* 11 no. 3 (2000).

Saavedra, Cinthya M. and Ellen D. Nymark. "Borderland-*Mestizaje* Feminism: The New Tribalism." In *Handbook of Critical and Indigenous Methodologies,* edited by Norma Denzing, Yvonna Lincoln and Linda Tuhiwai Smith, pp. 255–276. Los Angeles: Sage, 2008.

Sadowski-Smith, Claudia., ed. *Globalization on the Line: Culture, Capital, and Citizenship at the U.S. Borders.* New York: Palgrave, 2002.

Saenz, Benjamin Alire. "In the Borderlands of Chicano Identity, There Are Only Fragments." In *Border Theory: The Limits of Cultural Politics,* edited by Scott Michaelson and David E. Johnson, pp. 68–96. Minneapolis: University of Minnesota Press, 1997.

Sahagún, Fray Bernardino. *Historia General de las Cosas de la Nueva España.* Vols 1–4. México: Editorial Robredo, 1938.

Saldívar, José David. "The Limits of Cultural Studies." *American Literary History* 2 (1990): 251–266.

———. "Frontera Crossings: Sites of Cultural Contestation." *Mester* 22/23 (Fall/Spring 1994): 81–92.

———. *The Dialects of our America: Genealogy, Cultural Critique, and Literary History.* Durham: Duke University, 1995.

———. *Border Matters: Remapping American Cultural Studies.* Berkeley: University of California Press, 1997.

Saldívar, Ramón. *Chicano Narrative: the Dialects of Difference.* Madison: University of Wisconsin Press, 1990.

———. "The Borderlands of Culture: Americo Paredes's George Washington Gómez and Chicano Literature at the End of the Twentieth Century." *American Literary History* 5, 2 (Summer 1993): 272–293.

————. *The Borderlands of Culture: Américo Paredes and the Transnational Imaginary.* Durham, NC: Duke University Press, 2006.

Saldívar-Hull, Sonia. "Feminism on the Border: From Gender Politics to Geopolitics." In *Criticism in the Borderlands: Studies in Chicano Literature, Culture and Ideology,* edited by Hector Calderón and José David Saldivar, pp. 203–220. Durham and London: Duke University Press, 1991.

————. Introduction to *Borderlands/La Frontera: The New Mestiza,* by Gloria Anzaldúa. 2nd ed. San Francisco: Aunt Lute Books, 1999.

————. *Feminism on the Border: Chicana Gender Politics and Literature.* Berkeley and Los Angeles: University of California Press, 2000.

Sampaio, Anna. "Transnational Feminisms in a New Global Matrix." *International Journal of Politics* 6, no. 2 (2004): 245–269.

Sánchez, George. *Becoming Mexican American: Ethnicity, Culture, and Identity in Chicano Los Angles, 1900–1945.* New York: Oxford University Press, 1993.

————. "History, Culture, and Education." In *Latinos and Education: A Critical Reader,* edited by Antonia Darder, Rodolfo Torres, Henry Gutiérrez, pp. 117–134. New York: Routledge, 1997.

Sandoval, Anna M. *Toward a Latina Feminism of the Americas: Repression and Resistance in Chicana and Mexicana Literature.* Austin: University of Texas Press, 2008.

Sandoval, Chela. "U.S. Third World Feminism: The Theory and Method of Oppositional Consciousness in the Postmodern World." *Genders* 10 (Spring 1991):1–24.

————. "Mestizaje as Method: Feminists-of-Color Challenge the Canon." In *Living Chicana Theory,* edited by Carla Trujillo, pp. 352–370. Berkeley: Third Woman Press, 1998.

————. *Methodology of the Oppressed.* Minneapolis: University of Minnesota Press, 2000.

San Miguel, Guadalupe Jr. *"Let All of Them Take Heed": Mexican Americans and the Campaign for Educational Equality in Texas, 1910–1981.* Austin: University of Texas Press, 1987.

Segura, Denize and Patricia Zavella, eds. *Women and Migration in the U.S.-Mexico Borderlands: A Reader.* Durham: Duke University Press, 2007.

Simon, Roger. "Forms of Insurgency in the Production of Popular Memories: The Columbus Quincentenary and the Pedagogy of Countercommemoration." In *Between Borders,* edited by Henry Giroux and Peter McLaren, pp. 119–144. Routledge: New York, 1994.

Simpson, Lesley Byrd, ed., *Cortés: The Life of the Conqueror by His Secretary Francisco López de Gómara.* Translated by Lesley Byrd Simpson. Berkeley and Los Angeles: University of California Press, 1964.

Sleeter, Christine E. *Multicultural Education as Social Activism.* Albany: State University of New York Press, 1996.

Sleeter, Christine E. and Peter McLaren, eds. *Multicultural Education, Critical Pedagogy, and the Politics of Difference.* Albany: State University of New York Press, 1995.

Soldatenko, María Angelina. "Made in the U.S.A.: Latinas/os?, Garment Work and Ethnic Conflict in Los Angeles' Sweat Shops." *Cultural Studies* 13 no. 2 (1999): 319–334.

———. "Justice for Janitors: Latinzing Los Angeles: Moblilizing Latina(o) Cultural Repertoire." In *Latino Los Angeles: Transformations, Communities, and Activism,* edited by Enrique C. Ochoa and Gilda L. Ochoa, pp. 225–245. Tucson: University of Arizona Press, 2005.

Somonte, Mariano G. *Doña Maria: "La Malinche."* Monterrey, Nuevo León: México,

Soto, Shirlene Ann. "Tres Modelos Culturales: La Virgin de Guadalupe, La Malinche y La Llorona." *Fem* 10 (1986): 13–16.

Spivak, Gayatri Chakravorty. *In Other Worlds: Essays on Cultural Politics.* New York: Routledge, 1988a.

———. "Can the Subaltern Speak." In *Marxism and the Interpretation of Culture,* edited by Lawrence Grossberg, pp. 271–313.. Chicago: University of Illinois Press,1988b.

———. *Outside in the Teaching Machine.* New York: Routledge, 1993.

———. "Disasporas Old and New: Women in the Transnational World." *Textual Practice* 10, no. 2 (1996): 245–269.

Sten, Maria. *Las Extraordinarias Historias de los Códices Mexicanos.* México: Grupo Editorial Planeta, 1992.

Stoddard, Ellwyn. "Frontiers, Borders, and Border Segmentation: Toward a Conceptual Clarification." *Journal of Borderlands Studies* 6 (Spring 1991): 1–22.

Tafolla, Carmen. *Curandera.* Texas: M & A Editions, 1983.

Tan, Amy. *The Joy Luck Club.* New York: Putnam, 1989.

Tatum, Charles M. ed. *New Chicana/Chicano Writing.* Tucson: The University of Arizona Press, 1992.

Taylor, William. "The Virgin of Guadalupe in New Spain: An Inquiry into the Social History of Marian Devotion." *American Ethnologist* 14 (February 1987): 9–33.

Téllez, Michelle. "Doing Research at the Borderlands: Notes from a Chicana Feminist Ethnographer." *Chicana/Latina Studies: The Journal of Mujeres Activas en Letras y Cambio Social* 4, no. 2 (2005): 46–70.

———. "Generating hope, creating change, searching for community: Stories of resistance against globalization at the U.S.-México border." In *Reinventing critical pedagogy: Widening the circle of anti-oppression education,* edited by César August Rossatto, Ricky Lee Allen & Marc Pruyn, pp. 225–234. Lanham, MD: Rowman & Littlefield, 2006.

———. "Community of Struggle: Gender, Violence, and Resistance on the U.S./ Mexico Border." *Gender & Society* 22, no. 5 (October 2008): 545–567.

Thelen, David. "Of Audiences, Borderlands, and Comparisons: Toward the Internationalization of American History." *Journal of American History* 79, 2 (September 1992): 432–463.

Todorov, Tzvetan. *The Conquest of America: The Question of the Other.* New York: Harper & Row Publishers, 1987.

———. "Dialogism and Schizophrenia." In *An Other Tongue: Nation and Ethnicity in the Linguistic Borderlands,* edited by Alfred Arteaga, pp. 203–214. Durham, NC: Duke University Press, 1994.

Torres, Eden E. *Chicana without Apology, Chicana sin Vergüenza: the New Chicana Cultural Studies.* New York: Routledge, 2003.

Torres, María de los Angeles. "Encuentros y Encontronazos: Homeland in the Politics and Identity of the Cuban Diaspora." In *The Latino Studies Reader: Culture, Economy, and Society,* edited by Antonia Darder and Rodolofo D. Torres, pp. 43–62. Malden: Blackwell Publishers, 1998.

Townsend, Camilla. *Malintzin's Choices: An Indian Woman in the Conquest of Mexico.* Albuquerque: University of New Mexico Press, 2006.

Trinidad Galván, Ruth. "Portraits of *Mujeres Desjuiciadas:* Womanist Pedagogies of the Everyday, the Mundane, and the Ordinary." *International Journal of Qualitative Studies in Education* 14(5), (September-October 2001): 603–621.

———. "*Campesina* epistemologies and pedagogies of the spirit: Examining women's *sobrevivencia.*" In *Chicana/Latina education in everyday life: Feminista perspectives on pedagogy and epistemology,* edited by Dolores Delgado Bernal, C. Alejandra Elenes, Francisca E. Godinez, and Sofia Villenas, pp. 161–179. Albany: State University of New York Press, 2006.

Trueba, Enrique (Henry) T. *Latinos Unidos: From Cultural Diversity to the Politics of Solidarity.* Lanham, MD: Rowman & Littlefield, 1999.

Trujillo, Carla. "Chicana Lesbians: Fear and Loathing in the Chicano Community." In *Chicana Lesbians: The Girls Our Mothers Warned Us About,* edited by Carla Trujillo, pp. 186–194. Berkeley: Third Woman Press, 1991.

———. "La Virgen de Guadalupe and Her Reconstruction in Chicana Lesbian Desire." In *Living Chicana Theory,* edited by Carla Trujillo, pp. 214–231. Berkeley: Third Woman Press, 1998.

Turner, Louise. "Ghosts of New Mexico: Benevolent or Malevolent." *El Palacio* 94 (Spring 1994): 38–43.

Valeriano, Don Antonio. *Nican Mopohua (Aqui se Narra).* Trans. Mario Rojas Sánchez. México: Editorial Hombre, nd.

Valencia, Richard R. "The Plight of Chicano Students: An Overview of Schooling Conditions and Outcomes." In *Chicano School Failure and Success,* edited by Richard R. Valencia, 2d ed., pp. 52–69. New York: Routledge/Falmer Press, 2002.

Valenzuela, Angela. *Subtractive Schooling: U.S.-Mexican Youth and the Politics of Caring.* Albany: State University of New York Press, 1999.

Varela, Felix. *Jicoténcal.* Edited by Luis Leal and Roldofo J. Cortina. Houston: Arte Público Press, 1995.

Varney, Joan A. "Undressing the Normal: Community Efforts for Queer Asian and Asian American Youth." In *Troubling Intersections of Race and Sexuality: Queer Students of Color and Anti-Oppressive Education,* edited by Kevin K. Kumashiro, pp. 87–104. Lanham, MD: Rowman & Littlefield, 2001.

Vasconcelos, José. *Hernán Cortés: Creador de la Nacionalidad.* México: Ediciones Botas, 1941.

———. *Discursos: 1920–1950.* México: Ediciones Botas, 1950.

———. *La Raza Cosmica.* México: Espasa-Calpe Mexicana S.A., 1992.

Vélez-Ibáñez, Carlos G.. *Border Visions: Mexican Cultures of the Southwest United States.* Tucson: University of Arizona Press, 1996.

Venegas, Yolanda. "The Erotics of Racialization: Gender and Sexuality in the Making of California." *Frontiers: A Journal of Women Studies* 25, 3 (2004): 63–89.

Vigil, Ralph. "Inequality and Ideology in Borderlands Historiography." *Latin American Research Review* 29, 1 (1994): 155–171.

Vila, Pablo. *Crossing Borders, Reinforcing Borders: Social Categories, Metaphors, and Narrative Identities on the U.S.-Mexico Frontier.* Austin: University of Texas Press, 2000.

Villenas, Sofia. "The Colonizer/Colonized Chicana Ethnographer: Identity, Marginalization, and Co-optation in the Field." *Harvard Educational Review* 66 (Winter 1996): 711–731.

———. "Latina/Chicana Feminist Postcolonialities: Un/Tracking Educational Actors' Interventions." *Qualitative Studies in Education* 19, no. 5 (September-October 2006a): 659–672.

———. "Pedagogical Moments in the Borderlands: Latina Mothers Teaching and Learning." In *Chicana/Latina Education in Everyday Life: Feminista Perspectives on Pedagogy and Epistemology,* edited by Dolores Delgado Bernal, C. Alejandra Elenes, Francisca E. Godinez, and Sofia Villenas, pp. 147–160. Albany: State University of New York Press, 2006b.

———. "Thinking Latina/o Education with and from Chicana/Latina Feminist Cultural Studies." In *Handbook of Cultural Politics in Education,* edited by Zeus Leonardo. Sense Publishers, 2010.

Villenas, Sofia and Douglas E. Foley. "Chicano/Latino Critical Ethnography of Education: Cultural Productions from *la Frontera.*" In *Chicano school failure and success: Past, present and future,* edited by Richard R. Valencia. 2nd ed., pp.195–226. New York and London: Routledge, 2002.

Villenas, Sofia and M. Moreno. "To *valerse por si misma* Between Race, Capitalism and Patriarchy: Latina Mother-Daughter Pedagogies in North Carolina." *Qualitative Studies in Education* 14, no. 5 (2001): 671–687.

Villenas, Sofia, Francisca E. Godinez, Dolores Delgado Bernal, and C. Alejandra Elenes. "Chicana/Latinas Building Bridges: An Introduction." In *Chicana/Latina Education in Everyday Life: Feminista Perspectives on Pedagogy and Epistemology,* edited by Dolores Delgado Bernal, C. Alejandra Elenes, Francisca E. Godinez and Sofia Villenas, pp. 1–9. Albany: State University of New York Press, 2006.

Viramontes, Helena María. *The Moths and Other Stories.* Houston: Arte Público Press, 1985.

Vizeñor, Gerald. "The Ruins of Representation: Shadow Survivance and the Literature of Dominance." In *An Other Tongue: Nation and Ethnicity in the Linguistic*

Borderlands, edited by Alfred Arteaga, pp. 139–167. Durham: Duke University Press, 1994.

Wallace, Michele. "Multiculturalism and Oppositionality." In *Between Borders,* edited by Henry Giroux and Peter McLaren, pp. 180–191. New York: Routledge, 1994.

Walraven, Ed. "Evidence for a Developing Variant of 'La Llorona." *Western Folklore* 50 (April 1991): 208–217.

Warren, Karen and Alison Rheingold. "Feminist Pedagogy and Experiential Education: A Critical Look." *Journal of Experiential Education* 16 (December 1993): 25–31.

Webb, Walter. *The Texas Rangers.* Austin: University of Texas Press, 1935.

———. *The Great Frontier.* Austin: University of Texas Press, 1951.

Weber, David J. *The Mexican Frontier, 1821–1846: The American Southwest Under Mexico.* Albuquerque: University of New Mexico Press, 1982.

———. ed. *The Idea of Spanish Borderlands.* New York and London: Garland Publishing, 1991.

Weber, Donald. "From Limen to Border: A Meditation on the Legacy of Victory Turner for American Cultural Studies." *American Quarterly* 47, 3 (September 1995): 525–536.

Weedon, Chris. *Feminist Practice and Poststructuralist Theory.* Oxford and New York: Basil Blackwell, 1987.

White, Hayden. *The Content of the Form: Narrative Discourse and Historical Representation.* Baltimore: Johns Hopkins University Press, 1987.

Winant, Howard. *Racial Conditions: Politics, Theory, Comparisons.* Minneapolis: University of Minnesota Press, 1994.

Wing, Adriane K., editor. *Critical Race Feminism: A Reader.* New York: New York University Press, 1997.

Wolf, Eric R. "The Virgin of Guadalupe: A Mexican National Symbol." *Journal of American Folklore* 71 (1958): 45–58.

Wyatt, Jean. "On Not Being La Malinche: Border Negotiations of Gender in Sandra Cisneros's *Woman Hollering Creek.*" *Tulsa Studies in Women's Studies Literature* 14, 2 (Fall 1995): 243–271.

Xicoténcatl. Translated by Guillermo I. Castillo-Feliú. Austin: University of Texas Press, 1999.

Yarbro-Bejarano, Yvonne. "Chicana's Experience in Collective Theater: Ideology and Form." *Women and Performance* 2 (1985): 45–58.

———. "The Female Subject in Chicano Theater: Sexuality, 'Race,' and Class." *Theater of Color* 38 (1986): 389–407.

———. "Gloria Anzaldúa's *Borderlands/La Frontera:* 'Difference' and the Non-Unitary Subject." *Cultural Critique* (Fall 1994): 5–24.

———. "Expanding the Categories of Race and Sexuality in Lesbian and Gay Studies." *Professions of Desire: Lesbian and Gay Studies in Literature,* edited by George E. Haggerty and Bonnie Zimmerman, pp. 124–135. New York: Modern Language Association of America, 1995.

———. "Laying it Bare: The Queer/Colored Body in Photography by Laura Aguilar." In *Living Chicana Theory,* edited by Carla Trujillo, pp. 277–305. Berkeley: Third Woman Press, 1998.

———. "Sexuality and Chicana/o Studies: Toward a Theoretical Paradigm for the Twenty-first Century." *Cultural Studies* 13, 2 (1999): 335–345.

Zamora, Margarita. *Reading Columbus.* Berkeley, CA: University of California Press, 1993.

Zavella, Patricia. "Feminist Insider Dilemmas: Constructing Ethnic Identity with 'Chicana' Informants." *Frontiers* 13, 3 (1993): 52–76.

———. "Living on the Edge: Everyday Lives of Poor Chicano/Mexicano Families." In *Mapping Multiculturalism,* edited by Avery F. Gordon and Christopher Newfield, pp. 362–386. Minneapolis: University of Minnesota Press, 1996.

Zires, Margarita. "Los mitos de la Virgen de Guadalupe: su proceso de construcción y reinterpretación en el Mexico pasado y contemporaneo." *Mexican Studies/Estudios Mexicanos* 10, 2 (Summer 1994): 281–313.

Index

About The Author

C. Alejandra Elenes is associate professor of women's and gender studies in the Division of Humanities, Arts, and Cultural Studies at Arizona State University. She is coeditor of the anthology *Chicana/Latina Education in Everyday Life: Feminista Perspectives on Pedagogy and Epistemology*, winner of the 2006 AESA Book Critics Award.

CPSIA information can be obtained at www.ICGtesting.com
Printed in the USA
269910BV00003B/33/P

As these popular Mexican figure are reconceptualized/transformative ↙ ✳
by border/pedagogies—
alternative reading (best way)

So we may need to walk into our classrooms and reconceptualize who sits before us, rethink the canon and consider again what constitute a "great" music program.

Moving away from binary constructions

Outline
① Hook
② Lit Review
   esp Third World
③ La Llorona
④ La Virgen
⑤ La Malinche
⑥ Why should this matter to music educators?
⑦ Conclusion